D0935728

Certain victory

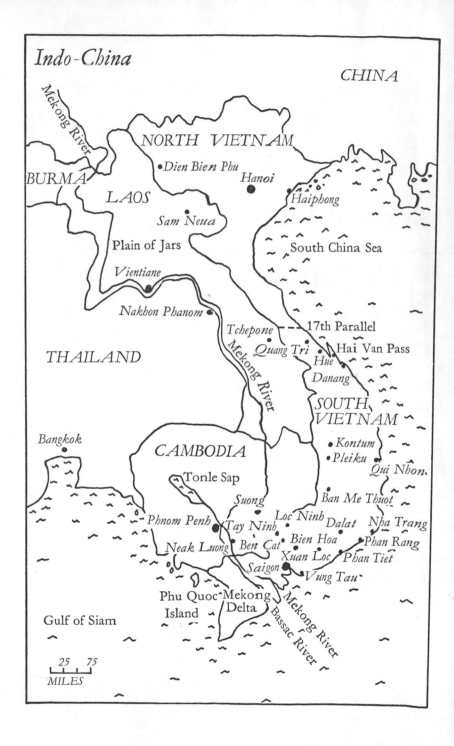

Certain victory

How Hanoi won the war

Denis Warner

Sheed Andrews and McMeel, Inc.
Subsidiary of Universal Press Syndicate
Kansas City

017102

Connetquot Public Library
760 Ocean Avenue
Bohemia, New York 11716

Certain victory: How Hanoi won the war Copyright © 1977, 1978 by Denis Warner. All rights reserved. Printed in the United States of America. No part of this book may be used or reproduced in any manner whatsoever, without written permission, except in the case of reprints in the context of reviews. For information write Sheed Andrews and McMeel, Inc., Subsidiary of Universal Press Syndicate, 6700 Squibb Road, Mission, Kansas 66202.

First published by Hutchinson of Australia in 1977.

Library of Congress Cataloging in Publication Data

Warner, Denis Ashton, 1917–
  Certain victory.

  First published under title: Not with guns alone.
  Includes bibliographical references and index.
  1. Vietnamese Conflict, 1961–1975. I. Title
DS557.7.W37 1977b   959.704´3   78–5648
ISBN 0–8362–6201–8

The single most important thing about Vietnam is to understand it.

Douglas Pike, Anatomy of Deceit

Also by Denis Warner
Out of the Gun
The Last Confucian
Reporting South-East Asia
The Tide At Sunrise, A History of the Russo-Japanese War, 1904-05,
    (in collaboration with Peggy Warner)

Contents

List of Maps

Introduction

The bombed and battered remains of a small French military encampment stand guard over the sluggish, brown waters of the Mekong at Neak Luong, twenty-four miles upriver in Cambodia from the Vietnamese border. A long time ago, in the brief period between the first and second Indo-China wars, it used to be a pleasant place to break the journey by road from Saigon to Phnom Penh. A little restaurant close to the river served baked crabs and long loaves of crisp French bread and mangoes of immense size and exquisite taste. Years later, Neak Luong was where the Russian and Chinese military supplies shipped through the port of Kompong Som, or Sihanoukville, as it was called then, used to be ferried to the North Vietnamese and Viet Cong forces in the Cambodian sanctuaries. It was here, also, in April, 1970, when war spread across the border into Cambodia, that the bodies of hundreds of men and boys, with their hands tied behind their backs, drifted down the Mekong on the tide. By 1975 Neak Luong had become Phnom Penh's absolutely vital strategic outpost, the one essential position that had to be held if the tugboats towing the barges of rice, fuel and ammunition, were to continue their run up the Mekong to the beleaguered capital. When Neak Luong fell, we knew that Phnom Penh would soon follow. He who commands Neak Luong also commands eastern Cambodia. In January, 1978, Vietnamese forces advancing through the Parrot's Beak again appeared to threaten Neak Luong.

There was not a day, nor apparently even an hour, between the end of the second Indo-China War and the beginning of the third.

While the last battles were being fought in the Mekong Delta between the ARVN and the North Vietnamese divisions, the Cambodians were striking in the Gulf of Siam. Fighting, according to Vietnamese refugees from the new battle zones, and to the quite detailed, though often contradictory, statements issued by both sides, has gone on intermittently ever since.

On October 31, 1977, the sixty-foot Vietnamese boat, *Hai Hung*, loaded down with salt to hoodwink the guards at the eight check points down river, slipped out of Saigon. Crammed into a two-deck secret cabin built into the engine room, and only fifteen feet long and five feet wide, were sixty-eight refugees.

The *Hai Hung* broke down fifty miles from Darwin and was towed into port on December 2 by an Australian patrol boat. Two of the refugees onboard came from the pear-shaped Vietnamese island of Phu Quoc, south of the south-southeastern corner of Cambodia, and one from Cu Chi, roughly halfway between Saigon and the Parrot's Beak area, where Cambodian incursions finally led to full-fledged Vietnamese counterattacks. They have helped to fill in the gaps in the official Vietnamese and Cambodian reports of the war.

The Khmer Rouge occupied Phnom Penh on April 17, 1975, and in the following days not only emptied the city but began the systematic liquidation of the Cambodian middle classes. Included in this pogrom were the Vietnamese citizens remaining in Cambodia. According to Pham Van Dong, the prime minister of Socialist Vietnam, the Cambodians massacred thousands of Vietnamese, seized their property and expelled to Vietnam those they did not kill. All of this began before the fall of Saigon on April 30. The day after the red flag went up over the Independence Palace, Cambodian amphibious forces attacked Phu Quoc. The *Hai Hung* refugees described this as a small raid, but it was only the first of many that continued through 1975, 1976 and 1977. The Cambodians appeared determined to drive the Vietnamese fishermen out of the waters near the island. Many—500 according to Hanoi—have been captured. None, according to the refugees, has been released.

As part of the programme to take control of all territories previously occupied by the Republic of Vietnam, Hanoi's forces took over the island of Puolo Way, which is nearly a hundred miles south-southwest of Phu Quoc. While they were thus engaged, the Cambodians seized Tho Chu, about thirty miles south-southeast of Puolo Way. All along the border from Ha Tien to Tay Ninh, Cambodian forces crossed into Vietnamese territory.

xii

The Vietnamese who had never abandoned some of their wartime sanctuaries in Cambodia, responded in kind, shelling and strafing the border areas and moving more deeply into the Cambodian provinces of Ratanakiri and Mondolkiri. 'In truth', said the Cambodian government in a statement released in Phnom Penh on December 30, 1977, 'these territories belong to Cambodia and were sanctuaries begged [by Hanoi] as refuge on Cambodian soil from 1965 to 1975 when they had nowhere to stay as refugees from South Vietnam at that time. This is their ungrateful nature'.

Attempts to settle the differences between the two countries by negotiation began in May, 1976, with a preparatory meeting in Phnom Penh. The meeting was broken off at Cambodia's request after it had been agreed that both sides would set up liaison committees to investigate and settle disputes when they occurred. The full-scale conference between the two countries did not materialize. The Cambodians suspected the Vietnamese of plotting against them through their agents in the Kampuchea (Cambodian) Communist Party. Early in 1977 Pol Pot, the secretary of the Cambodian Communist Party, and the Politburo began a massive purge of those suspected to be working secretly with the Vietnamese. At the same time, Cambodian forces stepped up their attacks on the Vietnam border and their harassing raids on the off-shore islands.

So little is known of the Cambodian leadership that it is impossible to identify those who have been purged as a result of what Phnom Penh describes as an attempted coup. The purge involved not only those in the higher echelons of the party leadership but provincial and district leaders and all ranks of the army.

Relations with Vietnam deteriorated to the point almost of open war in April, 1977, when the Cambodians thrust deeply into Vietnam from the Parrot's Beak, following the Phnom Penh-Saigon road as far as Trang Bang, which is almost one third of the way to Saigon.

Here, the Cambodians behaved in the same sort of ruthless way that characterized their forays across the Thai border and in dealing with all those who had been associated with the Lon Nol regime. They simply killed everyone they came across, men, women and children. A flood of refugees, from the region, headed toward Saigon, carrying with them the stories of the atrocities.

The Vietnamese immediately reinforced the border area. Through Cu Chi, Molotova trucks carrying troops and supplies, T54 tanks, and artillery passed in constant succession. From July through the end of October, the sound of heavy artillery could be heard day and night in Cu Chi, and ambulances carrying the wounded back to the hospital was a daily sight.

Refugees in Australia speak with first-hand authority only of events to the end of October, 1977. They claim to have later reports from refugees who have not reached Australia of heavy fighting in November. If their scarcely credible accounts can be believed, the Cambodian Air Force, using MIG17s and MIG19s, together with naval forces repeatedly attacked Phu Quoc, which had been reinforced with a division of troops. If these reports are true, the MIGs can have come only from China or North Korea, both of which have been supplying weapons to the Cambodians. Pyongyang was the first capital to send an aid mission to Phnom Penh after the end of the war in 1975, and North Korean small arms have been turning up among the captured weapons following Cambodian incursions across the Thai border.

Oil in particular and the continental shelf in general are the causes of the trouble in the off-shore islands. The Thieu government divided the off-shore areas into forty separate leases and put some of them up for auction in 1973 and again in 1974. Drilling began in August, 1974, and quickly resulted in the discovery of oil in what was regarded as encouraging commercial quantities. One well was estimated as having the capacity to yield 1500 barrels of oil and 58 million cubic feet of natural gas per day.

The first strike occurred east of the southern tip of South Vietnam, but the potential around the three islands, over which Vietnam and Cambodia have since been warring, was also regarded as encouraging.

Vietnamese land grabbing appears to have been the cause for the border fighting, or this, plus the natural animosity that exists between the Vietnamese and Cambodian people, and the unwillingness of the Khmer Rouge to accept the primacy of the Communist Party of Vietnam. Laos has become an obedient satellite; Cambodia has turned to China. These were matters that could have been conveniently left for time to resolve if the Vietnamese had not established a sort of tenancy claim to the areas they occupied inside the Cambodian border during the Vietnam War. It was their refusal to vacate these areas that led to Lon Nol's singularly unwise ultimatum to Hanoi in March, 1970: Leave the sanctuaries, or we will push you out. No one ever learns the lessons of history, it seems, and the Khmer Rouge leadership, though it did not issue an ultimatum, tried to push the Vietnamese out by sheer force when the negotiations in Phnom Penh ground to a halt. The effort was bound to fail, just as Lon Nol was bound to fail in 1970.

xiv

Three months after the Cambodians had taken the military initiative along the border in 1977, General Vo Nguyen Giap visited the area to complete his battle plan. According to the Cambodians, he threw six of his twenty-five divisions into the action. Whatever the force, it was sufficient to throw back Cambodian forces along the border. If it had followed up and captured Neak Luong, Phnom Penh would have been Hanoi's for the asking—if it wanted to strain its relations still further with China.

The likely outcome is that Vietnam will use the threat of its military strength to force a political accommodation. Inevitably, if slowly, Cambodia will shift into the Vietnam orbit.

Laos is already installed within the orbit. In the middle of 1977, Vietnam signed a treaty of friendship and cooperation with Laos. The effect was to turn the former kingdom into a de facto satellite of Vietnam. By the end of the year, Vietnamese forces in Laos had been reinforced and had begun extensive mopping up operations against the remnants of the Meo forces, once financed by the c.i.a. Thousands of Meo refugees fled across the Mekong to swell the numbers in the over-stretched camps in Thailand.

Thailand, with yet another change of government, is doing its best to bend with the breeze, but, in the longer term, all of Bangkok's current efforts to establish a *modus vivendi* with Hanoi will not put an end to Vietnam's aid for the Thai insurgency. Hanoi is frank enough to admit that one of the reasons why it wants the policies of the three Indo-China states coordinated is because of the importance to the 'revolutionary interest of South-East Asia'. This is an expression that needs no explanation.

So much for the zone of peace in South-East Asia. So much for the illusion of stability in the region. Every new development heightens the danger of serious confrontation between the Soviet Union and China in the region. There is at least an element of truth in the claim that the Soviet Union and China are fighting on the Vietnamese-Cambodian border through proxies. The Malayan Communist Party owes allegiance to Peking, and looks to it for ideological guidance and propaganda aid. The Burmese Communist Party wants—and receives—Chinese hardware. Peking keeps the remnants of the Indonesian Communist Party alive. There are interesting dilemmas to be resolved here in the years ahead.

It would be unwise to assume that there will be no more Vietnams, in South-East Asia and beyond, however improbable it may be that the United States will be directly involved. The Vietnamese have gone far beyond the theories they borrowed from Mao Tse-Tung. They have perfected the principles of protracted war against the world's most powerful nation. This is their contribution, and it is a great one, to world revolution. Deeply conscious of what they call their 'internationalist obligations', the Vietnamese, though beset with problems of unification, control, the restoration of war damage, growing enough food, coping with the Cambodians and helping the Lao to crush the Meo tribesmen, are also willing to share their knowledge.

I have written this book for several reasons, not the least being that since the first and second Indo-China wars occupied my professional attention for more than a quarter of a century, I feel impelled to tell it as I saw it and knew it. At the same time, the book leans heavily on General Van Tien Dung's own extremely frank and detailed account of the final North Vietnamese offensive. There was much more to the war, of course, than that last offensive, and to ignore what went before it, and all the other factors involved, would be to distort and oversimplify. At the same time, I have not attempted to write a history of the war. I pity any historian trying to find a way through the clouds of obfuscation. In giving the background, I have drawn on my own extensive records of the war, including my previous writings. In essence, I have tried to write an often quite personal account of happenings, some of them strange, some perhaps even incredible, but all of them in their own way part of Hanoi's ultimate victory. I have gone through my notebooks, dog-eared, worn and hard to read, that contain one man's Indo-China observations, using incidents and anecdotes drawn from a thousand sources.

Denis Warner
January 1978

Part one

The beginning of the end

---

*1 January 1975
to 31 March 1975*

1. General Dung's beautiful road to war

It was just after five o'clock in the afternoon of 5 February, 1975. I was running late for an appointment with an old friend at the Continental-Palace Hotel in Saigon. The streets were choked with motor scooters, cyclos and cars, and my taxi, a rickety little Renault almost as old as the war itself, had been caught in the noisy hot smog of the traffic jam.

Outside the hotel the usual street urchins, prostitutes, crippled war veterans, shoeshine boys, drivers of hire cars, vendors of books and paintings, beggars and the giggling pair of endlessly cheerful and ferociously successful girls, hawking their garlands of wild jasmine, were waiting in ambush. 'You buy, you buy now', said the elder flower girl. 'Later', I said. 'No, now', echoed the younger. 'You buy from me now. You always buy from other girl.' It was a pantomime we played every day, the preliminary skirmishing that always led to my ultimate capitulation.

Tet, the lunar New Year, was approaching with all its festivities, and when I escaped into the lobby garlanded with the inevitable flowers, it was crowded, as it had been for days at this hour, with wedding guests going to the little interior garden with its frangipani petals, thatched shelters, potted palms and turquoise-coloured china elephants. In three weeks I had seen more wedding receptions at the Continental, one of Asia's best and most lovable masterpieces of colonial discomfort and absolute charm, than I remembered in all the twenty-five years I had stayed there. Haunted by the ghosts of thirty years of war, and

3

raped by the raffish throng outside who preyed on the weakness of the flesh, or the softness of the heart, of its clients, the hotel had unforgettable character. It also had an ageless, unchanging, splendid and abominably treated staff, one of whom, a Chinese from Hainan Island, had been there since 1917. Most of the others were not much his junior.

The hotel was always full in times of crisis, but somehow portly Monsieur Loi, bowing from the waist, could always find just one more room for an old friend, even if it meant throwing someone out. Number 32, with its eighteen-foot high ceiling, a vast expanse of tiled floor, a springless double bed with a mattress filled with flint, cane chairs, yellow walls, enough heavy French wardrobes to accommodate the accoutrement of a battalion of guests and a bathroom partitioned off with its bidet, an immense porcelain jar of cold water, and cockroaches of unparalleled dimensions, was mine.

The room was cooled by a large ceiling fan that could be made to whirl like the propeller of an aeroplane, and an overworked air conditioner, whose wheezing in the hotel's more recent years had made unnecessary the acres of mosquito netting that once hung from a grappling hook above the bed. It looked out on the National Assembly building, and the open square in front where, in their time, rockets, mortars, grenades, rifles and machine guns had all exploded without damaging either the Continental, or the curiously detached way of life that went on behind its walls.

I pushed through the wedding guests clustered in the lobby–the young men with sleeked hair and dark suits who had somehow dodged the draft and the slender girls in their diaphanous *ao dais*, the most discreetly seductive garment ever worn by women–apologized for my late arrival and remarked on the number of weddings. My friend, a noted astrologer, said the young were seeking whatever good fortune was left in the Year of the Tiger, making their nuptial vows before the Year of the Cat. 'It is natural', he said. 'The tiger is the king of the forest. The cat is sly and untrustworthy.'

Not much luck was left in the Tiger for the Republic of Vietnam, and Senior General Van Tien Dung, Chief of Staff of the People's Army of North Vietnam, the man who was to ensure the untrustworthiness of the Cat, was at that very moment making his way upstream along the Ben Hai River, once the dividing line between North and South Vietnam, with the plans that would soon bring the war to its climax and Saigon to the austerities and discipline of Communist rule.

It was just two years since the Paris Agreement had theoretically brought the war to an end. The two years had seen the pendulum swing wildly to the disadvantage of South Vietnam. Saigon had been desper-

4

ately unhappy about some of the terms of the agreement. President Nguyen Van Thieu had rejected one draft, presented almost as a *fait accompli* by Dr Henry Kissinger in Saigon in October 1972, and thereafter had hammered out what he and his advisers hoped would be watertight assurances from President Nixon. The exchange was not merely by cable but also by several letters. 'What happens if we are attacked?' Thieu asked. 'We will have no defence at all.' Nixon replied by letter that if the North Vietnamese attacked, the United States would respond vigorously and immediately. There were also assurances of continuing and substantial military and economic aid.

Tran Van Lam, then South Vietnam's foreign minister, was in Paris at the beginning of January 1973, when the North, after twelve days of heavy American bombing, indicated that it was willing to resume serious negotiations again. He was instructed to see Dr Kissinger to discuss two major points of concern. The first was the provision of a clause in the agreement to prevent the North Vietnamese from using Laos and Cambodia as bases from which to attack South Vietnam.

'Laos and Cambodia can't stop them', Lam said to Kissinger. 'The United States with B52s couldn't stop them. How can we stop them? They will just go on infiltrating. We would like to have a guarantee that this will not happen.'

Dr Kissinger took a paper from his brief case and showed it to Lam. It was a record of conversation between Kissinger and Le Duc Tho, Hanoi's negotiator. It contained Tho's firm assurance that fifteen days after the agreement was signed the North Vietnamese would withdraw from Laos and Cambodia and stop infiltrating into South Vietnam.

'They won't attack you through the 17th parallel', Dr Kissinger said. 'You've got plenty of strength to hold them there. There is nothing to worry about. If they attack you, we will react.'

Lam asked for confirmation of this in writing.

Kissinger agreed, and it was duly given in another Nixon letter.

Saigon's second concern was that although South Vietnam had been restricted by the terms of the contemplated agreement to replacing its arms on a one-for-one basis if weapons became worn out or lost and ammunition was expended, no restrictions of any sort were contemplated for North Vietnam.

'Don't worry', Kissinger told Lam, 'I have a deal with the Soviet Union and China. From now on they will stop supplying all offensive arms to North Vietnam.'

Kissinger said that he had been to both Peking and Moscow to arrange this and he had firm assurances from those two powers that the flow of offensive weapons would stop.

5

Presented with this good news, Lam cabled Saigon and was told to go ahead and sign the agreement. He did so with many reservations. He regarded Dr Kissinger as a very clever man, and also as a very clever liar. He simply did not believe that Hanoi had suddenly abandoned its *guerre sacrée*, as Prime Minister Pham Van Dong called it. Fighting and negotiating were both part of Hanoi's plan. Both had the same goal: victory. But he also knew that the United States wanted out, and that nothing South Vietnam could do would prevent its ally from turning its attention to other affairs.

Thieu and the military hierarchy in South Vietnam read into the American assurances flights of B52s winging their way back to the battlefields to save the situation for Saigon as they had saved it before against the Communist Easter offensive in 1972. Lam knew that the bombers had gone for ever, and he urged on Thieu the need for political initiatives instead of continuing military confrontation. Thieu spurned the advice, although for years, in fact until the moment he resigned, he authorized a continuing secret dialogue with a man representing the Southern Communists in the National Liberation Front. On the South Vietnamese side, the discussions were entrusted to General Tran Van Don, onetime commander-in-chief of the Vietnamese armed forces, Senator, a leader in the coup that overthrew Ngo Dinh Diem and, in the last Thieu-appointed government, minister of defence.

Don was good looking, gregarious and, in his days as commanding general of I and II Corps, a leader with real charisma. Born in France in August 1917, the son of a Vietnamese physician serving in the French Army, he helped defend a French Army cavalry school against the attacking Germans, and was promoted to the grade of reserve officer candidate in the French Army. After the Second World War, he attended the General Staff School of the Ecole Supérieure de Guerre in Paris, France's most advanced military school. Back in Vietnam, he rose quickly in the newly-formed Vietnamese Army. Although always regarded with some suspicion by Diem because of his French background and associations, he continued to serve him loyally until 1962 when, along with many others, he became disenchanted.

As early as 1970, Don, long since retired from the Army, felt it was wise to establish some sort of bridge with the National Liberation Front. When the opportunity presented itself, he sought French advice and was told he ought to go ahead. He also cleared his activities with Thieu, who, though he approved, did not take the discussions very seriously. Because the Front contact is still in Vietnam and holds an official post in reunified Vietnam, I have been asked not to mention his name.

I met him for the first time with Don at lunch at the My Canh Floating Restaurant in Saigon in October 1973. I was aware of his connections with the Front at that time, and was still in touch with him just before the fall of Saigon. For the purposes of this work he is identified by the alias 'Nguyen Van Tri'.

In 1971 'Nguyen Van Tri' proposed that an intermediary should be sent to Hanoi to negotiate a peace settlement, bypassing the negotiations that were then dragging on in Paris. The proposal was passed on to the American Embassy and Thieu. Nothing came of it.

Late in 1972, when the Paris peace talks were at a critical stage, he suggested the partition of Vietnam, with Thieu controlling all areas south of Quang Ngai and the National Liberation Front (not Hanoi) the northern part of South Vietnam. Again there was no response.

My first meeting with Don and 'Nguyen Van Tri' came just before the first, and subsequently aborted, Paris Agreement. Don had come to the lunch with a brief case containing, among other things, the horoscopes of all the principal Vietnamese leaders, and an overlay map of the real situation on the ground in South Vietnam. My eyes popped. In the areas conceded to the North Vietnamese it differed fundamentally from the maps officially recognized by the government.

'I must have a copy of that', I said.

'You can't', Don replied. 'It's top secret.'

But, later in the day, he relented. After all, if the NLF had seen it, it could scarcely remain top secret and, in Don's presence, I copied it at the house of a mutual friend.

At the time of the ceasefire agreement in 1973, 'Nguyen Van Tri' again proposed partition, this time claiming a much larger area. Again, the proposals were put to the U.S. through Don's contacts with the C.I.A., and to Thieu. Again there was no response.

When the Paris Agreement came into force, there was not even one hour of peace. With the assured expectation that American military and economic aid would continue at a level sufficiently high to replace losses and worn out equipment on the one-for-one basis permitted by the agreement, the South Vietnamese took an eye for an eye in the early exchanges. The Viet Cong had hoisted the flag in 350 contested hamlets. The South Vietnamese tore them down. They won the battle of the flags. It was their last victory.

For a time, however, they seemed to have it made. This was the view of the Hungarian and Polish members of the International Commission for Control and Supervision set up under the Paris Agreement with the impossible, and never seriously attempted, task of keeping the antagonists apart. In anticipation of continuing American military aid for South Vietnam, they made no secret that they thought the North would be wise to abandon its attempts to win by force of arms and to work for a political solution based on the Paris Agreement. This was the advice they continued to offer Hanoi long after the old guard revolutionaries there had decided to revert to all-out war. For in October 1973, less than nine months after solemnly signing the Paris Agreement, the Central Committee of the Laodong (Workers) Party of North Vietnam, on the recommendation of its eleven-man Politburo, had decided that South Vietnam should be taken by armed force. Thereafter, all plans were directed to that end. The first and second Indo-China wars were over. The third was in the making.

By February 1975, the official optimism that had been so widespread in Saigon a year before, and only relatively muted by December 1974, had turned into bleak pessimism. With the crunch coming, the Americans, coldly and calmly, under irresistible pressure from the Democratic liberal left wing in Congress were walking away from the Nixon commitment. In 1972-73 the South Vietnamese received $2,167 million in military aid from the United States. In 1973-74 this was cut to $964 million. In 1974-75, when Soviet aid to North Vietnam quadrupled, the South got only $700 million from an unsympathetic Congress, which removed $900 million from the figure recommended by the American Embassy in Saigon as the irreducible minimum. (The quadrupling of petroleum costs after the 1973 Arab-Israeli war and similar inflationary rises in the cost of military material caused, in real terms, a cut of 80 per cent in American military aid.) Almost as damaging as the cuts in aid were the increases in local costs that followed the escalation in the price of oil after the Arab-Israeli War in 1973. Even if there was no major North Vietnamese offensive, it was obvious by the beginning of February 1975 that South Vietnam could no longer hope to hold vast stretches of territory where small and isolated garrisons continued to fly the flag.

Realizing belatedly that military disaster lay ahead if the war continued without American military and economic aid in substantial quantities, Saigon had proposed the creation of four committees to study the special issues which were essential to a permanent settlement: the setting up of the National Council for Reconciliation and Concord, as required by the Paris Agreement; the assuring of democratic liberties; the reduction of armed forces; and the organization of general elections in July 1974. There was no answering call. Captured documents setting out the general goals of the North Vietnamese in the 1975 campaigning season exuded optimism. 'The current contest of strength between us and the enemy . . . . is highly favourable to our side and greatly disadvantageous to the enemy', said Directive 08 from COSVN, the Central Office for South Vietnam, as Hanoi's southern command post was called. The directive was now being read and re-read by the General Staff in Saigon. In December the appreciation of the enemy's intention was that only fairly limited attacks were in the offing. Now there were much deeper apprehensions. For years Hanoi had maintained the fiction that its troops were not fighting in the South, that the war there was purely a civil war between the indigenous Viet Cong and the 'puppet' government in Saigon. All pretence was now abandoned. The North Vietnamese were now described as the 'fulcrum of the effort'.

Late in 1974 the American Embassy also learned from what were regarded as impeccable intelligence sources that the Soviet Union had advised the North Vietnamese to 'go for broke' before South Vietnam used its gold reserves to buy arms from sources other than the United States. Support for honouring the American commitment to South Vietnam had been irretrievably eroded in Congress, the Russians said.

Morale in South Vietnam had also eroded almost beyond the point of no recall as troops found themselves short of ammunition, spare parts, or the gasoline to move all the vehicles they had inherited from the road-bound American military system. It was always a good indicator of the war to measure the ratio of weapons lost to captured. A year earlier the ratio had been two to one in the government's favour. Now the ratio had been reversed. Helicopter missions had dropped from 16,000 a month to about 3,000 because of the lack of spare parts and the gasoline ration. A quarter of the armed forces were non-existent phantoms, there in name, rank and serial number and useful only as a source of food and pay that could be distributed, not always fairly, among the others so that they might manage the better to feed and clothe their families. Intelligence estimates were that the North Vietnamese had accumulated enough supplies to maintain an all-out offensive for at least twelve months. They had so many supplies, in fact, that they no longer bothered to conceal their vast dumps. These were well protected by anti-aircraft guns but, in any event, the fixed-wing aircraft of the Vietnamese Air Force, like the helicopters, had had their flying schedules so drastically reduced that you could drive for hundreds of miles through the countryside without ever seeing a plane overhead.*

Government ground patrols were still cautiously pushing their way

---

*Even in its hey-day, the Vietnamese Air Force was never more than a light-weight, short range, ground attack force. At no time did it have the capacity adequately to interdict the convoys of trucks on the invasion routes because it had neither the range nor the fire power to do it.

into territory controlled by the North Vietnamese. Their reports were sensational. The Ho Chi Minh 'trail' had been paved with a mixture of limestone and packed dirt, and was now a myriad of all-weather roads along which thousands of trucks were pouring men and supplies into the South. An oil pipeline ran for more than 600 miles from Vinh in North Vietnam to Loc Ninh, eighty miles from Saigon, to fuel the tanks and trucks now using the thousands of miles of strategic roads either built by, or under the control of, the North Vietnamese in the South.

Down in the Mekong Delta, a government battalion was destroyed almost in its entirety when it ran out of ammunition. For the first time North Vietnamese tanks had moved out of the Cambodian sanctuaries into the Delta. The vital brown water fleet was tied up for lack of spare parts and money and once again, as they had been in 1962, 1965 and 1967, the rivers and the canals of the Delta were in Communist hands. Villages under Communist control were cheek by jowl with villages where the government flag still flew.

In Central Vietnam, artillery batteries that once used to fire a hundred rounds a day were sometimes rationed to four. There were reports, credible reports, of helicopter pilots who refused to fly medivac missions unless the wounded paid. And the artillery sometimes demanded cash from the infantry to pay for supporting fire.

This was the scene on the eve of the Year of the Cat. With or without weddings, or a new Communist offensive, it was going to be a frugal and an anxious Tet, though Saigon did its best to go about its business and pleasures without paying too much attention tò the war. Free-spending Americans had brought undreamed of prosperity to many Vietnamese in the late 1960s and early 1970s. They created a way of life built around their wealth. Like a balloon, it was easily inflated and even more easily burst. The u.s. withdrawal threw hundreds of thousands out of work. Indirectly, almost everyone was affected. A million new jobs were needed to provide full employment, and those lucky enough to be employed were struggling against inflation that defied control. Not for years had there been less money to spend, and Tet demanded lots of money, not just for the celebration of the national holiday and everyone's birthday, but to buy flowers and plants and new clothes and good food and to pay debts and homage to ancestors and to visit family and friends.

Apart from its impact on the fighting capacity of the armed forces, the energy crisis had precipitated crippling increases in the price of fertilizer, gasoline and even electricity. Every town needed its own oil-generated supply, for although there were excellent hydro-electric generators in the mountains, they were of no use. The Viet

Cong habitually blew down the transmission poles. What the government built, the Viet Cong destroyed—bridges, schools, clinics, and water and power plants.

Peasants, once encouraged by the Americans to use tractors and rotary hoes to work their fields, found they could no longer afford to run their machines. Along the coast of Central Vietnam even the fishermen were hungry. It cost them more each day to run their boats on gasoline or diesel oil than they received for their catch. Corruption had not just become a way of life but a necessity to live. The senior officer in charge of the 35,000 regional forces in Central Vietnam was married with nine children to support on a monthly salary of $50. 'What can I do?' he asked, making a gesture of despair with his hands.

A million refugees 'generated', that awful word, by the 1972 Communist Easter offensive had been moved out of the squalor and moral degradation of the camps and given new building materials, plots of land, seeds and hope. But there was often not much hope. 'I begin to despair that we will ever conquer, for no one seems willing to pay the price', lamented a rural social worker. 'For a people who are scratching the surface to keep alive, there is a strange softness of spirit. Unlike the Spartans of old, they nurture their children on softness and they are ill-fitted to come into the terrible world in which they must live. The American USAID is a strange monolith. It pours in millions, but I never received any of this help beyond an occasional Coca-Cola, or some minor thing. I am beginning to believe God chastises not only the ones he loves, but beachcombers like me.'

To many people God was synonymous with Uncle Sam. They clung to their belief in him like the followers of the cargo cult in New Guinea. He had too much to lose not to intervene, they said. When the moment was right, the B52 bombers would be there. All would be well.

But all was not well. Early in January, the province of Phuoc Long, only a hundred miles north of Saigon, had fallen to two North Vietnamese regiments armed with tanks and the very long range, and even harder hitting, 130-millimetre guns. In area, Phuoc Long was one of the biggest provinces in Vietnam, but its population of about 40,000 was the smallest. The provincial capital of Phuoc Binh was an overgrown village of about 20,000. The district capitals were tiny and life generally was hard for the Vietnamese and the montagnards who lived there. Strategically, the province was significant because its denial to government forces dispensed with any threat to the new North Vietnamese road system in Military Region 3 and facilitated the movement of troops and supplies for an eventual attack on Saigon. The government, already heavily over-extended, was not willing to pay the price to take back Phuoc Long, hoping in vain that its fall would soften Congressional hearts in Washington when they appreciated that for the first time a province had been lost in its entirety. But Saigon had cried 'wolf' too often and its own failure to react simply reinforced the views of those who believed the South Vietnamese would not fight whatever aid they received.

Even closer to Saigon, the provincial capital of Tay Ninh, a comfortable sixty miles away along a flat black-capped highway, was under daily rocket and artillery attack. The heavily bunkered and sandbagged provincial headquarters in the centre of the town of some 30,000 inhabitants, and the American compound towards the outskirts were the principal targets, but neither the shells nor the rockets had eyes and most of the inhabitants had fled to Saigon.

I drove there one day with Bob Tamarkin, a young *Chicago Daily News* correspondent making his first foray into the Vietnamese countryside, and Paul Burnard, the son of the Australian military attaché in Saigon. We had to clear the debris from the road before the car could get through, a task we might not have attempted at all if we had known that the shells which had scattered it in our path had only just preceded our arrival.

Outside the city in the Cao Dai temple, it was business as usual. The Seeing Eye, the symbol of the faith that blends Catholicism, Buddhism, Confucianism, ancestor worship and spiritualism, discreetly looked away from Black Virgin Mountain, which rises like a pyramid from the flat fields of rice and vegetables just a couple of miles to the north. The mountain had fallen and it was taken as an ill omen that pilgrims could no longer approach the shrine of the Black Virgin who, centuries before, had jumped off the peak to save herself from a predatory mandarin.

Battered, smoking and rumbling with the sound of artillery and mortar fire that threatened to drown the chants of the colourful collection of archbishops (of both sexes), bishops, priests and acolytes who were praying among the dragon-entwined pillars of the Holy See, the mountain was to prove beyond the army's capacity to recover. In their best days, the Americans maintained only a precarious foothold on top, and they frequently pulled off and brought in the B52s to drench the slopes with bombs. It worked for a time, but what the B52s could do then, the emasculated Vietnamese Air Force could not do now.

A Washington mission had arrived in Saigon to report on prospects. One of its members, an old Vietnam hand, heard I was in town and came by the Continental to let me know how they had assessed the situation. A political accommodation now was the only hope, he said.

An increasing number of people, including the Prime Minister, Tran Thien Khiem, were ready to settle for something like a Laotian solution, or the Vietnam equivalent thereof.

By the side of a crystal-clear swimming pool in a white painted villa not far from the presidential palace, the contingency solution had been worked out several months before. Its author was one of the more remarkable of the men who lived in the shadows of the Vietnam War–Ted Serong, a retired brigadier, onetime commander of the Australian Army Training Team in Vietnam, subsequently employed by the Central Intelligence Agency to set up a police field force, later a RAND consultant, and now an independent adviser to the government of Vietnam. He met with a small group of senior Vietnamese officials to think the unthinkable. What they thought was that South Vietnam should abandon the Highlands and Central Vietnam in an effort, by negotiation preferably, but, if not, by force of arms, to hold the rest. Serong was brave, brilliant, patronizing and well informed, with a matching ego. His latest report had been sent to the government. 'I would propose', he wrote, 'that Vietnam set for itself a deadline on which to base the timing of the major strategic decision–14 February 1975, two weeks from now. If by that date $300 million is not granted [the sum urgently being sought from the u.s. Congress], or is only partly granted, or is tied to unworkable strings, implement the decision to amputate Military Region 1' [Central Vietnam]. ($300 million was the balance of the aid that had been appropriated by Congress but not yet authorized for expenditure.)

Serong recommended the abandonment of Hue and Danang and much else besides, including most of the Central Highlands. He envisaged it both as a military operation designed to shorten lines and as a basis for new negotiations. Seven of the government's thirteen divisions of main force troops were defending one-sixth of the population, and an unproductive one-sixth at that, he said. The strength of the North Vietnamese, either in the two northern military regions, or immediately available in Laos, or North Vietnam, was so disproportionately high as to make the area indefendible unless adequate ammunition supplies were ensured. They were not.

Negotiations for the southern boundary, he believed, should be based on an initial offer by the government of Vietnam on the 15th parallel, just south of Quang Ngai city. If that was unacceptable, and there was little likelihood that it would be, the government should be prepared to negotiate back as far as the 13th parallel, just north of Ban Me Thuot, a line that would have cut South Vietnam into two almost equal parts. An interesting, and extremely important, part of the

Serong plan was that the deal for switching territory should be made with the Provisional Revolutionary Government, and not with Hanoi, a concept that ended ironically whatever chance the South may have had for a twilight period of independent existence before being taken over by the North. One of the reasons for Hanoi's accelerated offensive after the fall of the Highlands was to avoid becoming involved with negotiations that would, of necessity, have resulted in a role of some substance for the Provisional Revolutionary Government.

Long before 5 February the government in Saigon had drawn up contingency plans to abandon Military Region 1 and Military Region 2, which embraced Central Vietnam and the Highlands, but the timing and the method had yet to be resolved. Thieu was very much his own commander-in-chief, and the Joint General Staff had been emasculated to the point where it lacked the machinery to undertake the sort of planning necessary in an operation such as this and had been given no instruction by Thieu to take the matter in hand. There was also a natural reluctance on the part of Thieu to give the Provisional Revolutionary Government, much less North Vietnam, something for nothing. Clutching at straws, Thieu had delayed making a move, well aware of the traumatic political consequences the abandonment of so many people and so much territory would have on the rest of Vietnam.

Toward noon on 5 February, however, it became apparent that Saigon would soon have to take into consideration another highly damaging factor. Up the Saigon River to berth at the end of the rue Catinat, or Tu Do as it was called after the French departure, half a dozen blocks from the Hotel Continental, came the tugboats *Geronimo* and *Wolverine*, two survivors of four that had tried to run the blockade down the Mekong River from Phnom Penh, the embattled capital of Cambodia, after delivering supplies there. The tugs looked as if Humphrey Bogart and Katharine Hepburn were sure to be aboard. Though dressed with sandbags, the tugs were both full of holes. Rockets, mortars and 50-calibre bullets had blasted through almost every cabin and passageway. 'I wouldn't go back up that river if the Holy Father himself offered me a place next to him in Heaven', said *Geronimo's* captain, a Filipino, who did, indeed, look a bit like Bogart. His was a unanimous view, I found. Phnom Penh and the troops now fighting desperately in its defence would have to depend on the airport at Pochentong, just outside the city, for all their needs. The end in Cambodia was clearly very near, and this could only compound South Vietnam's awful problems.

All of this was well known to Senior General Van Tien Dung when he made his way to Gialam airport outside Hanoi on the morning of 5 February. Dung was now fifty-seven, four years younger than General

Vo Nguyen Giap, the Defence Minister and Commander-in-Chief, and younger by a substantially greater margin than all the other ten members of the Politburo of the Laodong Party which he had joined in mid-1972. Many years before, Dung had distinguished himself for the brilliance of his military planning at Dien Bien Phu, and for having arranged the establishment of the arms caches used by the Viet Cong when, in 1959, they began the war in the South. Now, on the eve of the last and greatest offensive against South Vietnam, he had not only supervised the planning and the vast movement of men and supplies to the South, he was also going to the field to take personal command.

The truism that great soldiers are born, not made, would not be denied by Dung. He had little formal education. While still in his teens, he worked in a textile factory in Hanoi. There, at the age of twenty, he joined the Indo-Chinese Communist Party. The French threw him into prison in 1939. He stayed there until 1944, when he escaped to join Ho Chi Minh in the mountainous Viet Bac region on the Vietnam-China border. He was just in time to join the fight against the 'terror campaign' then being carried out by the French with the intention of wiping out Ho Chi Minh's still very small band.

Dung attracted attention by his work in one of the anti-terror volunteer committees and his rise in the fledgling Communist army was meteoric. In 1946 he became head of the Military Political Department, a post of great importance, though the Army itself was still little more than a loose collection of guerrilla units. When the 320th Division was formed he took command and led the division in some of its more spectacular operations against the French in the Red River Delta. In 1953, at the age of thirty-six, he became Chief of Staff and second only to Giap.

I saw him for the first time at Trung Gia, outside the northern French defence line in Tongking on 4 July 1954, when he led the Viet Minh ceasefire delegation to negotiations with the French. He was small, stony-faced and very much the victor when he entered the long bamboo-matting and corrugated iron conference hut decorated with French parachutes captured at Dien Bien Phu. Dung stretched out his hand to greet Colonel Marcel Lannuyeux, the principal French delegate.

Confident, assured and dignified, Dung spoke about the 'eight years of patriotic war' and the 'enlightened leadership of Ho Chi Minh'. Colonel Lannuyeux thanked him for his remarks and talked of studying a concrete plan about 'how to remedy certain problems born of war'. Seven days later, in Geneva, the Indo-China War came to its end, and Dung moved to Saigon, where he led the North Vietnamese delegation with the International Control Commission. This had been set up under the Geneva Agreement to police the peace, a task far beyond its competence, especially with Dung actively making sure that weapons and ammunition would be available when the time came again to make war.

Now, nearly twenty-one years later, when he boarded his AN-24 plane in Hanoi precisely at 10.30 a.m. on 5 February, he was about to set in motion events that were to win the war in a shattering 51-day campaign. For more than a year Hanoi's war plans, aided and abetted by a well-orchestrated international psychological warfare campaign, had been in the making. 'Throughout the war there was no finer example of *dich van* (literally, action among the enemy or, more mundanely, psychological warfare) than the parade of America's self-proclaimed best and brightest making their guilt laden pilgrimage to Hanoi, the New Jerusalem of the New Left', wrote Douglas Pike in his unpublished Anatomy of Deceit. Now, in the place of actress Jane Fonda posing in a steel helmet beside the crew of a North Vietnamese Russian-built surface to air missile and describing American pilots as 'professional killers', or Ramsey Clark, former Attorney-General of the United States, who was 'particularly touched' by the hygienic conditions he found in prison camps (which were as bad and as brutal as those unfortunate Americans and others were imprisoned in during the Korean War), Bishop Thomas Gumbleton, of the Archdioecese of Detroit, fresh back from his pilgrimage to Hanoi, was making the running with a group of clerics who wanted Congress to veto any further aid to Vietnam. 'We must communicate to our leaders an urgent demand that this nation live up to its pledged word at Paris both by implementing its unkept promise and by ceasing current actions, such as massive military aid to the oppressive Thieu regime, a living denial of the pledged word', he argued.

Dr Colin Williams, dean of the Yale Divinity School, was among the thirty-five interfaith members who put their signature to the pastoral letter calling for a national assembly to advocate an end to American aid for Vietnam.

The clerics were treading an already established path. Just three months after the Politburo had decided to launch its full force against the South, Hanoi reported that Congressman Ronald Dellums, after a meeting with Jane Fonda and her husband, had declared he would urge the U.S. Congress to put an end to support for the Saigon administration.

The campaign was quickly orchestrated in Washington and around the world through the World Peace Council and its affiliates, including the Congress for International Co-operation and Disarmament in

Australia, under the presidency of the deputy prime minister, Dr J. F. Cairns. The Congress distributed a broadsheet, 'Vietnam: It's Still America's War' to members of parliament in Australia, and asked them to recognize the Provisional Revolutionary Government and to 'undergird the Paris Agreement by vigorous protest against the Thieu regime's callous and anti-democratic programme of repression and intimidation involving serious violations of the Paris Agreement'. The Congress also took a half page advertisement in the *Australian* newspaper to publish a petition containing hundreds of signatures condemning continued American military support in South Vietnam.

In its own way the international campaign to put a stop to the flow of aid to Saigon was as important as the endless flow of Russian ships unloading war materials in Haiphong for the new offensive. The world, grown weary of Vietnam, could no longer separate fact from fiction. Once it was an outcry against the American bombing of the dykes in North Vietnam. But, though much else was bombed, the dykes were not. Now it was Thieu's 'tyranny' and the charges, backed by Amnesty International, that the prisons in South Vietnam were filled with a hundred thousand, or even two hundred thousand, political prisoners. The island of Phu Quoc off the southern coast was said to be stuffed full of prisoners whose only offence was that they didn't like Thieu. On other business, I found my way there and saw evidence only of former prisoner of war camps fallen into decay because of disuse. There were no political prisoners on the island.

In a campaign of this sort, fact or fiction was immaterial. What Hanoi needed was a climate of international opinion, but especially American opinion, to ensure that the u.s. Congress did not rise in the defence of its ally when the guns started firing, and this was as good as any, though the total number of all prisoners, according to what seemed to be a fairly thorough u.s. Embassy investigation, totalled about 35,000. Of these no more than five hundred to a thousand were detained for political reasons. The Australian Embassy looked at the island of Con Son and found no evidence of the political prisoners who were said to be there.

By the time General Dung was ready to move into his offensive, however, international opinion had been conditioned to believe that the Thieu regime was tyrannical, oppressive and responsible for all major infringements of the Paris Agreement. The facts did not support the charges. The Thieu regime was illiberal, but it was also extraordinarily lax and ineffective. Far from being aggressive, it had been so seriously denied assistance from the United States that it was in many areas hopelessly over-stretched and incapable of defending itself.

17

For convenience in command, Hanoi during the Indo-China War and again in 1960 divided South Vietnam into four separate military regions. Nam Bo, the southern part of South Vietnam and neighbouring areas in Cambodia, came under control of COSVN, the Central Office for South Vietnam. Its headquarters were secret and mobile, sometimes in the western part of South Vietnam, sometimes in Cambodia. The Central Highlands were known as the B3 Front. Military Region 5 extended along the central coast and the Tri-Thien-Hue Military Region covered the extreme north of South Vietnam. Because of its distance from Hanoi, COSVN had a great deal of autonomy, although its leadership was always entrusted to a senior Party man from the North. The other regions came under Northern command, although their leaders occasionally sat on COSVN's current affairs committee and maintained close liaison. COSVN directives, cleared with Hanoi, applied to all areas of South Vietnam.

Early in 1974, just after Tet, Hanoi called in its leaders from COSVN and regional military commanders in the South for a meeting at 33 Pham Ngu Lao Street. Thirteen years before, Le Duan, the first secretary of the Laodong Party and head of the Politburo, the supreme decision-making authority, had made the initial decision to start the war in South Vietnam. Again, Le Duan and Le Duc Tho, who had so patiently negotiated the Paris Agreement with Dr Henry Kissinger to get the Americans out of the war and to pave the way for an ultimate military victory, sounded the call to colours.

The Central Military Party Committee, presided over by General Vo Nguyen Giap, translated the order into the planning stage. The decision necessitated a large increase in the North Vietnamese army from seventeen divisions to twenty-four and the movement of vast additional quantities of equipment from the North to the South. Let General Dung take up the story:

> Large mobile armies composed of various armed branches were needed to serve as powerful fists which could be used at the most important opportunities to operate along the main directions and carry out the main tasks with a view to destroying the enemy's regular forces. The Politburo and the Central Military Party committee agreed with this assessment and ordered that it was necessary immediately to organize mobile armies subordinate to the High Command. In 1974 army corps were gradually formed and deployed in strategic areas most vital to ensuring mobility. Along with organizing forces, another urgent task was to replace the army's equipment with good, modern equipment. Great quantities of material such as tanks, armored cars, missiles, long-range artillery pieces and anti-aircraft guns, which the U.S. imperialists had unsuccessfully sought to destroy during their twelve-day B52 blitz against the North, were gradually sent to the various battlefields. For the first time our

mechanized long-range artillery and good tanks made their way to the very rubber forests in Nam Bo.

As I have noted, vast road building operations had begun in the occupied areas of South Vietnam as soon as the Paris Agreement was signed in 1973. Throughout 1974 a much larger army went to work. Says Dung:

> Aided by thousands of vehicles and various types of machinery, tens of thousands of troops, workers, engineers, youth volunteers and civil labourers braved untold difficulties and hardships. . . working day and night to hack away at the mountains, broaden mountain passes, move rocks, build roads, lay slucies and build bridges. . . . This 8-metre wide, all-weather road permitted the two-way passage for rapidly moving large trucks and heavy military vehicles and was used night and day to transport hundreds of thousands of tons of materials of all types to insure powerful attacks.

A telegraph line connected Hanoi with the district capital of Loc Ninh, where new tank formations crouched to spring for the kill on Saigon, and with all the other battlefields. A vast recruiting campaign in the North emptied hamlets and villages of their youth.

Through all of this period the North Vietnamese forces gave the South no quarter. Much of their fighting in the past had been limited in scope and intention. The Northern field commanders were infinitely painstaking in their attention to detail and meticulous planning. This was essential in the sort of quasi-conventional, quasi-guerrilla war they had fought in the past, using regular, regional and local force units at the same time. They lacked experience in quick exploitation, and had proved themselves unable to co-ordinate infantry and armor. These, and the fallacious belief that the population would rise up to support them in a mass general uprising, were the fundamental weaknesses of the 1972 offensive. They had abandoned the tactics that had served well, but not decisively, in the past when the guerrilla and regional component of the effort was an essential part of the whole. They had now switched to full conventional war, with massive armoured columns, radar, missiles, heavy artillery and a highly-sophisticated communications network. The indigenous Communist forces were no longer required, or able, to play a primary role, or even a role of any real significance, since the local force units were now filled with recruits from the North.

For the coming offensive the North Vietnamese troops needed to sharpen themselves against the toughest Southern troops, to learn how to hold ground against a counter-offensive and how to attack again, quickly and without inhibition, improvising as circumstances dictated. They began in August 1974, with a tactical exercise against some of the best government forces in the remote district of Thuong Duc, guarding the approaches to Danang in Central Vietnam. 'We. paid special attention to the outcome of the battle which destroyed the district capital of Thuong Duc in the 5th Region', Dung wrote. 'This was a test of strength with the best of the enemy's forces. We destroyed the enemy forces defending the Thuong Duc district capital sub-sector. The enemy sent in a whole division of paratroopers to launch repeated and protracted counter-attacks in a bid to recapture the position, but we heavily decimated the enemy forces, firmly defending Thuong Duc and forcing the enemy to give up.'

Similar actions followed in rapid fire succession, now in Quang Ngai province, now in the Highlands. In the next six months the government lost ten district capitals to North Vietnamese forces engaged in tactical training for the big battles that lay ahead. Explained Dung: 'Evaluating the Thuong Duc and other annihilating battles against the enemy's main forces ... the General Staff reported to the Central Military Party Committee that the combat capability of our mobile main force troops was now altogether superior to that of the enemy's mobile regular troops, that the war had reached its final stage and that the balance of forces had changed in our favour'.

Incredulously, but with mounting satisfaction, Hanoi watched American aid to South Vietnam dry up. 'Nguyen Van Thieu was forced to fight a poor man's war', Dung exulted. 'Enemy firepower had decreased by nearly 60 per cent because of bomb and ammunition shortages. Its mobility was also reduced by half due to lack of aircraft, vehicles and fuel. Thus, the enemy had to shift from large-scale operations and heliborne deep-thrust mounted attacks to small-scale blocking, nibbling and searching operations.'

The North, on the other hand, was preparing to fight anything but a poor man's war. Russian aid continued to flow into North Vietnam in 1973 and 1974 in ever increasing quantities. A report dated 5 March 1975, drawn up by the Central Intelligence Agency, the Defence Intelligence Agency and concurred in by the Bureau of Intelligence and Research in the State Department, said bluntly: 'Total Communist military and economic aid to North Vietnam in 1974 was higher (in current dollars) than in any previous year; in 1974 the delivery of ammunition to Hanoi markedly increased over 1973 and reached a level as high as that of 1972 [the North Vietnamese Easter offensive]; North Vietnamese forces in South Vietnam, supported by record stockpiles of military supplies, are stronger today than they have ever been.'

By October 1974, the vast inflow of military assistance from the Soviet Union had reached a stage where the General Staff in Hanoi had been able to complete its strategic plan on the basis that enough military supplies were now available to sustain an all-out military offensive for two years, the anticipated length of time that the North Vietnamese military believed it might take to win the war. Only one really major question needed to be resolved: Would the United States send its troops back to the South when the North launched the offensive?

This was considered urgently and at length at a meeting of the Politburo and the Central Military Party Committee. Again, Le Duan, who more than any other man was responsible for the key decisions–including the decision to go to war in 1959, the Tet offensive in 1968 and the Easter offensive in 1972–shrewdly and presciently assessed the situation. 'Having already withdrawn from the South', he said, 'the United States could hardly jump back in and, no matter how it might intervene, it would be unable to save the Saigon administration from collapse.' His statement became a resolution and from this day forward Hanoi pushed ahead with its plan to win the war with overwhelming force.

A month later Don Luce, former International Volunteer Service worker in South Vietnam, and Bishop Gumbleton arrived in Hanoi and by their public statements reinforced the campaign in the United States against further aid for the Saigon government. In an emotional and bitter despatch to the State Department, Ambassador Graham Martin described the interfaith's statement following the Gumbleton-Luce visit to Hanoi as a 'tissue of lies from beginning to end', and said that 'its clear and obvious design is to intervene massively on behalf of North Vietnam. . . The memories of Pontius Pilate washing his hands are too fresh in our minds this Christmas season.'

The cable was heartfelt but scarcely diplomatic. To do battle with clerics you need to have a firm stance, and Martin's own credibility had already been eroded in Washington. Once again there was an unfortunate tendency within the Embassy to suppress bad news and to exaggerate good news. As consul-general in Can Tho, Wolfgang Lehmann, deputy chief of mission in Saigon, had misreported the news of the deterioration in the Delta. In Saigon, he was again overoptimistic. Washington could scarcely be blamed for its doubts.

Le Duan's resolution did not entirely preclude the possibility of American air intervention, and clearly it was desirable to insure in every practicable way against any disruption to the strategic plan. International pressure on the United States to end the bombing of North Vietnam at Christmas 1972, had been extremely helpful. All contingencies were being guarded against now.

Where to launch the offensive was also important. The Tet offensive in 1968 had alternative aims. It was a gamble based on the ideologically-inspired belief that the massive nation-wide onslaught coupled with a mass uprising could lead to victory at one stroke or, failing that, it was designed to deliver such a psychological blow that the United States would throw in the towel and negotiate its way out of the war. The North Vietnamese grossly over-estimated mass support in the South, and there was no mass uprising in support of the indigenous Southerners and supporting Northerners who fought their way into almost every city. Because of faltering and inept military leadership in Vietnam, the self-deceit the Americans had practised in assessing enemy strength and capabilities, and the strength of the anti-war movement in the United States, however, the offensive succeeded in persuading Washington to negotiate.

The Easter offensive in 1972 attempted a blitzkrieg offensive down through Quang Tri province to Hue and Danang, and east from Cambodia to An Loc and on to Saigon. Because of the Northerners' lack of experience, unpopularity, and the B52s, it failed.

At the beginning of 1975 the Saigon government was strongest in Military Region 1, around Hue and Danang, where it had deployed five divisions, including the superb 1st ARVN, the élite Marines and the Airborne, to discourage any overt invasion over the 17th parallel. It was weakest in the Central Highlands, where its two divisions were seriously over-extended.

Early in December 1974, Pham Hung, the COSVN secretary-general and fourth ranking member of the Politburo, and Tran Van Tra, then commanding the Northern forces in the South, arrived in Hanoi to discuss the plans with the General Staff. These deliberations led to another meeting of the Politburo. It began on 18 December and continued until 8 January 1975. While it was still in session, Hanoi floated its trial military balloon–the capture of Phuoc Long province. The United States made noises off, but it did not move. Two days later the Politburo meeting came to an end, highly encouraged by the Phuoc Long victory, and immensely gratified by Le Duan's correct prediction of the U.S. reaction. 'The world supports us', said Le Duan. 'Never before have the military and political conditions been more propitious.' It was decided to launch the offensive at the earliest possible date, that if need be it should last two years but that if opportunities presented themselves early or late, South Vietnam would be taken in 1975.

The final decision of where to launch the offensive had not yet been taken when the Politburo adjourned, although it was agreed that it should be in the Central Highlands, where heavy concentrations of North Vietnamese were now in place, outnumbering the Southern forces by more than two to one.

Next day the Central Military Party committee went into session and learned that the South Vietnamese had dispatched additional troops from the Highlands to reinforce Danang in Central Vietnam. Saigon, it was assumed, knew that an offensive was in the making but had erred grievously in thinking it would come immediately south of the former demilitarized zone. Le Duc Tho, the peacemaker, and Le Duan, the warmaker, joined the conference, and advocated that the first target of the offensive should be Ban Me Thuot, capital of Darlac Province, and headquarters for the 23rd Division of the Army of the Republic of Vietnam.

Ban Me Thuot is sleepy French tropical, with scarlet and green flame trees shading the streets and its clip-clopping mountain ponies from the sun. It stands on a vast flat expanse in the Central Highlands, and is surrounded by centuries-old jungles with scattered small concentrations of Rhade montagnard tribesmen. About 150 air miles north-east of Saigon, its economy depended on the coffee that grew under the trees and the banana plantations that had sprouted up around the town in recent years. The forest areas were kept as a game reserve. Despite the war, a plentiful number of tigers, panthers, leopards, elephants, antelopes and even, it was said, the occasional rhinoceros, had survived. There were so many panthers and leopards that the GIS used to keep the babies as pets, tying them up by bits of string. When stroked, they purred with deep and noisy content.

The Rhade lived in longhouses and did not care for the pushing Vietnamese who came crowding into their homeland after 1954. Under the French the whole area had been denied to the Vietnamese for resettlement. Bao Dai, the Chief of State and former emperor, liked to use the province for hunting. The Viet Minh were active during the Indo-China War among the Rhade, and after the Geneva Agreement in 1954 a Polish ship carried some tribesmen, including three of the four Rhade doctors, to North Vietnam.

Later, when Saigon began 'land grabbing', as the Rhade called it, relations between the tribesmen and Saigon grew bitter. Many turned to the Viet Cong–and were turned back again largely because of two Australians, Serong and a young Army captain, Barry Petersen.

Petersen, a member of Serong's first Australian Army Training Team in Vietnam, went to the Highlands first in 1963, and there, under the umbrella of the Central Intelligence Agency, commanded a force of more than a thousand montagnards. Few men, and certainly no Australian, was ever better known or more highly respected in the Highlands. He lived with the forces he led and, as he puts it, he 'developed quite a deal of empathy for them'.

Relations between the montagnards and the Vietnamese were rarely

23

good and raising a people's army in the Highlands presented delicate problems which were aggravated by the North Vietnamese and Viet Cong, who were constantly urging the montagnards to revolt. Petersen could answer for his own people, but his writ did not run in adjacent areas, or over the border in Cambodia, where tribal allies dwelt.

In September 1964, montagnard forces being raised and trained by American officers rose in revolt against the Vietnamese authorities. They imprisoned their American advisers and marched on Ban Me Thuot, and at the same time tried to persuade Petersen's men to join in the revolt. His main camp, Boun Enou, some miles outside Ban Me Thuot, had become designated as revolt headquarters, though its force was still uncommitted. Four battalions of mutineers had grouped around Ban Me Thuot, the airfield was in their hands and all hope of saving the town depended on the loyalty of Petersen's group.

At dusk one day, in heavy rain, Petersen and Serong, then chief of the Australian Army Training Team, drove through the last government defences and on into a rubber plantation–into the middle of a montagnard ambush. Petersen got out of the jeep, leaving Serong sitting alone.

For half an hour Serong sat there, and then Petersen emerged from the trees. 'They're ours', he said. 'We can go ahead.' Ahead meant the stockaded wired and wooden walls of Boun Enou, with its double gates and high fortified towers on each side, manned, alert, suspicious and nervous.

Again Serong stayed in the jeep and Petersen went forward. An hour passed. Then Serong heard scraping sounds, and the gates opened. Serong drove through and the gates closed behind him, while armed montagnards in battle dress swarmed silently up to the jeep and surrounded it.

Half an hour later in one of the longhouses the council of peace began. Petersen based his argument on the undertaking given by the government forces not to fire the first shot. Would the montagnards also agree? For hours the talk went on.

As Serong recalls it, 'It was Petersen who turned the edged phrases into harmless corners, who smoothed the jangled nerves of tribal leaders all too conscious of the death they faced for revolt, all the time well aware that in the desperate mood of these desperate men, a single misplaced phrase would be the end for them all, and for the government's position in the Highlands and perhaps for the Allied effort in Vietnam'.

Late that night Petersen and Serong led the montagnard leaders back to Ban Me Thuot for talks with the Vietnamese commander. It was long after midnight. The rain had stopped, but torrents were flowing down the rutted tracks.

Part of the agreement they had reached at Boun Enou was that the montagnards should be allowed to carry their guns to the conference at Ban Me Thuot. But when the Vietnamese commander saw the guns in the tribesmen's hands, he reacted with horror.

'Take it easy', Serong said to him, and tossed his own gun into the corner, waving to it and the montagnards. One by one, as they reached the top of the stairs, they followed his lead and stacked their guns. The talk went on till dawn–and the revolt was over.

Thereafter Ban Me Thuot was loyal to Saigon. The North Vietnamese attacked the city during the Tet offensive in 1968 but were driven off by the 23rd Division with heavy losses. To the west, however, and across the Cambodian border, there were small tribal groups under Communist control.

In attacking Ban Me Thuot with the bulk of his forces assembled in the west and moving through the Cambodian border, General Dung could be assured of good jungle cover. As he got closer to Ban Me Thuot, however, the problem of security would become increasingly serious.

General Giap, who presided over the meeting, talked in detail of the tactics to be employed, the need for security and surprise and of persuading Saigon to concentrate its forces in the Hue-Danang region. The operation in the Highlands was code-named 275 and on the instruction of Le Duan and Le Duc Tho, General Dung became field commander.

The 320th Division, which General Dung had led more than twenty years earlier, was already in the Highlands and had been joined by the 10th and 968th divisions. The 316th Division was readying to move. Two weeks later in North Vietnam the general travelled to Ninh Binh province in the southern part of North Vietnam to give his battle orders to senior officers and to address the troops. 'I hope the battle drums of this army corps as well as its victory bugle calls will be heard majestically in this symphony of the entire army and people', he said. 'I would like to ask whether you "musicians" here are capable of this or not. If you say "yes" the conductor–the Central Military Party Committee and the High Command–will be ready to raise the baton at the right moment when the opportunity arises.'

'We can do it. We can do it', the troops answered.

General Dung chose his staff with care from among his old colleagues. It included Major-General Dinh Duc Thien, who had become Minister of Machinery and Metallurgy in 1960, but who was also head of the General Logistics Department of the Army. Twenty-one years before, Thien's logistical brilliance had made possible the extraordinary movement of supplies across the mountains of Tongking that so shocked the French at Dien Bien Phu in 1954. Old, grey and short-tempered, he had been close to Dung since 1939, when they were together in a French prison. Next in order was Major-General Le Ngoc Hien, a deputy chief of the General Staff, who had wide experience against the American forces. He had also fought under Dung in the 320th Division in the early 1950s. Between them there was a close affinity. 'He understood not only my views on active offensives against the enemy, conduct in combat, faithful observance of orders and my attitude towards cadres, combatants and the people, but also my personal ideas concerning the application of combat to each particular circumstance', said Dung. Hien did not need instructions. As soon as he was informed of his appointment, he led the advance party to the Highlands, and was already there when he learned that Ban Me Thuot was to be the initial target.

Diplomats stationed in Hanoi regard the city as one of the world's most secretive capitals. They have almost no substantive access to government officials. If they have issues to discuss, they are required to list these in writing, and when meetings are arranged these issues, and these issues alone, are discussed. In an endeavour to break the system, diplomats repeatedly try to take advantage of national day celebrations to lie in wait for senior officials whom they try to engage in conversation. They are not often successful.

Even more elaborate security arrangements than usual were made to ensure that Dung's departure for the front was unkown. On 5 February, when he went off to the airport, he gave the impression that he was leaving on an inspection of troops in North Vietnam by wearing full uniform instead of the black pyjamas habitually worn by even the most senior officers going to the war zone. After his departure, it was arranged that his Volga sedan would make its usual trips from his house to general headquarters at 7 a.m. and 2 p.m. and from general head-quarters to his house at noon and 5 p.m. Late in the afternoon each day troops would go to the courtyard at his house to play their usual game of volleyball with the absent general. Daily the press carried reports of his 'activities' as if he was still in Hanoi.

Dung himself prepared messages to send to friendly countries on their respective army days and bought lunar new year presents and cards for friends and members of his staff. All the equipment needed by the general and his staff, operating under the code name of A75, was prepared in an office at general headquarters. Dung's personal secretary even feigned illness and was carted off in an ambulance, so that no one would guess that he, too, might have left for the war. For the duration of the campaign Dung was to have the code name 'Tuan' and Giap that of 'Chien'.

From Hanoi, General Dung flew to Dong Hoi, immediately south of the former demilitarized zone and, since 1972, in North Vietnamese hands. By car he went to the Ben Hai River, where he boarded a motor launch to take him up-stream. That evening he met General Hien whó had travelled north by car.

Dung spent a restless night and next day, 6 February, was heading south along the new highway built by more than 30,000 troops and men and women 'shock youths'. The general's security fetish seems to have left him once he entered the war zone, and as he drove south he cheerfully gave away hundreds of hairpins to the girl labourers and cigarettes to the men.

As if intent on helping to be an instrument of its own destruction, the Thieu government had just closed down five newspapers and detained eighteen journalists accused of being Communist agents. Most of the eighteen were well-known either as journalists or writers—and for their left-wing sympathies. The list included one of Vietnam's best known playwrights and also one of the leading historians. Many had been arrested before, some two or three times, and there was probably reason enough to detain them again. But since their principal crime now appeared to be their charges of corruption in Thieu's own family, Saigon was sceptical. Father Tran Huu Thanh, naive, and egotistical, but with a growing following for his People's Anti-Corruption Movement for Salvation of the Country and Restoration of Peace, had just distributed a 'political indictment' of Thieu. 'Corruption is the basis of the regime because it is the leader who uses corruption as a means to command the others', he said. Thieu did not dare to arrest Father Thanh, one of the priests responsible for the creation of the late Ngo Dinh Diem's ideology, Personalism.

In the Saigon view, however, by trying to silence the Press, Thieu was also trying to stifle opposition to himself. Father Thanh's charges, and much of what the Press had to say, were exaggerated. Some of it was false, but there was now evident for the first time the signs of total public disaffection with Thieu. In 1972 when the nation was threatened by the Easter offensive, those who opposed Thieu closed ranks with the government. In the mounting crisis now he had lost all capacity to provide the leadership, and to bring about the unity, that the country so desperately needed.

I attended a reception at the palace at this time. Among those present was a former senior official. We were standing about six feet from Thieu when I remarked, 'So the President is going to run for office again'.

'Yes, the son of a bitch', he replied venomously and loudly. Thieu may not have heard my question. It was inconceivable that he did not hear the answer. Sleek haired, trim and all but expressionless, Thieu made the round of his guests. A man of little talent, he had fallen back on deviousness and cunning to win, and keep, office. Surrounded by cronies and relatives, his regime allowed a surprising degree of public expression and debate, rare in Asia. Nevertheless, it remained divorced both from the people and from reality.

Thieu's position apart, the attack on the Press at this time could only play into the hands of those who were so stridently denouncing South Vietnam. With Tran Van Lam, now President of the Senate, on his way to Washington to seek the additional $300 million in military aid so urgently needed, and with Congress and the American Press hostile to South Vietnam, the timing could not have been worse. Nevertheless, as Ambassador Graham Martin later told a Congressional committee, the American people sometimes overlooked the fact that 'what we required of the Vietnamese in a war situation in which their very survival was at stake was that they observe all the forms that we, ourselves, have found somewhat difficult to observe when we have been in similar circumstances'. He added, pointedly, that he had been almost court-martialed during the Second World War, when he described the removal of Japanese living in California as a shocking disgrace.

If Thieu had any understanding at all of the critically dangerous feelings that had been aroused in America, he would have known that it would have been better to allow the newspapers to operate in any way they wished in Saigon rather than to occasion further violent criticism on Capitol Hill. It is difficult, it seems, to shake off a death wish.

On 6 February, just as General Dung was starting his trip down the Ho Chi Minh trail, the Government of Vietnam called a press conference in Saigon to explain itself. Fox Butterfield, of the *New York Times*, came into the crowded auditorium and took his place next to me in the front row. On the top of his pad in bold letters he had chalked the letters 'c.i.a.'. Naively, I failed at first to see the connection. But, sure enough, when the time came, Butterfield was on his feet to ask about c.i.a. involvement. Dissatisfied with the answer, the *Washington Post* took over the questioning. Once, when a senior North Vietnamese defector, who in other days had been authorized to write a biography of Ho Chi Minh, explained the Communist penetration of the Press, a Western correspondent, name unknown, applauded. 'Who was that? Do you know his name?' Butterfield asked me, pencil poised. Out of Saigon to the United States that night went stories that would have delighted General Dung if he had been able to read them on the Ho Chi Minh trail.

On his way south, Dung passed the 316th Division, travelling aboard five hundred trucks. From the time the division left North Vietnam it had been under instruction to maintain radio silence. An intercepted message that the 316th could no longer be seen and no one knew where it was going was further good news for the general. The South Vietnamese were already becoming confused. 'Our combatants in the trucks were strong, healthy and joyful', he wrote. 'They waved their hats and hands and sang to the roar of tanks and armored cars and the thud of long-range artillery guns, anti-aircraft guns and trucks of all types which followed one another, forming an endless line like a big waterfall to the front. The road to the front at that time of the year was very beautiful.'

In the forest to the west of Ban Me Thuot, General Dung established the Central Highlands Front Command under the leadership of Lieut-General Hoang Minh Thao. Although it was about four hundred miles by road from Saigon, Ban Me Thuot seems in retrospect to have been an obvious choice. Pleiku and Kontum, larger and seemingly more important towns to the north, were watched and guarded with some care by Thieu's forces. Thieu himself was concerned about Ban Me Thuot, but his warnings were not taken very seriously. Yet if it fell to a major force, Pleiku and Kontum would, in the existing state of the South Vietnamese Air Force, be indefensible. Moreover, Ban Me Thuot was important in a psychological sense as a provincial capital and a focal point for montagnards in the Highlands.

By 25 February General Dung had assembled a force of nearly three divisions outside Ban Me Thuot against one regiment of the 23rd ARVN (Army of the Republic of Vietnam) Division, and three second-quality regional force battalions. With this overwhelming force, Dung had sufficient troops not only to occupy the town quickly but to keep a substantial group in reserve for use when the government forces attempted to counter-attack.

Surprise remained the key to the campaign, and it was brilliantly maintained, not merely by the preservation of secrecy in the jungles outside Ban Me Thuot but by highly effective diversionary actions.

On 1 March, the 968th Division destroyed two government posts along the highway west of Pleiku, thus reinforcing the view held by General Pham Van Phu, commander of Military Region 2, that Pleiku was still the main target. Four days later, however, a group of North Vietnamese artillery officers on reconnaissance west of Ban Me Thuot brushed with a patrol and a wounded officer fell into South Vietnamese hands. The next day the 23rd Division moved swiftly to cover the northern approaches to the town, with the 3rd Battalion of the 53rd Regiment, an armoured company and a regional force battalion. This was accompanied by renewed reconnaissance patrols that forced the North Vietnamese tank, engineer and artillery units to pull back to avoid detection.

The intelligence that a wounded North Vietnamese was being nursed to life so that he could be interviewed personally by Brigadier Le Trung Tuong, commander of the 23rd Division, persuaded General Dung that he had to move quickly if secrecy was to be preserved. On 7, 8 and 9 March his forces blocked all roads north and south and had effectively isolated Ban Me Thuot.

By this time Thieu knew that an attack was coming and warned General Phu that Ban Me Thuot might be the target. Phu called an emergency briefing at his headquarters in Pleiku on 9 March. Among those present were Brigadier-General Tran Van Cam, deputy commander of II Corps, and General Tuong, the commander of the 23rd Division.

The Corps staff had identified three North Vietnamese divisions in the area, with one close to Pleiku and another outside Ban Me Thuot. General Cam proposed that Ban Me Thuot should be strengthened. He was supported by General Tuong, who wanted to rush the 45th Regiment there. Phu disagreed. He said that as soon as Ban Me Thuot came under attack he would move in reinforcements by air, but that until the main attack could be identified the reinforcements ought to be kept at Pleiku. One by one his subordinates agreed. Dung's secrecy had paid off. The Corps staff had no idea that three North Vietnamese divisions were in position outside Ban Me Thuot.

On the night of 9 March, Dung sent a message to the Central Military Party Committee and to the Politburo in Hanoi with the details of the battle plan. The attack on Ban Me Thuot was to begin at 2 a.m. the following day.

'At 0200 sharp on the morning of 10 March, the offensive on Ban Me Thuot was heralded by the fire from sapper units directed on the Hoa Binh and city airfields', the general wrote in his report of the battle: 'Long-range artillery began destroying military targets in the city. From a point forty kilometres from Ban Me Thuot, our tank unit started their engines, knocked down trees which had been cut halfway in advance, and headed for Ban Me Thuot. On the Srepok River, modern ferryboats were rapidly assembled, while tanks, armoured vehicles, anti-aircraft guns and armoured cars formed queues to cross on the ferries. The mountains and forests of the Central Highlands were shaken by a fire storm.'

General Dung aptly described the South Vietnamese as stunned. Since Route 14 connecting Ban Me Thuot with Pleiku had been cut,

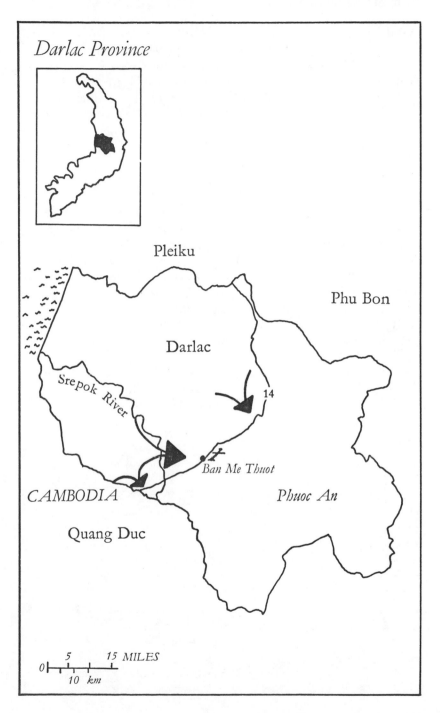

Darlac Province

Pleiku

Phu Bon

Darlac

Srepok River

14

Ban Me Thuot

CAMBODIA

Phuoc An

Quang Duc

5   15 MILES
0
10   km

reinforcements could not be sent by road. Pleiku airport was under heavy artillery fire, a move designed to prevent reinforcement by air. On 10 March, the government had only four Chinook troop-carrying helicopters at Pleiku and, because of the lack of spare parts due to the reduction in American aid, only one was airworthy. Dodging shells and flying a shuttle service to Ban Me Thuot, fifty soldiers to a load, it moved some 500 reinforcements into the battle. They were far from enough. The North Vietnamese claimed a superiority of 5.5:1 in soldiers, 2.2:1 in heavy artillery and 1.2:1 in tanks. There could be only one outcome: a Northern victory. By 10.30 a.m. on 11 March Ban Me Thuot had fallen. Among the prisoners was Colonel Vu The Quang, deputy commander of the 23rd Division, the former mayor of Cam Ranh, whose pessimistic conclusions about the state of the government forces encouraged Dung to send a message to Giap in Hanoi. 'If we extend operations to eastern Phu Bon [the adjoining province], we can either annihilate or encircle the enemy and from there we can extend operations northward to Pleiku to encircle and annihilate the enemy and isolate him at Kontum', he telegraphed.

Back came the reply: 'The victories . . . indicate that we are capable of winning great victories more quickly than initially planned . . . We must rapidly extend our operations toward Phu Bon to destroy all vital forces of the enemy and seize Pleiku with a view toward capturing the province. We should isolate and destroy Kontum later and finally march south.' The message came both from the Politburo and the Central Military Party Committee.

2. The Highland rout

Over the years of war a few dedicated South Vietnamese nationalists stood out above the rest. They worked tirelessly and hard for the country under whatever regime happened to be in office, seeking no preferment for themselves, labouring only for the creation of a Vietnam that would be independent, non-Communist and free. One of these was a short, rotund Cochin-Chinese named Tran Van Lam, whose attributes included a batch of daughters of extraordinary beauty, even for Vietnam, home of Asia's most delicate, graceful and charming women.

Lam, a Buddhist turned Roman Catholic, was the first president of Ngo Dinh Diem's National Assembly in 1956. Nineteen years later, after a period in the 1960s as ambassador to Australia, he was president of the Senate, serving Thieu as he had once served Diem. Two of the most important, and difficult, tasks had fallen to his lot. The first, in 1973, was to sign, as Foreign Minister, the Paris Agreement, and the second, in February 1975, to persuade Washington to give the additional aid South Vietnam so desperately needed if it was to have an outside chance of surviving.

As Lam travelled to the United States, General Dung was making his way down the Ho Chi Minh trail to Ban Me Thuot. And as Dung manoeuvred his tanks and guns into position, Lam was being shot down by the blind and disillusioned warriors of Capitol Hill. His report to Saigon at the beginning of March was just as shattering in its own way as the fall of Ban Me Thuot.

'After all, barely six years ago, the Vietnam War required the participation of nearly 600,000 American troops and an annual expenditure of $30 billion', Lam pleaded in Washington. ' $30 billion per year, that was a little less than $100 million per day. Next to such figures, the requested $300 million increment of aid for a whole fiscal year does not appear exorbitant, if one allows that the job has to be done.'

Congress did not allow that the job had to be done. Lam saw Vice President Rockefeller, John Sparkman, chairman of the Senate Foreign Relations Committee, and John McClellan, chairman of the Appropriations committee, and Hubert Humphrey. Mike Mansfield and several others were too busy. 'I got the feeling that there was a kind of *revanche* of the legislature against the executive', Lam told me after his return. 'What the executive said the legislature did not want to accept, including those in the President's own party. The United States was too deeply involved in its own domestic worries to be concerned with Vietnam any longer. Everyone was much more concerned with how to reduce inflation and unemployment and how to get oil'.

The Congressmen told him South Vietnam was not fighting well. 'I said, "We fought well in 1968 and 1972 and these are the same people"', Lam recalled. 'They held An Loc [held against heavy North Vietnamese attacks in 1972] for years. The North Vietnamese have ten times more shells than we have. If our troops have ten bullets and know they will get ten more when they need them, then they will fight. But, inevitably, when soldiers have no bullets, no equipment, no means of transportation, it is only natural that morale will suffer.'

Lam was talking not only to the blind but also to the deaf. He returned to Saigon early in March, just as General Van Tien Dung was beginning to fire his preliminary shots. His message was that South Vietnam would not get the $300 million it sought, and that with the 1975-76 financial year it might get no aid at all.

Thieu was still digesting this most disastrous of intelligence when Ban Me Thuot fell. Unlike Phuoc Binh, which was only lightly held, Ban Me Thuot was a divisional headquarters. Its loss was a major blow. Thieu fought for time, witholding the news of the fall of Ban Me Thuot while assembling enough forces for a counter-attack and the means to convey them into action. But so heavily infiltrated were the ARVN forces that Dung knew every move in advance. In Hanoi, Giap was on the end of the telegraph line to tell him just where the ARVN reinforcements would be sent and in what numbers.

For years the North Vietnamese had been perfecting a new-old tactic borrowed straight from the game of Vietnamese chess. It called for an overt feinting attack covered by a well-concealed ambush. Many

34

years before I had seen the tactic in play in the Mekong Delta. The Viet Cong launched simultaneous assaults against a post held by thirty-eight civil guards and a nearby watchtower manned by seven militia. News of the attack went to the district chief, who decided to use M113 armoured amphibious carriers to move his troops, thus avoiding the possibility of a road-side ambush. This was just what the Viet Cong had anticipated. The M113s drove across the rice fields straight into a horseshoe-shaped ambush and came under heavy attack from recoilless rifles. One M113 was set on fire and burned along with its seven occupants. Viet Cong fire also damaged four other carriers and prevented the relief column from reaching the civil guard post, or the watchtower, which had already been destroyed. In their own good time, the Viet Cong broke off the operation and dispersed. They were not followed.

They learned to be patient. If a relief column failed to show up quickly, they were prepared to wait for it. On another occasion, in Kien Hoa province, also in the Delta, two civil guard companies waited a full day before going to a hamlet that had come under attack. For maximum security, they chose separate routes to approach the hamlet. The Viet Cong staged two ambushes. The first ambush pinned down one company, the second wiped out the other.

The government began to use helicopters flying at thirty feet to inspect the ground before ordering troops in to counter-attack. One day the all-clear came and a government battalion started to make its way through the ricefields to a beleagured post. Suddenly the rice got up and ran. While Viet Cong machine guns took the battalion under cross fire, heavily camouflaged Viet Cong infantrymen, rice sheaves over their heads and shoulders, tore across the paddy fields to deliver the coup de grâce.

Similar preparations, but on a corps scale, were in the planning stage at Dung's headquarters in Darlac province. Tipped off by Giap that the 45th Regiment of the 23rd Division was to be airlifted from Pleiku to Phuoc An, one of the provincial districts of Darlac, just to the east of Ban Me Thuot, Dung made his arrangements to meet the troops on arrival. At noon on 12 March, the North Vietnamese troops encircled the little town of Ea Yong and its small airfield, while other forces consolidated around the Ban Me Thuot airport to await forces known to have been assigned to land there. Another message from Giap told Dung that the government forces would attempt to regroup north and east of Ban Me Thuot with parts of the 53rd Regiment and the 21st Ranger multi-battalion unit, supported by two new regiments of regular troops.

In Hanoi, the excitement was mounting. Although the Politburo and the Central Military Party Committee had already given the green light to Dung to exploit the situation as quickly as possible, Giap, Le Duan and Le Duc Tho now sent their own personal endorsement. For thirty years this trio had had their sights on Saigon. Now they could draw a bead.

All of them had been immediately and importantly involved with the war from the very first day. While Giap had had overall command in the war against the French, Le Duan and Le Duc Tho had alternated in running COSVN. All three had been strongly in favour of resuming the war in 1959. In 1966, when the doves in Hanoi were arguing that the war could not be won against the United States, Le Duc Tho had led the hawks in furious and virulent attacks against the 'defeatists'. Those who had known Le Duan in the South described him as a 'ruthless commissar'. Others who had encountered Le Duc Tho during the peace negotiations had found him 'charming'. But, as Dung was well aware, there would have been no resumption of the war in the South without their direction. When their message came in, he could be reassured that boldness and decisiveness were what was required of him.

Dung directed the war from his forest headquarters, linked by telegraph with Hanoi and by phone and radio to his combat forces. The most alarming event in the course of the battle was not caused by enemy action but by a herd of elephants, terrified by gunfire, which raced through the forest, ripping up telephone lines and carrying them away. Everything else went according to plan. 'Throughout Darlac province enemy troops were like snakes that had lost their heads', said Dung. As Giap had predicted, waves of helicopters landed troops in Phuoc An district and west of Ban Me Thuot airport, but in both places Dung was ready. 'No sooner had they [the South Vietnamese troops] touched the ground–even before they could regroup–they fled in disorder to avoid the high trajectory direct fire of our infantry', he said. 'They panicked when they saw our tanks and armoured cars rushing toward them.' The enemy airborne units were annihilated one by one and the remaining troops ran away, mixing with one another and gradually withdrawing toward Route 21 (the highway running east from Ban Me Thuot to Nha Trang, on the coast).

The fleeing regular soldiers were followed by the militia, the civilian authorities and the civilians. By dawn on 14 March, Dung was in a position to report new victories to Hanoi. The main force of the 23rd Division, including the 44th and 45th Regiments, had been destroyed in two days of fighting. The remnants of the 53rd Regiment and the 21st Ranger multi-battalion had also been smashed.

In the Khai Doan Buddhist pagoda in Ban Me Thuot the North Vietnamese found a number of government soldiers mixed with civilian refugees. All of them were arrested. The monks were led to the marketplace, where they were told to sit down together with a crowd of people who had been seized elsewhere in the town. Local Viet Cong cadres then walked through the crowd pointing out government employees and police. About three hundred were separated from the rest and taken to the other side of the marketplace where they were harangued by a northern official who accused them of being American lackeys, spies and enemies of the people. All of them were shot and killed.

After the shooting, the families of those known to the local cadres were placed under armed guard and marched a short distance out of town. One of the monks from the Khai Doan pagoda was following the procession along the road when he saw the guards open fire on their captives. Those who were not killed or wounded ran into the trees on either side of the road, with the monk following. He was among the few who eventually reached the coast and found his way to Saigon.

By 14 March Dung had concluded that the victory had been so spectacular and so overwhelming that the strategic plan could be telescoped and that total victory in 1975 might now be achieved. Yet Dung was not happy that his forces had demonstrated their ability to move swiftly enough to maintain momentum after seizing the initiative. 'We detected shortcomings requiring rapid solutions', he wrote.

Understanding of the situation and working methods had not yet caught up with new circumstances and requirements and were still affected by old-fashioned practices. Persons able to make decisions and organize swift action had not yet emerged conspicuously. There were still cases of failure to direct troops firmly and to use radio sets, although they were available. Instead, secret codes continued to be used, and telephone lines were clumsily dragged along. Though the enemy troops were confused and were disintegrating . . . our side, before launching an attack, still proceeded according to the full routine, made night-time preparations and waited until morning to attack. Though the enemy air force launched only limited attacks, flew at a high altitude and dropped bombs inaccurately, our troops were not allowed to move about in daytime but were compelled to wait, delay and waste time . . . Local party committee echelons were confused by all the tasks that had to be done, like working in broad daylight instead of moonlight and moving from dense forests to cities.

Dung was also concerned that too little use had been made of captured equipment and captured troops. He believed that provided prisoners were carefully watched and guarded, it was practicable to use captured truck, tank, and armoured car drivers, and even artillerymen. Dung was in a hurry. The wet season was approaching, and before the rains came he wanted to press the attack against Pleiku and Kontum.

The notion that the Provisional Revolutionary Government might have a part to play in the administration of liberated territory did not for a moment enter into the calculations of either Hanoi or Dung and his staff in the field. Earlier, Douglas Pike had written of the PRG that 'it had none of the appurtenances of a government or a foreign ministry ... As a governmental organization conducting foreign affairs it existed only in the minds of its planners and of those outside the borders of Vietnam whose own purposes were served by playing out the pretence'. Hanoi had never bothered to recognize the 'government', and now even the pretence was abandoned. Ban Me Thuot was turned over to a military management committee, a procedure followed in all other cities, including Saigon, as they fell into North Vietnamese hands. What Hanoi seized, it intended to hold.

Saigon had now identified four North Vietnamese divisions in the Highlands. They were heavily protected with anti-aircraft guns, but in their haste to exploit the initial success at Ban Me Thuot they made little attempt at concealment. Bunched together on the new roads with hundreds of trucks and tanks, they made an ideal target for the B52 bombers. Many were sure the B52s would come.

By 13 March, however, it was clear to Saigon that its attempt to retake Ban Me Thuot had failed. 'The shock effect on Saigon was immediate', according to Brigadier Serong, who to all intents and purposes had become one of the military hierarchy. 'A group of generals threatened Thieu that if he did not move quickly to order implementation of the plan to abandon MR1 and MR2 (Central Vietnam and the Highlands) they would remove him.* He complied, with disastrous alacrity.'

On the 13th Thieu met his four regional commanders in Saigon. They were surprised by the North Vietnamese mobility. This was greater than they had expected. At this meeting Thieu gave no direct warning that he intended to abandon Central Vietnam, but he told Lieut-General Ngo Quang Truong, the regional commander, that he wanted to withdraw the Airborne Division, which would necessitate the removal of the Marines from Quang Tri and their redeployment in the place of the Airborne outside Danang. Faced with this major blow

---

* Serong's version surprised one former member of the Joint General Staff when he read this manuscript. He was not only unaware of a threatened coup, but, as late as 12 March, was working, under Thieu's orders, on plans for a counter-attack.

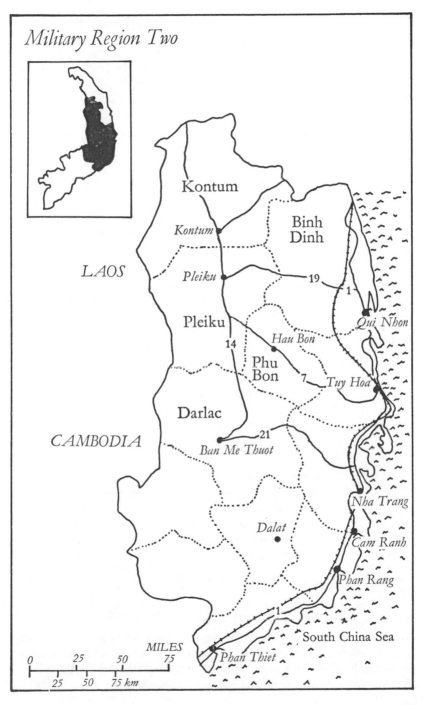

Military Region Two

Kontum

Kontum

Binh
Dinh

LAOS

Pleiku

19

1

Pleiku

Qui Nhon

14

Hau Bon

Phu
Bon

7

Tuy Hoa

Darlac

21

CAMBODIA

Ban Me Thuot

Nha Trang

Dalat

Cam Ranh

Phan Rang

1

South China Sea

MILES

0   25   50   75

Phan Thiet

25   50   75 km

39

to his defences, Truong, like the other regional commanders, spoke pessimistically about the situation.

Next day Thieu flew to Cam Ranh Bay with Tran Thien Khiem, the Prime Minister, General Cao Van Vien, the Chief of Staff, and other military advisers to talk to General Pham Van Phu.

Thieu asked Vien, 'Do we still have reserve forces to reinforce II Corps?' 'No', Vien replied.

Thieu then turned to Phu and asked him how long he would be able to defend the area without reinforcements. Phu replied that he could defend for a month if he got sufficient airborne materials, weapons, ammunition and also reinforcements to compensate for his heavy losses.

Over-extended on the ground, short of ammunition, spare parts, oil and gasoline, and with Lam's dire predictions of no further aid, what was Thieu to do? Vien said there were no further reinforcements available for the Highlands. Serong had told him to pull out no later than 14 February. Now it was a month later–and a month too late.

Thieu told Phu that his condition could not be met. 'We must withdraw from Kontum and Pleiku so as to preserve our forces and use our troops to defend the Delta and the coastal area', he said. 'There, we will have more convenient access to supplies.'

But how to withdraw? Thieu asked about Route 19, the main highway from Pleiku to the coast. But it was on Route 19 in June 1954, that the French Mobile Group 100, trying to effect just such a withdrawal as this, had been ambushed and destroyed. Vien replied, 'In the history of the Indo-China War, no forces have been able to withdraw along Route 19 without being badly mauled'.

'What about Route 14?' Thieu asked rhetorically, since he knew it had already been cut.

'It would be worse', said Vien.

Since an evacuation by air was impossible, the only alternative was along Route 7, a disused road running through Phu Bon province. It was in very bad repair, but at least its use would constitute a certain measure of surprise, which was about the only capacity the government forces in the Highlands had left.

Tran Van Lam, in his capacity as President of the Senate, was one of the first to hear of the decision from Thieu, who had withdrawn more and more from contact with senior colleagues and subordinates. He told him that after the fall of Ban Me Thuot the defence of Pleiku and Kontum would be impossible. Ban Me Thuot was the essential rear base to support the other two positions in the Highlands. All attempts to retake Ban Me Thuot had failed. The arrival there of the 316th North Vietnamese Division had changed the balance of forces overwhelmingly in North Vietnam's favour. The only hope of holding Pleiku and Kontum was to have strong air support to attack the four North Vietnamese divisions now available for the attack. This was not available in Vietnam. The Americans were not willing even to provide more ammunition and Thieu could get no assurance whatsoever of air support. Moreover, even if American air support were forthcoming, both Pleiku and Kontum would be cut off by land and would have to be supplied by air. Thieu added bitterly, 'I don't have enough fuel for the planes and the Communists are very strongly equipped with anti-aircraft guns.'

Thieu said he had to save what was left of the 23rd Division and the Rangers. If they stayed they might be able to fight for ten days to two weeks. 'If I had had assurances of support and enough means to supply by air, I would maintain the forces in the Highlands', he said. 'As neither of these conditions are met, I must redeploy the 23rd Division and the Rangers to fight elsewhere. If I leave them in Pleiku and Kontum, it will become another Dien Bien Phu.'

Thieu was preoccupied with the lessons to be learned from the French experience in Tongking after the fall of Dien Bien Phu. With the loss of the garrison, the French in North Vietnam were over-extended in much the same way as the South Vietnamese were over-extended in the Highlands. They solved their problems by shortening their lines. What Thieu forgot when he gave the strategic orders, and Phu overlooked when he gave the tactical instructions, were the families of the soldiers and the civilian population. The French troops in the Red River Delta had no families to leave behind, and the civilians were not so much in love with the French that many wanted to go. But in the Highlands the troops had their families with them, and if not to a man, then at least to almost every woman and child, the population was determined not to remain under the North Vietnamese.

Though the military kept their secrets to themselves, in Pleiku and in Kontum fear rippled through the regional forces and the civilian population. Saigon had now admitted the fall of Ban Me Thuot and no one needed to be a strategist to know that Pleiku and Kontum would be next. Members of General Dung's staff sat glued to the radio for whatever intelligence they might be able to glean from it. They learned that the price of a Pleiku-Saigon air ticket had risen to 40,000 piastres, about three times the normal fare. The next day they intercepted messages from aircraft taking off from Pleiku instructing them to land at Nha Trang on the coast. Reliable Giap weighed in with the intelligence that the forward command post of the Military Region 2 had moved to Nha Trang, and at 4 p.m. on the same day an observer reported that a large convoy of vehicles was making its way from Pleiku to Phu Bon.

In Saigon, however, not all attention was rivetted on the Central Highlands. The strategic contingency plan called for the evacuation of Central Vietnam also. Here, there were ominous-looking signs as the North Vietnamese feinted to persuade Saigon that it was in this direction that the main thrust would come. The 1st ARVN Division in the mountains west of Hue had been fighting heavily for months, and now General Truong was as pessimistic as anyone else. Tran Van Lam flew to Hue to see him and asked him in confidence how he could cope with the five North Vietnamese divisions known to be either in the region, or in a position of readiness just across the border. 'If they fight with their five divisions, I confess it will be difficult', said Truong. Then he added, 'I will fight, but I confess I will be beaten'.

Up the Mekong the situation looked much worse, as I was personally well aware. Late one night early in March I was at home in bed in Australia when the phone rang. The introduction of STD on an intercontinental basis is one of the most retrograde developments in the newspaper business. It means that editors and foreign editors are tempted to phone far-away correspondents at any hour simply on whim. 'George Evans here', said the voice of the London *Sunday Telegraph* at the other end. 'Sorry to trouble you at this hour [it was about 2 a.m.] but what about going to Phnom Penh? We'd like a profile of the city. And the war, too, of course. Four thousand words.'

'You can't get into Phnom Penh', I said. 'The river's closed and the airport is under fire.'

'You'll make it', he said. 'And by the way, we'd like to run the story two weeks from Sunday.'

I went back to bed and murmured quietly to my wife that I was going to Cambodia the next day. She made no reply, and rather reluctantly I offered the information again the following morning. 'I heard you last night', she said rather sharply.

Three days later and 5,000 miles away, I was comfortably ensconsed at the rear of the Air Cambodge Caravelle, sipping champagne (graciously delivered free to economy-class passengers) and marvelling at the ease with which these things could be arranged. I had no idea as we began to make our descent that this was to be the airline's last scheduled flight, or that Phnom Penh, the most exquisite of all the towns the French built in Indo-China, was so soon to be a city in name only.

One day not quite five years earlier, I had driven from Phnom Penh to Svay Rieng near the Vietnam border behind a battery of old, long-barrelled Russian 76mm guns which were being towed by two even older-looking trucks. Two of the trucks broke down, leaving the guns stranded for the night in the countryside, where the North Vietnamese, the enemy of the day, moved unmolested.

Not by any stretch of imagination could the column have been expected to promote any fear in the hearts of the North Vietnamese, but the people in every village and town reacted to the troops as if they were some miraculous answer to their prayers. It was flowers and fruit and smiles and tears and the Lord Buddha care for one and all. Never in the history of war have so many mangoes been showered on so few.

It was an enthusiasm born of ignorance and a sudden upsurge in national pride. If the Americans and the South Vietnamese together could not defeat the North Vietnamese across the border, the 32,000-man Cambodian army, trained for ceremonial appearances in the make-believe court of Prince Norodom Sihanouk, had no chance of putting them to flight in their sanctuaries.

Now, in the final agony and humiliation, the coup de grâce to the government forces was about to be administered, not by the North Vietnamese, who had performed their tasks in Cambodia and turned back for the final fling in South Vietnam, but by the Khmer Rouge–the Red Khmers, the Communist-led insurgents.

What they and their allies were was still largely an unknown factor, for the army with its grip around Phnom Penh was faction-filled and faceless.

Sihanouk, deposed as ruler of Cambodia in 1970 and then in far-off Peking, was a figure-head. The expectation, quite correctly, was that he would be cast aside by the rebels as soon as he had outlived his usefulness.

Stoically, fearfully, many people in Phnom Penh were waiting for the end. 'We are suffering from melancholic depression', said a school-teacher who, in the very first days of the war, had worked for me as an interpreter. 'We are too sad even to cry.'

More than a quarter of the country's perhaps seven million people were now jammed into the city, by far the greater number refugees who had fled from the provinces and the Khmer Rouge. They told stories of obedience exacted at the point of the gun, of hideous atrocities and of dissenters who did not go before a people's court, but simply disappeared. Their stories may have been exaggerated, or perhaps even untrue (although subsequent events have indicated that no one could exaggerate the cruelty, or the ruthlessness, of the Khmer Rouge), but for the people of Phnom Penh these were the reality. They knew the war was lost, not today or tomorrow or even next week or next month, but inevitably; that there would be no more convoys up the Mekong with food, ammunition and oil; that Battambang, where the home-grown rice came from, was about to fall; that the escape routes were closed; and that, whatever the outcome of the battles raging north and west of the city and the cynical deliberations of the u.s. Congress about continuing aid, the time would soon come when there would be no more American money, no air lift, and the Khmer Rouge would take over.

Day after day leading members of the Ford Administration in Washington went before Congressional committees to plead for another $220 million in aid to keep the ammunition up to the government forces. They were using 600 tons a day at a cost of $1.4 million. On 6 March, Philip Habib, Assistant Secretary of State for East Asian and Pacific Affairs, told the House of Representatives Committee on Inter-national Relations that, unless supplementary assistance was provided to the government in Cambodia, it would not be able to resist the military onslaught it was facing. 'I would go further', he added, 'and say that I cannot promise you, and no one can assure you, that the provision of military assistance will lead to a political settlement, but I can say with a degree of certainity that the failure to provide sup-plementary military assistance will assure that you don't get a politi-cal settlement. There will be no political settlement unless the people in Phnom Penh have the capacity to resist what they are up against.' Congress had passed the point where it cared about working for a dubious political settlement. It wanted out.

Phnom Penh was a spectator to its own trial. The witnesses for the defence were the tired and spent men in the fields outside the city. If their efforts with their dwindling supplies of ammunition failed to persuade the Khmer Rouge to abandon their attempt to seize, or interdict, Pochentong airport, nothing the people of Phnom Penh could do would alter their fate. If there was hope, it was for a stay of execution of sentence, that the Khmer Rouge would run out of men first, that the current offensive would die at the city gates, and that the wet season would flood the Mekong and, for another brief period, drown the war. But the wet season was July or August, and this was only March. Even if the army could fight for so long, the government could not fight another round like this. The army was still going through the motions of recruiting new troops, but there was no general mobilization. There would be no last ditch stand in the city.

Largely because of this, Phnom Penh managed to maintain an air of serenity and outward calm. In fact, provided he did not see or hear the incoming rockets that greeted the arrival of the Caravelle, and was whisked through immigration and customs without noticing the *Journey's End* flavour of the heavily-beamed processing bunker and the nervousness of the officials in their steel helmets and flak jackets, the newcomer might have been excused if at first he wondered whether there was a war at all. Phnom Penh was a city of grace and shade and dignity. Though it was built to reflect French culture, it was tailored, as if by accident, to the Cambodian character. The flame trees that lined almost every street provided the proper setting for the Cambodian women. In their trim white blouses and long, graceful *sampots* reaching to their ankles, they looked as if they were forever bound for a night at the opera.

The city streets were still kept clean and every day gardeners sprayed water on the boulevard lawns. The cinemas with their own generators were still in business. The Cercle Sportif was conducting its annual championships and the most menacing noise usually heard there was that of racket and ball. A rocket had closed the Lycee Descartes, where the French used to send their children, but the university and the Cambodian schools were still open. Students were excused the draft.

Once there used to be slogans denouncing Sihanouk painted on the walls, but the rains had washed them away. Except around government offices and military installations, no one had bothered much about sandbags. The only defence against the Chinese 107-millimetre rockets that came whistling overhead in brackets of three was to keep off the streets and away from the areas where they fell most heavily.

Like people trying to ward off a chill winter rain, the Cambodians walked with hunched shoulders and went quickly when they passed the bloodstains on the ground by the Monorom Hotel, its doors and windows shattered, or the Phnom, with its lawns and trees and fortune-tellers on the slopes. It used to be the favourite place for a Sunday outing. It wasn't any longer.

The 107-millimetre rocket was a murderous weapon, intended to terrorize. It was aimed haphazardly from a framework of sticks or half a drum in the ground. Its fragments were small and razor sharp. They did not just kill, they minced.

The rockets' course here brought them across the mile-wide waters of the Mekong, roughly over the Post and Telegraph office, the Ministry of Information complex, the fruit and flower market and the Chinese quarter. Walk around there and you quickly forgot the illusion of normality.

Artificial wreaths marked the spot where the rockets had struck the fruit and flower market. The outer stalls had closed, boarded up with

45

charred wooden beams. Ninety per cent of the Chinese shops in the city and most of the Cambodian shops were no longer open.

For the Chinese there was no road out, and Air Cambodge's single Caravelle, which had been sweeping in and out of Phnom Penh like a frightened seagull unwilling to come to rest, had lost its zeal for the rockets and 105-millimetre shells at Pochentong. The Taiwanese pilot who brought us in also took the plane out, and announced that he had made his last flight.

'A week ago I thought I might get out through Battambang and into Thailand', said the Chinese proprietor of an antique shop whose porcelains I had envied for years. 'But Battambang is all but lost. What do I do?'

It was a question that many Cambodians were asking also. They derived no comfort from the knowledge that the Khmer Rouge were Cambodians. And they did not share the complacent Western assumption that there would be no bloodbath. Thousands were being killed and wounded outside Phnom Penh, but almost no prisoners had been taken. There was no quarter on the battlefield. No one in Phnom Penh could be sure there would be any quarter there.

The Khmer Rouge had announced a death list of only seven, headed by President Lon Nol and including Prince Sirik Matak, Prime Minister Long Boret and others who had been principally concerned with the direction of the government and the war. People in Phnom Penh believed there would be many, many more, though if there was nothing else left to barter, they hoped the Americans might be able to negotiate the feeding of the starving populace in exchange for promises of humanitarian behaviour by the Khmer Rouge. It was a vain hope.

Chang Song, the Minister of Information, was one who expected a massacre. I suggested that if the Khmer Rouge forces were disciplined, they would not kill.

'Their discipline is to kill', he said. 'There will be all killings with the Khmer Communists. That is how they will get their discipline–[by killing] the monks, the students, the middle class.'

I asked him whether he intended to go. 'I would rather stay here and do what I can', he replied. 'It's not a duty. It's not an honour. It's just the thing you do.'

'It sounds trite, but I have been watching this city die', said Australian-born Dr Barry Robinson, World Health Organization chief, who had trained Chinese guerrillas in Kwantung during the Second World War. Figuratively, and literally, that was true. The streets were emptying not because of the petrol shortages–soldiers'

46

wives were doing a roaring trade in gasoline from their huts behind the French Embassy, and children were flogging bottles of the stuff in the streets–but because of unhappiness and inertia. There was nothing to live for any more.

The war had been a very personal tragedy. Scarcely a family had not had one or more killed. 'I have lost three sons in the war', said a woman who was buying one gram of pork in a market outside a Buddhist pagoda where she lived with her surviving four children. 'My money and my life are both spent.' She laughed apologetically, as if ashamed of herself for having given me this glimpse of her soul.

Buddhism had been both a comfort and a shelter for the people. The affinity between the monks and the people had always been close, but never closer than it was in those final few weeks. As everyone knew, in Khmer Rouge country the monks had been stripped of their saffron robes and put to manual labour. Not just Phnom Penh was in its death throes but a whole way of life.

The curfew began at 9 o'clock in the evening, but long before that those lucky enough to have homes retreated behind closed doors. Electricity generated by airlifted fuel lit their houses–and perhaps their lives–for about three hours three times a week.

There was little charcoal for cooking, and what there was was very expensive. People had begun to strip the bark and the twigs from the trees in the streets to heat their pots. Rice was available thanks to the airlift, but the ration per person was only two kilos every ten days, enough for two days.

CARE, the Roman Catholic Relief Service, and other voluntary organizations, had fed tens of thousands of undernourished children every day, and a World Vision team headed by five British doctors worked desperately to save the lives of the dying. In the month of February alone they treated 26,000 patients who should have been in hospital.

On the ground floor of the Cambodiana, the never-completed hotel that Sihanouk planned to run in conjunction with the casino on the banks of the Mekong, a family of nine refugees lay listlessly on the concrete. They had come from the embattled garrison at Neak Luong, down the Mekong, four days earlier. Only on the first day had they been given any rice. They had no food, no money, no possessions other than their clothing, and no hope.

Some non-refugees were just as badly off. For many, many thousands there was no work. There were no ships to load or unload, and the scarred companions of *Geronimo* and *Wolverine*, which I had seen on the Saigon waterfront, were trapped by the blockade, and seemingly

47

deserted and at anchor in the Tonle Sap, which joins the Mekong at Phnom Penh. There was no import or export. There were no homes or factories to be built. A cyclo-driver earned less than enough to buy his meagre rations. Some military families were among the worst off. The military were meant to look after their own. If they were away and could not send money, the families went without.

The soldiers themselves were short of food and close sometimes to starvation. 'I always feel hungry', a sergeant of an artillery battery on the western front told me. Because the three 105-millimetre guns were parked near a pond from which the troops could supplement their rice with lotus stalks and roots and an occasional very small fish, the battery had elected to remain dangerously close to the line. The 105s were elevated like anti-aircraft guns to fire against Khmer Rouge forces less than two miles away.

On every hand there was sickness, pain, grief, hunger and despair. A hundred thousand polio cases was the World Health Organization's estimate; 30,000 lepers receiving no attention; malaria back in the city.

The human flotsam of the war had drifted into every habitable, and uninhabitable, place in Phnom Penh. Four or five families crowded into a house. Tens of thousands slept in the city's three hundred Buddhist pagodas and their grounds, and the less fortunate in the streets. The hospitals, civilian and military alike, were the refuge camps for the maimed and their families. The wounded were twice as numerous as the beds, and by boat, by helicopter, by ambulance and by truck they poured in, an endless stream of human suffering.

On the street once called Boulevard Mao Tse-tung, the former Chinese Embassy had been taken over as a military hospital. It was peculiarly appropriate, since the Khmer Rouge weapons almost all came from China.

The concrete basketball stadium in the National Sports Complex, another gift from Peking, was the reception centre for the wounded. It was cool under the high arched concrete roof, and quiet except for the groans and cries of pain from the badly wounded. Here, a team of military doctors worked round the clock, making up to 600 critical decisions a day, amputating shattered limbs and performing other major operations. There was, of course, very little time for reflection, or consultation. Those with lesser wounds were passed quickly to the four military and seven civilian hospitals. Because there were so many, they were delivered by truck.

Between 1 January 1975, when the Khmer Rouge offensive (synchronized to coincide with the North Vietnamese attack on Phuoc Binh) began, and the end of the month, more than 10,000 wounded and

3,149 sick–beriberi and polyneuritis were increasing among the under-fed troops–passed through the centre. It was a quiet day when I was there. By noon only forty-eight wounded had been admitted. Some came by stretcher, with their wives mute and stricken by their side. Others walked slowly to where the rows of stretchers waited to receive them, nursing their own wounds.

The processing was quickly done. Late that same afternoon in the 'Russian' hospital–it was part of the Soviet Union's pre-war aid pro-gramme–I met a man who had been wounded in the morning in a distant battlefield. The bullet in his side had been extracted and the wound bandaged. He had found no bed.

The hospital, which was typical, had 600 beds, 1,200 patients and an in-built village of 5,000 sleepers. Through the corridors the wounded lay on stretchers, on mats, or on bare tiles, among their wives and families and cooking pots. It was expecting too much of young children that they would know where to find the lavatories in strange new sur-roundings like this. The institutional odour was not that of antiseptics. No one was to blame. Phnom Penh was just not geared for a crisis like this.

More than ever the wives were a tragic but essential part of the war. Once they lived with their husbands at the front lines. Now they stayed more discreetly at battalion headquarters growing extra food and cooking the rice, for the army provided no such service. Since there were no nurses to do the job, the wives were also required to wash and care for their men when they were wounded and in hospital. It followed that the badly wounded soldier with no wife might fare badly.

Yet morale, incredibly, remained high. There were plenty of com-plaints in the hospital about army life–not enough ammunition, not enough food, not enough pay. 'If I got 50,000 riels a month with my family of six, I could manage', said a sergeant wounded for the second time. 'I get 23,000 [less than $12] and cannot.'

Only a boy, just out of primary school, was unsure. He carried his bandaged hand as if he could still feel the impact of the AK47 bullet. He was fifteen, he said, though he looked an undersized twelve. If his commanding officer called for him, he would go back to the front.

Both sides had thrown in children like this. Many of the Khmer Rouge dead on the battlefield looked like young Boy Scouts. On the northern front Khmer Rouge women platoons, with women officers, had joined the men and boys.

Ever since the beginning of February, when the tugs *Wolverine* and *Geronimo* had made their dramatic escape and the last of the Mekong River convoys was turned back under blistering fire, the government forces had faced disaster. Trying to do too much with too little, they fed battalions into the battle to keep the Mekong open and lost them one by one. Now, on the lower reaches of the Mekong, the government flag flew only over Neak Luong, which was under constant rocket, mortar and artillery fire.

Around Phnom Penh, the critical battlefield was a rough quarter circle based on the centre of the city and with its circumference covering Prek Phnau on the Tonle Sap, seven miles to the north, and Toul Leap, eleven miles due west.

Toul Leap was thought to be strongly held by the government. It fell at the beginning of March. The brigade charged with its defence ran for a mile and then, recovering its discipline, stopped. The Khmer Rouge protected their gains with mines and slashed again at the government forces, creeping up to within five miles of the all important airport at Pochentong.

This also threatened to outflank the headquarters of the 3rd Division, and of course it brought Pochentong within easy range of the 105-millimetre guns. Worse, it meant that the 107-millimetre rockets, which had been fired at the airport previously with little accuracy, sporadically and at maximum range from the 'rocket belt' north of the airport, would henceforth be used much more accurately and effectively.

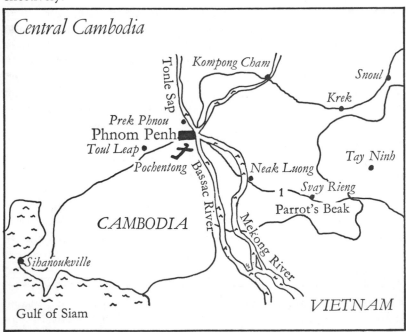

Central Cambodia

In a weatherboard hut to the west of the airport I found Brigadier-General Uk Sauv, who had just taken over the 3rd Division after its previous commanding general had been wounded for the fifth time. The hut had been built on stilts and the spaces between were filled with ammunition boxes packed with dirt. The walls extended to include a messing and working area lined with hundreds of captured Chinese weapons. Outside, as we talked, a yellow bulldozer was prudently piling more dirt against the ammunition cases. Like the divisional commander and the brigade commanders in the north who were already besieged, the general knew he had to be ready not merely to direct the division but even to stand off a ground attack against his own headquarters.

'We are getting replacements', he said, fingering a yellow handkerchief around his neck. 'We are getting them, but they are coming too slowly. It will be okay unless we have a big attack.'

Though the Khmer Rouge had lost by count 1,910 men killed by the 3rd Division since the beginning of January, they still had two divisions, or 12,000 to 16,000 men, on his front, the general believed. Three days after I had seen him they did make their big attack–with predictable results.

The situation was no less fragile at Prek Phnau, just a quick ten-minute drive up the Tonle Sap from Phnom Penh. If the 3rd Division's role was vital because it controlled the western approaches to the airport, Prek Phnau was the anchor for the whole Phnom Penh northern defence line, or what remained of it.

Two dirt roads lead west from the Tonle Sap at Prek Phnau and without them the fate of the two brigades encircled to the west would be sealed. It had to be held. And the Khmer Rouge had to take it.

As villages go in Cambodia, it did not amount to much: a market-place on the banks of the Tonle Sap and two rows of simple houses set among coconut and banana palms and fruit trees. The Khmer Rouge infantry attacked on the night of 7 March and the defenders of Prek Phnau held their ground. Most of the fighting took place about three hundred yards west of the road, but the Khmer Rouge once got to within thirty yards of the marketplace. The 5th Brigade killed more than a hundred Khmer Rouge and lost only three killed and thirty wounded. As evidence, the brigade doctor, bare to the waist and wearing only a sarong, produced for me the notebook in which, in clear strong writing he had recorded the name of every man killed and wounded in the brigade since the offensive began. There were not many pages left.

After the infantry attack came hours of an intermittent but heavy

51

mortar barrage that was still going on when I was there two days later. Villagers who came back to look for their missing were themselves shot down. Beyond the regimental aid post, where the doctor waited for the next wounded, there was a body covered with rusty corrugated iron. When there were no mortar bombs falling people came and lifted the iron sheets to see if these remains belonged to them.

Half a mile back along the road toward Phnom Penh, small taxi trucks waited safely beyond the firing line. People looking for their dead, or what they had left, went forward on foot. Once two truckloads of reinforcements and their families drove past on the way to the front. There were no cheers, no smiles, no fruit, no flowers. It was not that sort of war any longer, and it had not been that sort of war for a very long time. Yet despite the hell they had lived through, the rank and file seemed prepared to continue until no one was left to fight. Bad as things were on the government side, they were sure things were worse for the Khmer Rouge. They were also sure that they had been killing more than they lost. In past years, when victory seemed to be within their grasp, the Khmer Rouge had always fallen back exhausted.

At higher levels, where there was a more realistic appreciation of the odds against the government, the dissent began. Senior officials questioned the whole strategy of the war, whether the generals knew what they were doing. At the captain and major level, I was told, though I did not encounter it personally, there was a disposition to question the wisdom of trying to protract the slaughter. After all, we are all Khmers, aren't we?

There was some residual hope that if the government could hang on to Pochentong and if the offensive subsided, as it had in the past, negotiations would be possible. 'If the offensive fades, you'll see some real progress', said Chang Song, the Minister of Information.

While the silver DC8s could continue to come climbing down their invisible spiral staircases to Pochentong with the rice, and the lumbering American C130s passed the fuel and ammunition, the government had a chance. And in Saigon there were moves afoot to exploit it. On 19 March Brigadier Serong, acting on behalf of high-level members of the government of Vietnam, wrote to Pok Sam An, the Cambodian ambassador in Vietnam, enclosing an *aide memoire* recommending 'one final conjoint blow to save our freedom from the Communists'. What Serong proposed was that the government in Phnom Penh should invite the government in Saigon to send a task force into Cambodia to clear the approaches to Phnom Penh and to guarantee the security of of the capital while the Cambodian government reorganized itself and its armed forces. 'Our two nations are now being liquidated by the U.S.

Congress, in spite of the efforts of the u.s. administration and the wishes of a large proportion of the u.s. people', he wrote. 'The position of GKR [the Cambodian government] seems to be worse than that of GVN [the government of Vietnam], but it is only a matter of time before the GVN's position becomes the same as that of GKR now. It is now clear that, without a violent shock to u.s. public opinion, enough to transmit the shock to the Congress, both the GKR and GVN are doomed.'

The key to the plan was that both Cambodia and South Vietnam should simultaneously and immediately ask Congress for continued support to sustain the operation. 'It will be appreciated', Serong wrote, 'that it is impossible for the GVN to initiate action with a task force unless GKR asks for such GVN assistance, otherwise u.s. and world opinion would react adversely. It will also be appreciated that there is a serious possibility that such joint action may be taken by the u.s. Congress as a reason for terminating all aid immediately. We believe that this latter point is a risk that must be taken, on the grounds that if aid is terminated we are indeed lost, but if we continue as we now are, we are also lost. This action gives us yet one good chance, at this late hour, to save both our nations. We are willing to dare the attempt. We ask the GKR to join us by inviting our action.'

The letter had not been in the ambassador's hands for more than a few hours before it became obvious that Saigon had no task forces left to help anyone, perhaps even itself. The retreat from the Highlands became a rout, and in Central Vietnam even greater calamities were in the making for the government of Vietnam.

3. The fall of Danang

The fort at the top of the Hai Van Pass, black, sinister and solid, looks as if it has stepped from the pages of Beau Geste. When the clouds lift from around it, the view is breath-taking, the green rice fields and the sand dunes stretching north along the coast to Hue and to the south a superb valley that gives way to the coastal plain and Danang.

The Foreign Legion impression is not all illusion. The French built the fort in 1945 and on and off for thirty years it remained an essential watchdog over the tenuous road link between Hue and Danang. In the very earliest preliminary skirmishing to establish positions for the 1975 offensive, the North Vietnamese began to put strong pressure on the Hai Van Pass, using five regiments in an attempt to seize it.

I went through it for the last time at the beginning of February 1975. Although Phu Bai, the Hue airport, remained under unobserved artillery fire, the North Vietnamese had been pushed back into the mountains, and the regional and popular forces in Thieu's army were consolidating their hold on the pass. They had brought their families with them and were camped in pup tents stretching along the roadside on the approaches.

Here, as in many other places at this time, one was constantly reminded of how the war had changed. Once the hamlets in Thua Thien province around Hue carried a high complement of indigenous Viet Cong insurgents. Now they were few in number. They came in from the mountains and forest, but they never spent more than a day or two.

In most hamlets, control over Viet Cong activities had become a matter of routine surveillance. In one hamlet, for example, the authorities noted that a woman whose husband had left her eight years earlier to join the Viet Cong had become pregnant. They watched and found not that she was unfaithful to her husband, but that he sneaked back for a night at home occasionally. His nocturnal visits ceased abruptly.

In a refugee resettlement village the Viet Cong entered on a recruiting drive and marched off four young boys to the hills. Pleading that they could arrange for rice supplies, two of the boys persuaded the Viet Cong to let them return to the village, where they had remained.

Because North Vietnamese money had no value in the South, and a small elephant was needed to carry a decent quantity of Southern piastres, gold and American dollars had become the favoured currencies of the Viet Cong and the North Vietnamese in their clandestine purchases. The police shadowed one woman agent and picked her up with $600 in her purse. The Polish and Hungarian members of the International Commission for Control and Supervision set up under the Paris Agreement turned a blind eye to Hanoi's breaches of the agreement and acted as its buying agents on the side. Their sudden interest in gold rings, ear-rings, other expensive jewellery and ARVN insignia, aroused suspicions and Hue's shops were under instruction not to sell when members of the ICCS arrived to buy. According to one defector, both the Poles and the Hungarians acted as Hanoi's active agents, even using their privileges to prepare maps for the North Vietnamese forces.*

Deep in the mountains heavy fighting continued all the time. Beyond the airport at Phu Bai which had been under direct rocket fire until toward the end of January, and which was still not being used by Air Vietnam, the 1st ARVN Division had killed four hundred North Vietnamese in two weeks' fighting. In fearful weather, without air cover

---

* The American attitude to the ICCS was curious. The Indonesians were interested in trying to stop the fighting. The Americans did not trouble to keep them adequately informed. When the ICCS was running desperately short of money, for example, the United States decided to pay all the arrears for the Poles and Hungarians, without advising the Indonesians, who, when they learned what had happened in September 1974, seriously contemplated withdrawing. On the erroneous assumption that by courting the Poles and the Hungarians they would be well informed about North Vietnamese intentions, the Americans, notably through the C.I.A., continued to maintain the closest liaison, with the result they were misled into believing until the very day they were forced to evacuate, that the appointment of General Doung Van Minh as head of state would bring about an immediate cease-fire and a negotiated settlement.

and with no ammunition to spare for artillery support, they outflanked the North Vietnamese and forced them back.

In 1968, when it became obvious that the Americans were determined to opt out of the war, *Look* magazine in New York asked me to undertake a major survey of the South Vietnamese forces and to assess their chances of going it alone. I began with the 1st ARVN Division, which had distinguished itself notably during the battle for Hue in the Tet offensive.

Once, when I was questioning Colonel Vo Huu Hanh, the commander of the division's 1st Regiment, an American adviser, Major Michael Ferguson, could no longer tolerate what he regarded as my impertinence.

'Sir', he broke in, his voice quivering with emotion, 'this is my last day in Vietnam, and I want you to know this: At Tet, when we met the NVA [North Vietnamese], they were better equipped than any American division, and we beat the hell out of them. This division has met the threat as it has developed and done more and better than any division in the country.'

For a division that only two years earlier, at the height of the Buddhist discontent with Saigon, was broken in morale, bitterly divided in its loyalties, and stricken by desertions, this was high praise. But it was also warranted. Between 31 January 1968, when it fought back and ultimately prevailed against two North Vietnamese divisions in Hue, and 10 October of the same year, when I was interrogating Colonel Hanh, the 1st Division killed 12,664 North Vietnamese and Viet Cong troops. It also captured 2,571 prisoners and picked up 5,662 weapons, against a total loss of 1,600 killed, 6,675 wounded and 238 weapons.

This was a performance that no other division in Vietnam–American, Vietnamese or Korean–could match. In the battle for Hue, 240 men in the division's élite Black Panther Company fought without rest or relief for seventy-two hours. At the end of that time there were only nineteen men left, and they were still fighting.

A forward artillery observer working with the hard-pressed 4th Battalion of the 2nd Regiment at the Citadel in Hue on 5 February 1968, was ordered by the company commander to bring down fire on his home and his family sheltering inside it. 'I watched him give the fire orders with tears streaming down his face', an Australian adviser with the battalion told me. 'Two days later he was killed in a North Vietnamese counter-attack. I saw him with a hole in his back and two other wounds. I daresay he was glad to die.'

In the months following the Tet offensive, the 1st ARVN secured the coastal plains around Hue. Of all its tasks, this had been perhaps the most worthwhile, difficult and, as far as future prospects were concerned, seemed to be the most encouraging. At long last a proper basis had been laid for real pacification. Deliberately, effectively, the Viet Cong hamlet infrastructure, the lifeline of the whole enemy effort to control the rural population, was being destroyed.

Phu Thu district to the south-east of Hue was a place of abandoned rice paddies and bomb craters. For six years, to my knowledge, and probably for much longer, it had been Viet Cong territory. Before 1968 ARVN patrols in battalion strength visited it fearfully and infrequently on futile search-and-destroy missions, which killed a few people who may or may not have been Viet Cong and alienated the rest. Pacification was a mockery, and the gap between the government forces and the people became so wide in places like this that nothing, it seemed, would ever bridge it.

Yet, by October 1968, even the furtive movement of fragmented Viet Cong bands along Phu Thu's dismal waterways and through its battle-broken hamlets had become difficult and sometimes impossible. A group of seventeen young men setting off for the hills to form part of a new Viet Cong battalion was ambushed five times. One hungry, dispirited fugitive, when he was dragged out of his hiding place in a lily pond, admitted that only three of the original seventeen survived.

Peasants who fled to refugee centres in Hue and Danang to escape Viet Cong rule, and the earlier punitive futility of the South Vietnamese armed forces, began to return. Once, almost everyone here was for the Viet Cong. But now the newly formed 54th Regiment, attached to the 1st ARVN Division, was not only clearly in command but welcome.

'How have you done it?' I asked General Truong, as we climbed aboard his helicopter after visiting Phu Thu.

'We used to go in quickly and return', he said. 'Now, when we go in, we stay.'

Minutes later, just after we had taken off, two bullets cracked through the cabin of the helicopter, a reminder that not all Viet Cong had been driven out, or converted, but it was a gesture, nothing more. In the next six years the improvement in local security continued. The hamlets had become safe. Nevertheless, the conclusion I reached for *Look* in October 1968, remained valid at the beginning of 1975. Not all of the ARVN in 1968 was as good as the 1st Division. Some of it was very bad, but there had been, I concluded, a general improvement.

'This improvement in turn raises once more the vital question of whether South Vietnamese forces could ever handle a full-scale war against both indigenous Viet Cong and the North Vietnamese Army', I wrote for *Look*.

Over a period of years, a phased American withdrawal now seems feasible. By a careful weeding-out process, some reduction of u.s. strength could be made now without prejudice to South Vietnam's security. Despite the material build-up of the ARVN forces and their improving esprit, however, they are not self-sufficient and cannot be made self-sufficient under present plans and existing conditions. Their performance during and after Tet would have been impossible without a contribution of United States forces, not only in ground fighting but in air, artillery and logistical support. The ARVN has become accustomed to the tactical use of helicopters (for which it is almost totally dependent on the Americans), and lists them invariably as a principal need. Even if enough helicopters were available, Vietnamese pilots are not and may never be in the numbers required for self-sufficiency.

This is also true when it comes to fire support and logistics. The additional eleven battalions of artillery that have been contemplated would give the ARVN much greater hitting punch, but not enough certainly to compensate for the withdrawal of American artillery and the whole array of air power, especially the B52s, which, used tactically, caused more havoc among main-force enemy concentrations than all other weapons in this war. *In the face of full-scale war, South Vietnam could not go it alone and survive.*

The 1972 Communist Easter offensive did not change my conviction. By this time the ARVN was a much better fighting force overall than it had been in 1968, although the 1st Division remained an outstanding élite: but, again, it was American air power that prevented the Northern blitzkreig from breaking through to Hue and Danang and helped so importantly to hold An Loc.

But now, switching the scene to late March 1975, the core of South Vietnam's armed forces, including the 1st ARVN, the Airborne and the Marine Division, all the absolute élites, had collapsed and had shown very little fight. The rout in the Highlands was duplicated, and worse, in Central Vietnam. One small battle at Ban Me Thuot had led to the disintegration of almost half the South Vietnamese Army. How on earth did it all happen?

At the conference at Cam Ranh Bay on 14 March neither Thieu nor Cao Van Vien had bothered to give General Phu, the commander of Military Region 2, any specific instructions about how to execute the withdrawal from the Highlands. Planning a withdrawal is just as complex as planning an advance. But in this case planning ended with the selection of Route 7 as the line of withdrawal. To have had any chance at all of success, the retreat from the Highlands had to be planned in detail, so that a rearguard could fight an effective delaying action, refugees could be cared for, and arms and equipment withdrawn. There was still no pressure on Pleiku. There was still time. But General

Phu behaved as if all was lost and, in so behaving, contributed measurably to the loss of all.

Thieu was scarcely back in his palace in Saigon when Phu called his staff together in Pleiku and informed them that there was to be an immediate withdrawal from the Highlands. The announcement came as a bitter shock. There were other shocks to come. Asked by one of his staff whether the province chiefs, regional forces and populace generally were to be informed, Phu replied, 'According to the President's order, the regional forces should be left behind, and no information about the withdrawal should be given to the province chiefs. Let them continue to defend. Let us complete our withdrawal, and let them continue to defend. The regional forces here consist only of Highlanders. Let them return to the Highlands.'

When Phu continued with his briefing and said that the evacuation would take place along Route 7, the long-abandoned Pleiku-Phu Bon road, there was utter confusion. 'We wondered what had prompted them to take this foolish decision, and very much doubted, with due consideration for military secrecy, the sagacity of choosing Route 7', said General Cam. He wondered even more when Phu said the retreat would begin on the following day and would be completed within three days.

Thus, an operation requiring long planning and sober execution was set in instant motion without any consideration of the effect on the population, without reconnaissance, and without concern for enemy reaction.

Phu was to move by air to Nha Trang with most of the staff to set up a forward command to plan the return to Ban Me Thuot, and the retreat was to be left to General Cam. His forces were to be organized in three columns. The first was to include three Ranger groups, one armoured regiment and an engineer group. Its mission was to protect the province of Phu Bon and to rebuild the road to Tuy Hoa on the coast. The second column was to consist of the bulk of the Corps command, three artillery battalions, the 21st Armoured Regiment with its M-48 tanks, two motorized companies and the infantry of the 23rd Division. The third column, to fight the rearguard, consisted of three Ranger groups, one armoured regiment and support artillery.

Why General Cam and the rest of the staff did not object to this precipitate, unmilitary conduct we may never know. They were tired, dispirited and probably not thinking very well. In Saigon, it was subsequently said of Phu that whereas Thieu was thinking in strategic terms, Phu interpreted him tactically.

Pleiku, and its surrounding district, had a population of nearly 200,000. In Kontum, immediately to the north, were another 70,000. Already after the fall of Ban Me Thuot the regional forces had become restive and some had started to disintegrate. Now, no one wanted to be left behind. General Phu's extraordinary decision just to pack up and leave, without notifying the regional forces who, though they were mostly montagnards, were just as anti-Communist as the ethnicVietnamese, was not only treacherous, it was bound to create both panic and rebellion.

Whether intentionally, or unintentionally, ARVN was now keeping the Americans in the dark. They had not been included in the contingency planning in which Brigadier Serong had a part, or even briefed on the plans. They had been given no hint, even now, that the Highlands were to be abandoned. Tom Polgar, the c.i.a. station chief, called at the office of Prime Minister Tran Thien Khiem on the morning of 15 March and was told that it looked like being a quiet day. He was given no hint about what was happening in Pleiku.

All was quiet in Pleiku, also, until the news spread that General Phu and his staff had already left for Nha Trang. The Americans were among the last to hear. By lunch-time they had been told to go.

An excited crowd beseiged the Air Vietnam office, offering almost any sum for an immediate booking to Saigon. The long queue outside the office started a new crop of rumours and added to the mounting panic. By early afternoon almost everyone knew that the government was abandoning the Highlands, and everyone was frantically preparing to go. Soldiers from ARVN units ordered to begin the withdrawal took off in search of their families to make sure they went' too. The result was every man for himself.

'No explanation whatsoever of the move was made to the population', Nguyen Tu, a correspondent in the Saigon newspaper *Chinh Luan* reported on 19 March. 'No organization of any kind was set up for the massive evacuation. No support of any kind was given to the poor, especially the poor oneṣ who have no transportation facilities. Since 1954 I have witnessed many mass evacuations. But what I have seen in Kontum and Pleiku has filled me with such disgust that I find the slight hope I have been nursing in my heart since 1954 has disappeared. Looking back at Pleiku city, I can still see black smoke belching from the innumerable fires.'

Orders were given to blow up the arms and ammunition dumps and the fuel tanks. Looters moved in as householders moved out, often setting fire to the houses they had robbed. Store owners loaded everything they could move into cars or trucks in competition with the looters. Since the police had thrown away their uniforms and had joined the exodus, law and order collapsed. All hospitals, military and civilian, ceased to function. The doctors when they fled left behind large numbers of in-patients who were incapable either of moving, or looking after themselves. The chaos could scarcely have been worse if General Dung with all of his divisions in the Highlands had been knocking at the gates of Pleiku.

The retreat began on Saturday 15 March, but did not get into full swing until late the following day, when the procession of cars and trucks and bicycles stretched for ten miles along the road to Phu Bon.

That evening, Dung got his first report of what had happened. Pleiku was being abandoned, he was told, and a mass of 4,000 vehicles and perhaps 100,000 people in buses, trucks, cars, carts, on motorcycles and on foot were heading down Route 7 to the coast.

Dung reached for his phone to call Major-General Kim Tuan, commander of the 320th North Vietnamese Division, and told him that he had made a grievous error in failing to anticipate the retreat along Route 7, despite its broken bridges, inoperable ferries, collapsed culverts and cratered surface. 'If the enemy escapes, you will be responsible', Dung told Kim Tuan.

But Dung, also, was staggered by the precipitate retreat and its lack of preparation. The enemy, he noted, had made another grave strategic mistake, and had presented him with a great opportunity. Hurriedly, Dung set his war machine in motion. He called on local forces (all local forces had been heavily stiffened with North Vietnamese troops prior to the offensive) in Binh Dinh province to move rapidly across country to block Route 7, sent the 320th Division in hot pursuit, ordered the 986th Infantry Division to march into Pleiku province from Laos, and left the capture of Pleiku and Kontum provincial capitals, which had been abandoned in the rush, to one engineer battalion, the 470th.

The ill-conceived, under-planned retreat never had a chance. As soon as General Kim Tuan finished talking to Dung, he gave the orders for a night march across Phu Bon province to block Route 7. Guerrillas hit the column for the first time west of the town of Hau Bon, killing and wounding hundreds and setting off a new panic. Montagnard regional forces quickly realized they were being deserted and threw away their uniforms. Some went back to their homes. Others attacked the fleeing columns and contributed materially to the delays. For hours at a time the columns failed to move.

Nguyen Tu, the local reporter who accompanied the retreat, gave the Vietnamese people–and the world–a moving day by day account. 'The exodus continues this morning under a blazing sun', he wrote from Pleiku as the city began to empty.

It's a pity to see those people who could not afford to ride on cars or trucks. They are miserable. They can use only their feet. They are the largest bunch–women, children, elders–walking as rapidly as they can and not even a drop of water to quench their thirst.

On the way to Phu Bon, all the villages, hamlets and Buon (montagnard settlements) appear deserted. The desolation of the highway gives me an impression I find hard to describe with words. If I had a friend by my side I would tell him: 'Dear friend, the sky has as many stars as the sufferings that wound my heart'.

One key pontoon bridge at the eastern extremity of Phu Bon was still intact when the first elements of the retreating forces arrived. Then the 320th Division artillery zeroed on the bridge, cutting off between one third and one half of the South Vietnamese columns in which soldiers and civilians were hopelessly mixed. With thousands of people bunching up close to the bridge, the North Vietnamese brought mortars and recoilless rifles to bear. Those closest to the river were forced into the water by the fire and the panic pressure of those behind them. None of those caught in this way succeeded in crossing the river. Several thousand were killed and all the rest captured.

At 1700 hours on 18 March, Phu from his new headquarters in Nha Trang got in touch with General Cam by radio. 'We're in a bad fix', he said. 'Don't linger, otherwise you'll be wiped out. Run if you can, and destroy your vehicles to facilitate escape.'

Cam himself was ordered out by helicopter, together with his staff of fourteen, leaving the retreat to a Ranger officer who had just been promoted from colonel to brigadier-general.

While the North Vietnamese were trying to sort out the soldiers and young men from the refugees, government fighter bombers appeared overhead and dropped bombs on the North Vietnamese forces outside the mass of people. The planes then bombed the crowd. Terrified, people fled toward the jungle and were shot down by North Vietnamese troops.

'When I flew low I could see bodies scattered along the road, burning with the trucks', said a helicopter pilot. 'The line goes back for miles.'

Next day General Cam flew back in an observation plane. Shooting had stopped, but all the vehicles, trucks, jeeps, tanks and armoured personnel carriers were pinned down and many were burning. Radio communication with the forces on the ground had become very difficult, but General Cam finally succeeded in making contact to learn that Colonel Dong, the armour commander, had abandoned his tank and was lost in the jungle. According to General Dung, six Ranger multi-battalion units, three armoured regiments, various headquarters groups from II Corps and 'many tanks, artillery pieces, engineering vehicles and trucks were subjected to virtual destruction' at this point.

At the head of the emasculated column the engineers built as they retreated. Their families were far to the rear. Not a single member of the families reached the coast. All were either killed or captured, or had fallen from exhaustion by the wayside.

Helicopters picked up the wounded where they could, often under fire, and carried them to the coastal ports. Mothers carried their often dead or wounded babies in their arms. Old men and old women with grubby home-made bandages around their wounds frequently fell down and were left to die. Shoes and boots wore out, and still the refugees stumbled on, their bloodstained feet worn through to the bone. In all the years of war there had not been so much personal disaster and tragedy as this.

A young man who left Ban Me Thuot on 10 March said that he joined a mixed army-civilian group of about 5,000 to 6,000 people trying to escape to the coast. Four days later they met a small group of Viet Cong, who were too few to stop them. Later on the same day in a clearing they were surrounded by fifteen Molotova trucks that drove at high speed through the crowd, killing fifty or sixty.

Bitterness travelled down Route 7 with the refugees and the troops. When they got to Phan Thiet one group of survivors made a visit to Thieu's ancestral graves, which they desecrated to show their hatred and contempt of their president in Saigon.

The North Vietnamese were now moving in three columns from the Highlands to the coast. The 968th Division raced down Route 19 from Pleiku into Binh Dinh province to attack Qui Nhon. The 320th Division continued its hot pursuit along Route 7. When the government forces abandoned their heavy weapons and took to the jungle they were followed by tens of thousands of civilians–and by the North Vietnamese. Without food, without water, without weapons, they received no quarter from their pursuers.

On Route 21, which runs from Ban Me Thuot to Nha Trang, the 10th North Vietnamese Division's mission was to destroy General Phu's new headquarters before he could organize effective resistance. Morale broke long before the North Vietnamese forces were anywhere near the town. As General Dung described the scene, 'Three thousand puppet troops at the Lam Son Training Centre and the school for non-commissioned officers in the northern part of the city fled to the city centre. Policemen guarding the city prison also took flight. Two thousand imprisoned puppet soldiers broke out of the gaol, seized weapons and began to fire indiscriminately and go on a robbery rampage, spreading still more confusion in the city.' General Phu, with what was left of his II Corps command, fled to Phan Thiet, far down the coast toward Saigon.

If the defeat here was disastrous for Saigon, there are no words to describe the degree of calamity in Central Vietnam. After all, in the Highlands, there was a very significant North Vietnamese attack with overwhelming forces against Ban Me Thuot. In Central Vietnam the South Vietnamese simply set themselves up to be knocked down.

Until the first week in March the security situation in the five provinces of the Centre was good. The regional and popular forces continued to have considerable success in their task of preserving law and order in the populated and cultivated areas. Only in Quang Ngai province, where the North Vietnamese had built a new road running almost to the coast, were there difficulties.

On 9 March the North Vietnamese launched what the government forces regarded as a 'high point' offensive. It was far from an all-out attack. On many occasions in the past the government forces had been hit in this way, and always they had given a good account of themselves. This time regular North Vietnamese forces in the mountains attacked the 1st ARVN Division, the 15th Ranger Group and the Marines. At the same time, using four or five Viet Cong battalions, they also attacked in the lowlands, in the more densely-populated areas.

Colonel Van Cao Dong commanded the 35,000 regional forces in Military Region 1. He had been in Central Vietnam for sixteen years and knew both the terrain and local Viet Cong forces in detail. Using tanks and armoured personnel carriers to support his infantry, Colonel Dong destroyed the Viet Cong battalions. He suffered only one major reverse. Two regiments of the 2nd North Vietnamese Division attacked the district capital of Tien Phuoc in central Quang Tin province. The town was held only by Colonel Dong's regional forces, who fled from the town after twelve hours' fighting. In the following days the 2nd ARVN Division and a Ranger group counter-attacked and tried to retake Tien Phuoc. They were not successful.

On 13 March General Truong flew to Saigon to attend the meeting called by Thieu. His report on the tactical level was encouraging. Despite the loss of Tien Phuoc, the situation on the ground was good. Strategically, however, General Truong had every reason for concern, and he expressed it. That Thieu needed the Airborne in the strategic reserve could not be denied. But Truong had the gravest doubts whether Hue and Danang could be held without the Airborne in the event of a major North Vietnamese offensive. He put his case bluntly and was told that the Airborne had to go. He returned to Central Vietnam, and moved the Marines out of Quang Tri province, where they had been holding the line against any attack from North Vietnam. The Airborne came out of the line west of Danang and plans were drawn up for them to be replaced by the Marines. The Airborne started to pack their bags and to prepare to go South.

This troop reshuffle, and the dangerous gap it opened in Hue's defences, caused no immediate incident. After the end of the 1972 Communist Easter offensive, in which the town of Quang Tri was levelled, and the former defence line south of the demilitarized zone fell into North Vietnamese hands, refugees had begun to go back to Quang Tri to start farming again. They were both defended and helped by the Marines. The population living under Saigon control in Quang Tri had grown to about 280,000. Of these about 20,000 were so alarmed by the withdrawal of the Marines that they packed their belongings and went to Hue. But at this time there was no panic. The people in Central Vietnam were watching with dismay the events in the Highlands, but there was no sense of impending disaster in Hue or Danang.

On 17 March, Prime Minister Khiem flew to Danang with several Cabinet ministers. Before the meeting, while the Cabinet ministers and provincial officials waited in the war room, Khiem talked for about thirty to forty minutes with General Truong, one-time commander of the 1st ARVN Division and now responsible for the defence of all Military Region 1. When it began, the meeting concentrated on refugees. It was decided that the refugees from Quang Tri and others without any possessions should be sent South. Refugees from populated areas who had been temporarily driven out by the 'high point' offensive were to be given enough rice to provide for their needs for up to fourteen days and then sent back to their homes. Quang Tri itself was to be abandoned, but there was no hint that President Thieu had decided to abandon all of Central Vietnam.

On 17 March, also, the Politburo and the Central Military Party Committee met in Hanoi. It decided to open a second front in Central Vietnam. It ordered that the road from Hue to Danang should be cut and that all forces should move as rapidly as possible from the mountains toward the coast.

The forward movement of the North Vietnamese and the new retreat by the South Vietnamese coincided. At 8 a.m. on 18 March all the civil service and local administrators in Quang Tri province packed up and left, without a word or a hint to the local population that they were being abandoned to the North Vietnamese. As in Pleiku, the move

65

precipitated panic. An estimated 130,000 people, who had fled once under fire during the 1972 offensive, took to the road and headed for Hue. Only those with relations in the North Vietnamese forces, or with the Viet Cong, remained.

On 19 March, without opposition, the North Vietnamese tanks and infantry crossed the river at Quang Tri to take possession of the land abandoned by the South. Thieu had shortened his lines in Central Vietnam, but he had also brought the front to within about twenty miles of Hue on the My Chanh River. Even more importantly, the refugees carried the seeds of panic which were soon to grow and spread down the coastal plains.

That night, apparently to justify the new withdrawal, Thieu announced that the North Vietnamese had launched a new general offensive in Central Vietnam. What had happened in Pleiku and Quang Tri was now repeated all over again in Hue which, since the Tet offensive in 1968, had been bitterly anti-Communist.

The educational, cultural and spiritual centre of Vietnam, Hue had become known to the outside world as the 'ancient' capital, which was not true at all. Some illiterate correspondent translated the French word *ancien*, meaning former, into ancient, and so it had become in newspapers around the world, although, in fact, it had become the capital of Vietnam only in 1802, when Emperor Gia Long put down the warring factions in the country, established the Nguyen dynasty, and began the construction of the Citadel walls, moat, canals and towers. Weather, not age, was responsible for their appearance of great antiquity.

Nevertheless, Hue, with its population of about a quarter of a million, had become a symbol of resistance in Vietnam. The North Vietnamese had occupied the city in its entirety during the Tet offensive and had been driven out by the 1st ARVN Division, whose families lived there. For six years the inhabitants had been uncovering mass graves of those slaughtered by the North Vietnamese during their brief occupation of the city. Proud, independent, and contemptuous of commercial Saigon, Hue had been affected less than any other Vietnamese city by Americanization.

If the North Vietnamese had, in fact, begun a new offensive in Central Vietnam, General Truong and his staff knew nothing of it. They were aware, of course, that Quang Tri had fallen but, since it had been abandoned by the Marines and all the administrative staff, what did Saigon expect?

'Victory Without Blood', said the North Vietnamese posters plastered through Quang Tri.

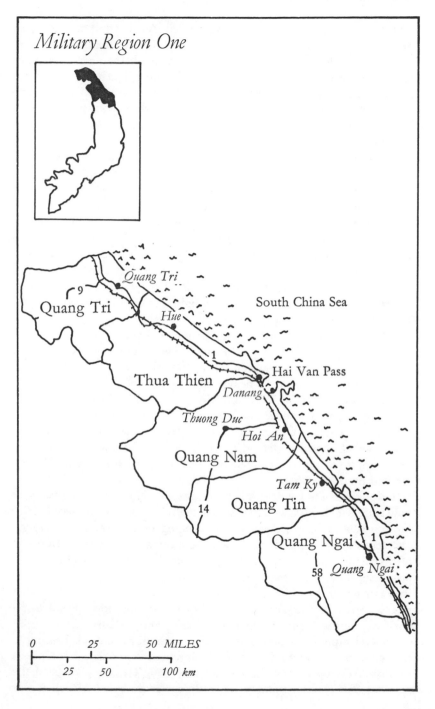

Military Region One

Quang Tri

Quang Tri

Hue

South China Sea

Thua Thien

Hai Van Pass

Danang

Thuong Duc

Hoi An

Quang Nam

Tam Ky

Quang Tin

Quang Ngai

Quang Ngai

0   25   50 MILES

25   50   100 km

For four days the inhabitants of Hue fled. All day and all night they moved along Route 1, over the Hai Van Pass, to Danang. They went by any means they could. For four days the North Vietnamese let them go. No one was ready to receive them in Danang. During the 1968 and 1972 Communist offensives there had been extensive barracks and other temporary wartime buildings. These had all been pulled down. There were no supplies of rice. No food. No medicines. No blankets. No shelter. No sanitation.

On 20 March the Politburo met again in Hanoi to assess the situation in the South. The withdrawal from the Highlands followed by the abandonment of Quang Tri led to the conclusion that Thieu was planning to carry out a large-scale strategic retreat in order to concentrate forces in the Saigon area, part of the Mekong Delta and perhaps also in Danang and Cam Ranh, with a view to the sort of negotiations for a new partition of Vietnam envisaged by Brigadier Serong and others when they had first drawn up plans for the abandonment of Central Vietnam and the Highlands. Everything, the Politburo decided, was now to be thrown into a lightning offensive to take Saigon before the wet season began in May.

On 23 March the North Vietnamese closed the road between Hue and Danang. Their forces attacking toward the coast occupied a small pass, Da Bac, between Hue and Hai Van. The 1st ARVN Division came under very heavy attack south of the airfield at Phu Bai. As was to be expected of this division, it resisted strongly.

But now there was only one way to go from Hue to Danang, by sea. On fishing boats, on sampans and on barges the exodus from Hue continued. Fishermen defending their boats with their lives against the human sea that descended on them counted hundreds of bodies washed up on the shore.

Throughout the Central Vietnam area, the North Vietnamese were now in full scale attack. They forced the bridge across the My Chanh River an hour before dusk on the evening of 22 March and added enormously to the alarm of those people remaining in Hue. Jumping off from their newly-captured position at Tien Phuoc in Quang Tin province, they also threatened the provincial capital of Tam Ky, and they cut Route 1 to Quang Ngai.

The terror that assailed the inhabitants of Hue now spread to all parts of Central Vietnam. Danang alone seemed secure and from all provincial capitals in the Centre refugees jammed the roads leading to this city, South Vietnam's second largest. Its population of about 450,000 grew by tens of thousands every day. The refugees filled the pagodas and churches and schools. By the night of 22 March it was estimated that there were 800,000 people in the city, and the inward flow was undiminished.

That day General Truong flew to Saigon to confer with Thieu. He returned the following day with orders to hold Hue at all costs, but looking, according to his staff, 'very sad'.

Truong met the commanders of the Marine Division and the 1st ARVN Division to work out plans. He repeated Thieu's instructions that Hue had to be held at any cost and that the city could be abandoned only on Thieu's personal order.

The 1st ARVN Division had been pushed out of the mountains by the North Vietnamese offensive and was now holding along Route 1. The men were tired and frantic for the safety of their wives and families. Their mothers and fathers and wives and children had all fled from Hue. Instead of responding to orders, the 1st ARVN began to break up as its officers and desperate rank and file began the fruitless search for their families. Instead of moving to the defence of Hue, many tried to get to Danang.

In January 1975 during a visit to Hue and Danang, I wrote about the situation in these terms for the *Daily Telegraph* in London: 'Trained by the Americans in the massive use of firepower, these South Vietnamese élites have had to be sparing and make every shot count. They have enough to deal with the two Northern divisions now on their front, but they wonder whether sufficient reserves will be available if and when the main attack comes. "Will we get the extra $300 million from the United States?" asked the deputy commander of the South Vietnamese forces in Central Vietnam, Lieut-General Lam Quang Thi, before he began his briefing. Clearly, in his mind, that was all important.' 'Don't bank on it', said Australian ambassador, Geoffrey Price.

Now, in March, when he knew that the aid was not forthcoming and that the Marines had been removed from the path of the invading North Vietnamese forces, General Thi ignored the order not to withdraw from Hue. He pulled out of his headquarters in the Citadel (General Truong's headquarters were in Danang), and Hue fell, with scarcely a shot fired in its defence.

In Quang Tin, the North Vietnamese took the provincial capital, Tam Ky, with no more than a show of force, and an unintentional show, at that. A lost North Vietnamese tank accompanied by a company of infantry strayed into the town, and Colonel Hoang Tich Thong, the assistant commander of the 2nd ARVN Division, and the province chief, Colonel Dao Mong Xuan, took to their heels, followed by the rest of the town's defenders.

Almost incidentally, in the continuing saga of disaster, Quang Ngai

Thua Thien Province

Quang Tri

South China Sea

Hue

1

Phu Bai

Perfume R.

Hai
Van Pass

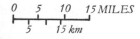

0   5   10   15 MILES

5   15 km

also fell. On the morning of 24 March, the province chief ordered that the town should be defended to the last man. Twelve hours later, under intense rocket fire, he was forced to retreat.

The news of these disasters from Central Vietnam had a devastating effect on Thieu, the Joint General Staff, and the public in Saigon. Thieu repeatedly called Truong on the phone in Danang and accused him of having given the order to withdraw from Hue. They spoke several times during the day but not again. 'Liaison between the President and Truong ended', said one of Truong's subordinates. 'Truong did not report again to the President.'

The rumour that Thieu really intended to abandon all Central Vietnam had reached Truong by this time. He suspected that Thieu had made a secret agreement to turn over the entire area to the North Vietnamese and that this accounted for the confusing orders he received. The withdrawal of the Airborne and the redeployment of the Marines from Quang Tri convinced him of the President's guilt. The general retreated deep into melancholia. He spoke little to his staff and not at all to his troops, all of whom were in urgent need of his leadership at this time.

The 3rd Regiment of the 1st ARVN Division had broken west of Route 1 and now fled to the beaches. Rangers and self-defence forces packed into two landing craft to escape and were attacked by Marines with grenades and machine guns. Both boats sank offshore, carrying down with them about a hundred men.

On the verge of a nervous breakdown, Truong, on 25 March, watched the remnants of his 1st ARVN Division attempt to escape from the trap that had now been sprung around it south of Hue. Somehow the division got its tanks, its trucks and its artillery to the long spit of low-lying sand that guards Thua Thien province from the sea. It is, in fact, an island entirely surrounded by water, with narrow and deep outlets to the ocean north of Hue and also about thirty miles to the south-east. Under constant artillery fire, the division had reached the southern extremity of the spit but was unable to cross the narrow gap that led to what might have been safety. Helicopters came in with bridging equipment, but the engineers broke under fire. The bridge was not put into position. There, on the sand dunes, South Vietnam's most admired division met its end.

Truong was a great soldier. He rose from battalion commander through to regimental, divisional and finally corps commander. His performance as a divisional commander during the 1968 Tet offensive was brilliant. He was no less distinguished in restoring morale and holding the line as a corps commander in the 1972 Easter offensive.

No hint of scandal was ever associated with his name, no breath of corruption. Sir Robert Thompson once described him as one of the finest soldiers in the world today, and it was an opinion that many Vietnamese–and Americans–shared.

What, then, were the reasons for the collapse? I put the question to Colonel Dong. 'So many reasons', he replied.

First Thieu's mistaken strategy. It was a grave error to pull out of Pleiku and Kontum after the fall of Ban Me Thuot. It was no less of a mistake to remove the Marines from Quang Tri and the Airborne from around Danang. He should have prepared well in advance and moved slowly. The Airborne was withdrawn without explanation. Thieu's explanation about the fall of Quang Tri was not correct. It was not lost by attack but by the reaction of the people (to the withdrawal of the Marines and the civil administration). Another reason is the panic caused by disorganized administration appointed by the President and the government. It did not have the capacity to deal with the situation quickly. Every decision had to wait orders from Saigon.

The ARVN units were trained during the u.s. stay here to fight with fire power and air power. With the big reduction in American aid they had to economize drastically. They had very little air or artillery support. Their effectiveness was much reduced.

Congress in the United States and the President and people have made us all very unhappy. I felt that we were beggars and had lost a lot of prestige. The Americans help us, but they make us feel like beggars.

The government itself tells lies. Thieu said we were recovering Hue when everyone knew that we had lost it and would not recover it.

Organized resistance to the North Vietnamese offensive in Central Vietnam ended with the collapse of the 1st ARVN Division. By 26 March General Truong realized that he had lost command and was no longer able to control either the situation or his own forces. He decided to send two of his most senior officers, including Colonel Dong, to Saigon to endeavour to arrange a meeting between himself and Thieu at Nha Trang.

The two officers left for Saigon on 27 March, saw Thieu and told him that two-thirds of the troops in Central Vietnam had either been lost, or had abandoned their posts. They conveyed Truong's urgent appeal for assistance and the meeting at Nha Trang. Thieu was not about to reinforce defeat, or to meet Truong. All trust between the two men was now entirely destroyed, and Truong in Danang sank deeper into depression.

General Dung seized his opportunity. On 26 March he telegraphed the Central Military Committee in Hanoi, requesting that Lieut-General Le Trong Tan, a deputy chief of the General Staff, should be sent immediately to Central Vietnam to take personal command of the attack on Danang. A Northerner by birth and a member of the Central Committee of the Laodong Party, Tan had been active for years in the South as deputy commander of the North Vietnamese forces and, for a time, as chief of staff of the COSVN military apparatus.

Dung sent another message to Lieut-General Hoang Van Thai, who had been responsible for the brilliant tactics that led the u.s. Marines into a succession of bloody actions south of the demilitarized zone earlier in the war. Educated at French schools in Hanoi and later at a Japanese naval college, Thai had also been through Russian and Chinese military schools and was highly regarded as the best trained North Vietnamese officer. Although he was now seventy years of age, he was still actively engaged in war planning. Dung needed him now to push the 130-millimetre artillery out of the mountains of Central Vietnam to within range of the airfield and wharves at Danang with the utmost speed.

General Tan boarded a helicopter in Hanoi and flew immediately to take command on the Danang front. The big guns started to move. Even in this moment of urgent action, the Central Military Committee in Hanoi did not forget its political and ideological responsibilities. At the same time, it appointed Major-General Chu Huy Man, yet another member of the Party's Central Committee, and for ten years military commander in B3, in the tri-border area command, to serve as political commissar. Of the Provisional Revolutionary Government not a word was heard.

Long before either man had reached the new command post west of Danang, Tan and Mao, who had his headquarters on the Quang Tin and Quang Ngai borders, had been in communication by phone. They had their troops and guns moving in a four-pronged drive on the city before they had had a chance to hang up their hats.

News that Hoi An, capital of Quang Nam province, had fallen to the North Vietnamese spread through Danang on the morning of 28 March. The headquarters of the 3rd ARVN Division at Phuoc Tuong, due west of the airfield, was preparing to make some sort of stand along Route 1 when two thousand soldiers in the nearby Hoa Cam training camp mutinied and attacked 3rd Division troops.

During the night of 28–29 March, a North Vietnamese force made a flanking attack along the coast to prevent the evacuation by sea. Other columns came from the west and south-west to seize the airfield and to drive on General Truong's headquarters. What remained of the 3rd Division's defenders threw away their guns.

More than a million people were now jammed into Danang. To cope

73

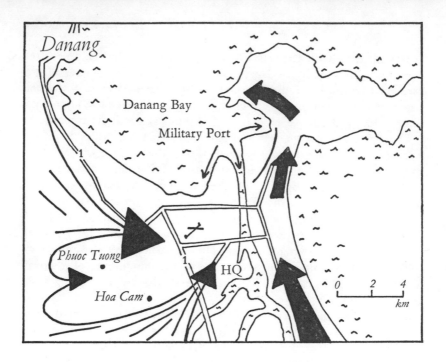

with the economic problems posed by the American withdrawal from the great air base the U.S. had built there, the mayor had put the unemployed to work painting and cleaning up the city. At the beginning of March it was the neatest and most spick and span city in all Vietnam. By the end of March it was a cesspit.

In 1972, during the Communist Easter offensive, the authorities had been able to take care of 280,000 refugees without too much difficulty. They put 150,000 under shelter in disued American barracks and installations and had at least enough food, clothing and medicines for the others. This time thay had no facilities and no preparation of any kind had been made to receive the refugees. There were so many people on the streets that on 26 March it took Colonel Dong four hours to walk from the centre of the city to General Truong's headquarters, a distance of no more than two miles.

The administration collapsed. Some dedicated men stayed by their posts and did their best. Most fled. Here, as in Pleiku, civilian doctors, who were most needed, were among the first to run.

The Marines ceased to take orders from General Truong. They made no attempt of any sort to defend Danang. On the contrary, they began the looting and the shooting and the violence that led a million people into hysteria. Some officers who tried to restore discipline were shot by their own men.

74

Tens of thousands swarmed to the airfield, fighting for places on outgoing planes. Soldiers used their weapons to demand places and fired if they were turned back. Women and children were flung aside, and even off the planes. Thus did the mob destroy the air lift designed to help it.

Hundreds of thousands went to the waterfront, hoping to escape by sea. Some got away, but very few. Of those who did many died of heat, exhaustion or thirst, or were drowned in overloaded boats and rafts, among them, it was said, the aged mother of Pham Van Dong, Prime Minister of North Vietnam.

Up to a thousand people crammed into ammunition barges that the Vietnamese navy towed out to sea. On none was there any room to sit down. Those who died lay where they fell and were trampled under foot. Professor Thao Le, of the Linguistics Department of the University of Hue, told me that the barge he escaped on was so crowded with people that many clung to its sides in the water and dropped off one by one. The barge had no food, no water and no shelter. Some of the women and men became insane from drinking salt water. Others, both men and women, were so weak when they were picked up by ship that they could not climb aboard. The professor's cousin, three months pregnant, was among those who died when she fell into the sea from the ropes thrown over the side of the ship. One woman was crushed to death between the ship and the barge.

I asked the professor how many he thought had died in the attempt to get away from Danang. He had heard a figure of 50,000 to 60,000, and from what he had seen he did not think the estimate seemed too high.

Trung Van Quang, a merchant, who left Danang on 28 March, climbed aboard a group of four sampans, roped together. Soldiers blew up one of the sampans, killing all aboard. The others cut their ropes and drifted for two days and two nights before they were picked up by a Filipino ship. About twenty people died in the two days on this sampan from exposure and thirst, or from drinking sea water. In another sampan that drifted not far away from his the death roll was about a hundred.

The North Vietnamese and Viet Cong infiltrated Danang with the refugees and had already begun to take over control of the city long before General Dung's marching columns were ready to attack. On the afternoon of 25 March, Colonel Dong's sister-in-law was pushing her way through the crowded streets when she met a man she had known in the past and identified as a high ranking Viet Cong cadre. Unabashed, her old friend told her what he knew of the plans for taking the city.

On 28 March Thieu appointed a Danang commander and many officers were detailed to restore law and order. By that time it was too late.

Rebuffed by a sentry at Marine headquarters, where the divisional commander refused to see him, General Truong waded from the beach in response to a call from Al Francis, the American consul-general, who was aboard a ship off-shore. The red and yellow flag of the Viet Cong flew over the City Hall. About 4,000 Marines escaped but were not worth anything again. The 1st, 2nd and 3rd ARVN Divisions were all destroyed.

Without pausing for a moment to consolidate, General Dung set his forces moving from all fronts toward Saigon. On 27 March he had given orders for 50,000 troops from the highlands to move South. This force was to be known as III Corps, and included the 10th, 320th and 316th Divisions. From North Vietnam yet another corps, the 1st, was already on the move. The Politburo and the Central Military Committee had about six weeks left before the wet season began around Saigon. By that time, they were determined, Saigon was to be theirs.

Part two

The end of the beginning

1940 to 1975

1. The French bow out

'During no war in which the United States has been involved has there been more detailed information available and less understanding of what it meant than in the long struggle over the future of South Vietnam', wrote Ellen Hammer, one of the leading authorities on Vietnamese nationalism, in a review of yet another batch of books on Vietnam. What was true in the United States was also true in Britain and Australia and pretty nearly everywhere else, including Vietnam, and I am not by any means sure that any attempted explanation now of what the war was all about will prove more successful than all the other attempts made in the past. There was not just one war, but a whole multiplicity of wars, some hot, some cold, in which protagonists disappeared from the field of battle, and even appeared to change sides. It lasted for thirty years, and during this period there were such changes in the international scene that what once seemed rational became irrational. Only one factor remained constant: the absolute determination on the part of the Democratic Republic of Vietnam to unify the entire country under its control. In opposition to this there were transient alliances that had great, but often brief, force. Over the long haul, however, the single-minded determination of the North was in sharp contrast to the divisive, uncertain, irresolute policies followed by those who sought to keep Saigon, the symbol of ultimate victory, out of the Northern grasp.

From the beginning, the Viet Minh, and only the Viet Minh, were ready to seize chance when it offered. Late in 1944, after an absence from his country of thirty-three years, Ho Chi Minh crossed the China border to join his Communist guerrillas in the mountains of northern Tongking. Outside the town of Cao Bang, on 22 December 1944, Vo Nguyen Giap formally created the first platoon of the Viet Minh army. It consisted of twenty-seven men. At the same time, Ho created a propaganda unit of similar strength. With the assistance of the American Office of Strategic Services, the small guerrilla bases around Cao Bang, Bac Kan, and Lang Son, which had hitherto concerned themselves primarily with espionage and intelligence, and with the extension of the underground apparatus through the rest of Vietnam, began to devote themselves to guerrilla work. According to Giap, within weeks these original forces had multiplied and become several thousands strong.

In March 1945, the Japanese ousted the French from nominal control of Indo-China. This left the way open for the Viet Minh to extend their authority through the rural regions of the North, where the French had hitherto exercised control. During the closing days of July, and early August, when rumours of a Japanese surrender were widespread, the Viet Minh guerrillas grew bolder. Several towns and many villages north and west of the Red River Delta passed into their hands. The Viet Minh were received with delight by the local population. The French had always been unpopular, and the Japanese, who had commandeered the rice supply as soon as they assumed full power, were now hated.

There were Viet Minh agents throughout North and Central Vietnam, and the organization had at least a sketchy framework in the South. The Japanese, while alarmed at events, were unable to do much about them. Japanese attempts to enlist the support of the Emperor Bao Dai and his puppet government to liquidate all known local Viet Minh agents leaked before they could be put to the test. American assistance for both the Viet Minh and rival guerrilla organizations was already beginning to make itself felt. Lu Conein, an American Office of Strategic Services commando, had been dropped into Tongking by parachute to link up with a small Gaullist group of Frenchmen fighting in the mountains. Between them they had a force of 148 men. Their target was a Japanese divisional headquarters at the town of Lang Son on the China-Indo-China border. They sent scouts into the city to reconnoitre but none ever returned. It was typical of Conein that the guerrillas decided to attack, anyway.

No more remarkable man ever appeared in Indo-China. He was in the Foreign Legion when the Second World War broke out, and, according to William Colby, who served with him in the French underground and later became his boss in the Central Intelligence Agency, he swam the English Channel to continue the fight when France fell. Parachuted back into France, he became an active underground leader, blowing up German ammunition dumps, wrecking trains and raising hell. In Colby's view, he was the single outstanding man among the partisans.

Although he could speak French fluently, he could not write or read a word. After France had been recovered by the Allies, he was sent to Yunnan and from there parachuted into Tongking.

'What the hell do you do when your scouts disappear?' said Conein, when he told me of the Lang Son raid. 'Sit around on your arse and wait until no one wants to do anything?' That was not the Conein way.

The raid almost ended in disaster before it was properly underway. The point scout threw a grenade, whereupon all the Vietnamese in the raiding party started firing and killed nine of their own men before the Japanese had fired a shot. Conein blasted his way to the centre of the headquarters with a tommy gun, killed the Japanese switchboard operator, and with the headquarters in an uproar, led the surviving members of his team in a massacre of the shocked Japanese. For the rest of the war, his forces heavily depleted by the raid, he contented himself with ambushes and blowing up bridges, minor stuff for this most amazing man.

Years later in Saigon an agitated Vietnamese officer called at Brigadier Serong's house late at night to tell him that a group of assassins were looking for Conein to kill him. 'God help them if they find him', said Serong and went back to bed.

In expectation of an early Japanese surrender, Viet Minh groups began to close around Hanoi early in August 1945. A hurried congress in the mountains appointed a National Liberation Committee to lead the coming revolution under the presidency of Ho Chi Minh. The Viet Minh guerrillas became the Vietnam Liberation Army under Vo Nguyen Giap. The call went out for a general uprising. 'The hour has struck for an offensive on all fronts', Ho ordered. Bao Dai's puppet government collapsed, and the Vietnamese people rallied to the ranks of the Viet Minh revolutionary committees which spread through the country.

Giap entered Hanoi with the vanguard of his troops, just a couple of companies strong, on 17 August 1945. The following day a Viet Minh provisional committee took over. Faced with a spontaneous and popular uprising, Bao Dai abdicated and took office as supreme counsellor under the provisional government led by Ho. It was a token post, soon to be abolished. The Communists held all the key posts in government and wanted advice from no one.

To the French, disarmed by the Japanese and fuming in their homes and hotels, afraid almost everywhere to be seen on the streets, this was all a monstrous joke. No one had ever head of Ho Chi Minh before, which was reasonable enough since the bearer of the name had scarcely grown familiar with it himself. It was inconceivable, the French thought, that this fragile little man with a wisp of a beard, and who liked to be called 'Uncle Ho' and wore an open-necked white shirt and khaki shorts, could seriously challenge the authority of France. He had the broad and calloused feet of a coolie, and his handshake was like the grip of an eagle's claw. It had taken Vietnam in its grasp and would never be persuaded to let go.

Many of the nationalists in the North bitterly opposed Ho. One of particular significance was a 27-year-old graduate of the Hanoi Medical School, Dr Phan Quang Dan, who was second to none in his opposition to French colonialism. Famine swept through the Red River Delta as the Second World War ended, and the hungry fled into Hanoi in search of food. They died on the streets in thousands. Dan organized the school children to go to every house in every street to collect leftovers for the famine victims. Before long his young recruits were collecting one full meal a day from thousands of families, and Dan had organized those well enough to work among the hungry to take the dead from the streets and to bury them in slit trenches that had been dug outside the city for protection against wartime American bombing raids.

On two occasions Ho offered Dan a seat in his Cabinet. Dan spurned both offers and occupied the district of Ngu-Xa in Hanoi, turning it into an autonomous anti-Communist zone, where he founded the anti-Communist and anti-French newspaper, *Thiet Thuc (The Realist)*. All through the latter part of 1945 and early into 1946 Dan extended his famine relief programme, at the same time fighting hard against the Viet Minh. He was dedicated, fearless, tireless and determined. Even in Viet Minh areas in the delta he began to gain ground before being driven into exile by a provisional agreement between the French and the Viet Minh, his common enemies.

In Saigon an altogether different sort of situation had developed. On 2 September, when Ho Chi Minh made his proclamation of independence in Hanoi, the proclamation was also made in Saigon. In the South, however, the Viet Minh had very little of the authority that Ho had succeeded in establishing in the North. Religious sects and nationalist groups did not accept Viet Minh primacy, and there were widespread incidents not directed specifically against the French or the Japanese, but by Vietnamese against Vietnamese. Initially, the British lacked the troops to keep order, and called on the Japanese to do the job. This was bad enough. In the eyes of the Vietnamese, however, the British then compounded their felony by bringing in French troops in British uniforms. General Douglas Gracey, the British commander, had no patience with, or understanding of, the deep anti-colonial emotions of the Vietnamese people. He had not come to Indo-China to preside over the liquidation of the French colonial empire, or to put a barefooted coolie in the palace.

From the day of the proclamation of independence there had been trouble. In the demonstration that accompanied the proclamation five Frenchmen, including a Roman Catholic priest, were killed. Incident followed incident, and there were brutal reprisals on both sides. On the night of 23–24 September 1945, a small force of Gaullist troops released French prisoners of war and armed civilians stormed the headquarters of the Viet Minh committee in Saigon. The committee fled and the French community, confident that victory was theirs, beat up any Vietnamese found in the French quarter of the city. The Vietnamese responded in kind, and on 24 September several Frenchmen were either killed or abducted near the Saigon River. An American, Colonel A. P. Dewey, head of the Office of Strategic Services in Saigon, was also ambushed and killed. Dewey, like his fellow members of the OSS who had been parachuted into Tongking to help train Viet Minh guerrillas, was sympathetic to the cause of Vietnamese independence, and there were widespread rumours that the French had had a hand in the killing.

This was followed on the night of the 25th by a bloody massacre, 'the night of the long knives', when some four hundred French and Eurasians were hacked to death. In thousands, the French converged on the Continental Hotel to seek security. By October, French forces had arrived in strength and were soon in active pursuit of the Viet Minh, quickly restoring their writ in the principal towns in the Mekong Delta and other parts of southern Vietnam with equipment, ammunition and stores made available from Lord Louis Mountbatten's South-East Asia Command in Ceylon.

Across the border in Cambodia, Prince Norodom Sihanouk–King, as he then was–had responded to Japanese encouragement and proclaimed his country's independence in March 1944. A little Anglo-French foray to Phnom Penh resulted in the arrest of the prime minister, Son Ngoc Thanh, a nationalist leader of integrity and capacity, whose supporters fled to the border regions where, for a time, they made common cause with the Viet Minh. Early in 1946 Cambodia acquired limited autonomy within the French Union.

About the middle of September Chinese Nationalist forces had arrived in the North to take the surrender of the Japanese. By an arrangement reached earlier with Washington, their area of responsibility covered all of Tongking and extended well south of Hue, on the Central Vietnam coast. The French received none of the co-operation from the Chinese that General Gracey had extended to them in the South. Although the Viet Minh carried guns, all returning Frenchmen were immediately disarmed.

To broaden his base, Ho had formally dissolved the Indo-China Communist Party and hastily organized elections, which were held openly in the North and Centre and clandestinely in the South. They resulted in a sweeping victory for Ho and, though their validity was open to question, they strengthened his position with the Chinese, who were, in any case, more concerned with looting than with the local political scene. They removed, among other things, the greater part of the Hanoi-Kunming railway line and all the plumbing fixtures in Hanoi and Haiphong.

Early in 1946, however, the French made a breakthrough. In return for the relinquishment of French extra-territorial rights in China and the promise of special conditions for Chinese living in Indo-China, the Nationalists agreed to withdraw their forces and to hand over control to the French. Because he felt he could not fight France and at the same time expedite the departure of the light-fingered Chinese, Ho also reached his preliminary agreement with the French under which he gained some measure of independence. The agreement did not satisfy any of his real aspirations. He signed it, he subsequently admitted, only because he had no alternative. He knew that he could not survive a joint French-Chinese offensive against him.

The Vietnamese people were surprised. But at this time in the eyes of many of his countrymen, Ho could do nothing wrong. Communist or not, he was a hero. Some Catholics even professed to see double pupils in his eyes, which they interpreted as signifying that he was a saint. To take advantage of this popular support, Ho announced the formation of an even wider national organization to be known as the Lien Viet front, or the League for the National Union of Vietnam. The idea was to conceal hard-core Communists under a liberal coating of nationalism. It worked with many, but not with all. Men like Dr Dan and Ngo Dinh Diem refused to join the Front. Bao Dai, an uncomfortable bedfellow, was soon exiled. Dr Dan went north to Shanghai. In the South, the alliance with the Cao Dai and Hoa Hao Buddhist sect, and with the Binh Xuyen river pirates, was uneasy.

In May 1946, Ho Chi Minh went to Paris to continue negotiations with the French, leaving Vo Nguyen Giap at home to mind the shop. Giap continued to eliminate the opposition and to reactivate the old guerrilla bases that the Viet Minh had used in the mountains during the closing stages of the Second World War.

On their side, the French were equally guilty of bad faith. While negotiations continued in France, they made all preparations to march north. Neither in Paris nor in Indo-China were the French prepared to bend before the winds of change. Negotiations broke down, and the main part of the Vietnamese delegation in France left for home. Ho stayed in Paris for a few weeks, continuing to plead for something in the way of an agreement to appease his more extremist followers. He got a *modus vivendi*, and the promise of another conference not later than January 1947.

The conference was never held. Giap's men clashed repeatedly with the French forces, and widespread incidents, some of them minor, but several quite serious, were reported from various parts of the country. By November relations had passed almost to the point of no return. The French, in the mistaken belief that a show of force would bring the Viet Minh to heel, used their navy and air force to bombard the Vietnamese quarter of the densely populated port of Haiphong. It was a monstrous act. The cruiser *Suffren*, firing at point-blank range, poured broadside after broadside into the port. Six thousand Vietnamese lay dead in the ruins when the order was given to cease fire.

The French followed the attack with military demands which, the Viet Minh at first seemed ready to accept. Gunboat diplomacy had worked again, the French thought. They were wrong. Giap issued his first Order of the Day on 7 December. This was merely an instruction to prepare for action. Troops were to be ready by 12 December. In a final effort to avoid war, Ho cabled Leon Blum, an acquaintance of his Paris days, whose election as premier of a Socialist Government in France appeared to offer some slight hope. But his cable lay for days in the French censor's office in Saigon. When at last it was sent and a reply came back, minor incidents in Hanoi had flared into all-out fighting. Ho Chi Minh and his government had fled to Giap's mountain bases north of the Red River Delta, and Indo-China was at war.

In those early days it was truly a colonial war. Very soon it was to become much more complex. The Vietnamese were not the only South-East Asians ready and willing to fight for their independence.

85

The Burmese and the Indians were hammering at the gates of White-hall. The Americans had already bowed out in the Philippines. The Indonesians were locked in battle with the Dutch. And then came the Cold War. The great wartime alliance between the Soviet Union and the United States split asunder. The Berlin blockade in June 1948 brought the allies to the brink of war. Communist insurgents in South-East Asia made war not only on their colonial masters but also on fellow nationalists. In China, Mao Tse-tung was leading his forces to victory against Chiang Kai-shek's Nationalists and eager to proclaim that henceforth China would lean to one side–toward the Soviet Union. And in 1950 North Korea invaded the South and inside two months had all but driven the American forces into the sea.

These were the great and profound changes in the international situation, and international perceptions, that helped to alter men's thinking about the situation in Indo-China. The French were no longer seen to be fighting a dirty little colonial war but helping to hold the pass for all of South-East Asia and beyond. Moreover, the view was not held exclusively by those who opposed the Communists: it was shared equally by the Communists themselves. As the Chinese Communist forces advanced closer to the Indo-China border, Ho Chi Minh began to shed the trappings of the united front of all nationalists and revived the Indo-China Communist Party, calling it now the Laodong (Workers) Party of North Vietnam. 'Only a party that has a vanguard theory can lead the revolution', Truong Chinh, a founder member of the old Indo-China Communist Party, told a meeting of political parties at a conference in the mountains north of Hanoi. 'A vanguard theory is like a compass. Without a compass, there can be no skipper. The Vietnam Laodong Party is the vanguard and general staff of the working class and the working people of Vietnam.'

Aware at last that concessions had to be made to genuine Vietnamese nationalists, the French tried what came to be known as the 'Bao Dai experiment'. Torn between left-wing demands in Paris to give Vietnam to Ho Chi Minh and rightist reluctance to relinquish anything, France finally compromised by asking Bao Dai, who had abdicated from the empire of Annam in 1945, to return as Chief of State of Vietnam, granting him, under an agreement signed in Paris on 8 March 1949, in-dependence concessions far exceeding anything offered to Ho Chi Minh.

Bao Dai, who returned with understandable reluctance–the Viet Minh had sentenced him to death in absentia–arrived in June 1949 to begin preliminary work associated with the transfer of powers from France to Vietnam. His hope of success lay in the rapidity with which those transfers were effected, his own popularity measured against that of Ho, and the effectiveness of French military action against Ho's forces, reinforced or rearmed through China.

I arrived in Saigon for the first time in October 1949, blissfully (and fortunately) unaware that Vietnam for the next quarter century was to occupy the greater part of my working life. I managed to find a room in the annex to the Continental, just across the rue Catinat, in those days filled with French boutiques and shaded from the sun by flame trees that finally succumbed to pollution. There was little traffic in the streets, and life–and the war–proceeded at a leisurely pace. For the noon aperitif and again in the evening, it was customary to sit on the sidewalk in front of the Continental. The road beyond was paved with metal bottle tops, discarded by the same 'boys' who were there twenty-five years later. On my very first night I was greeted with a mortar shell, fired from across the Saigon River. It was an appropriate baptism.

There was, I found, precious little optimism that the French had any intention of honouring their agreement with the Vietnamese, or that Bao Dai was likely to prove the man of the moment. I called on Nguyen Phan Long, the Minister of Foreign Affairs, who stared at me through his one melancholy-looking eye and expressed qualified doubts about how the rest of the world would receive the new state. He was even more pessimistic about the transfer of authority in Saigon. 'The French government and the High Commissioner have goodwill', he said, 'but the French heads of department here are fighting foot by foot to delay the transfer of power'. In particular, the French were fighting grimly to hold on to justice and the police. And, in fact, the French never let go until they were forced by circumstances, and the Viet Minh, five years later.

I flew to Dalat, a superb mountain resort in those days, at the southern end of the Central Highlands. Bao Dai had his headquarters in a small modern office building set among pine woods and closely guarded by Vietnamese troops. Here, to the annoyance of the French and a good many Vietnamese–who felt that his place was in Hanoi or Saigon and not in Dalat–he conducted his affairs of state.

I was shown into a small, pleasantly decorated office, with parquet floor and a big cupboard of books, where the director of the imperial cabinet handed me the replies to a written questionnaire I had been required to submit. The emperor sat opposite me. He was dressed in a neat sports .suit, turned-down bobby socks and two-toned shoes. In twenty minutes he contributed nothing to the conversation other than 'oui' or 'non'. Heavily-set and stolid, he slumped disinterestedly in his seat. 'He may be the man to win Indo-China from

Communism', I wrote, 'but he gave no indication of this or anything else in the interview'.

In the end, he not only failed, he did not even try. Since his grandfather had had three hundred concubines, it was not to be expected that Bao Dai would bring the morals of the monastery to his task. But, in the words of a British diplomat in Saigon, 'some of his women were pretty bad'. 'A thoroughly cynical man, he apparently trusts or confides in no one and he has continually surrounded himself with an entourage of nonentities and sycophants', said a confidential u.s. government report. His final act of cynicism before quitting Vietnam for the last time in 1954 was to take a bribe of 40 million piastres, then worth $1,142,857.14, for issuing a directive placing control of the police and Sûreté (which his more loyal subordinates had at last succeeded in wresting from the French) in the hands of the Binh Xuyen, river pirates and gangsters who thereafter ran both the police and the organized vice in Saigon.

I returned to Singapore, where I was then making my home, and talked to Mr Malcolm MacDonald, British Commissioner-General for South-East Asia, about what I had seen and heard in Saigon. I told him that I thought the independence promised Vietnam was a myth and that the emperor himself had neither the qualities to win people to his side, nor the intention of trying. Yet a week later Mr MacDonald followed me to Saigon and returned a convincing champion of Bao Dai's chances. He persuaded President Truman's roving ambassador, Mr Philip Jessup, that here was the South-East Asian rock that could stand firmly in the path of the Communist tide. On 8 February 1950, Britain and the United States recognized the independence of Vietnam within the French Union. Years later Mr MacDonald told me his belief that Bao Dai had more than a 50 per cent chance of success was based on the assumption that the French would quickly develop a policy of giving Vietnam self-government similar to that of a self-governing dominion in the Commonwealth, a provision which, in spite of British efforts at persuasion, was never met. France wanted a puppet in Vietnam and such pressures as were applied in Paris by Mr MacDonald and others to produce a more realistic internal policy in Indo-China proved fruitless. The French were not interested in giving Vietnam independence, or in establishing an effective nationalist government. Their principal concern was with the dangerous reaction dominion status for Vietnam might have on the North African colonies, and not at all with pushing more independence on Bao Dai than he asked for. But because the Russians and the Chinese had already recognized the Democratic Republic of Vietnam, Britain and the United States, in the Cold War context of the times, probably had no alternative but to support their French ally. In the end, only the Vietnamese suffered. Millions couldn't bear the Communists and their rule: but they also could not swallow the pretence, and the corruption, of the 'government' in Saigon.

As for the war . . . Some of the treasures from my notebooks have not lost their capacity to shock me, even after the passage of so many years. An interview with General Chassin, the French Air Force commander in Indo-China at the time of one of my first visits to Indo-China: 'We're now going in for night bombing on the lowlands, forcing the Viet Minh to turn the lights off, breaking down efficiency', he said. His targets included buffalo in the countryside. 'Buffalo? For God's sake, why?' 'Because they are the Viet Minh's tractor, their truck and supply column.'

Imagine fighting to win peasant support in a guerrilla war by shooting his buffalo by day and his cottage lights by night! I thought I'd heard the ultimate in insanity but the war, alas, was just beginning.

Early in 1952 I flew from Hanoi to Ninh Binh in the Red River Delta of North Vietnam with the Hanoi editor of *Vietnam Press*, a limping young man named Bui Anh Tuan. Tuan had just escaped from six years in a Viet Minh labour camp where he had seen 4,500 detainees die. When we got to Thai Binh, where battered mud and plaster houses, roughly thatched with rice straw, clustered around a huge Roman Catholic church, I was told to go to the officers' quarters, Tuan to the sergeants'. I refused to be separated from him. 'We are both correspondents', I said. 'Yes, but he's Vietnamese', said our escort officer with contempt.

I held out and Tuan came with me to the officers' quarters, beginning a deep friendship that has lasted ever since. The operation we were to watch was as revealing as General Chassin's choice of targets for his air force. The Viet Minh had carted off great chunks of the road that ran on an embankment above the sea of rice, and the French drove east toward the coast using the debris of villages knocked down in the advance and steel matting to make a new road alongside the old. In the course of one morning they demolished a complete village, loaded it into trucks and rolled everything from kitchen utensils to iron bedsteads into the mud to make a new path for their tanks and armoured cars. Occasionally, a spotter plane saw movement in a village ahead and fighter-bombers and artillery would begin work again, perhaps killing a few Viet Minh but doing nothing to win friends among the local people who, in this area, were all Catholic.

On the Viet Minh side, the weapons and the techniques all came from China, which was still deeply involved with the United States in the Korean War. The French relied on the Americans, and victories were signalled by the number of ships that unloaded at the Saigon waterfront. There were no other victories to count.

By the end of 1952 it had become apparent that the French were unlikely to continue indefinitely to hold the line. They had lost their hold on the mountains in the North and had been pushed back into the heavily infiltrated Red River Delta. All that remained in Tongking outside the Red River Delta were scattered, isolated and vulnerable outposts, almost all of which were under attack. To talk of the Viet Minh as guerrillas was no longer correct. General Van Tien Dung, for example, had taken command of the 320th Division and had attacked in the heartland of the delta. Giap was looking for the set-piece battle that the French always claimed they wanted. To conventionally trained Western soldiers plunged into Indo-China, the large-scale and small-scale revolutionary warfare they encountered was a mixture of magic and sleight of hand, shocking, fascinating and quite impossible. It was asking too much of a St Cyr graduate to believe that a peasant army still at least partly dependent on captured French weapons could pit itself successfully against an expeditionary force of 250,000 men built around the élite of France.

Toward the end of 1952 the French baited a trap, seventy-five miles west of the Red River Delta, at a place called Nasam. No less than three Viet Minh divisions, the 308th, the 312th and the 316th, plus an independent regiment, were loose on the board and French outlying posts had fallen like ninepins. The French flew in a full division of troops to hold a circle of low lying hills, with an airfield in the centre of the amphitheatre. I spent a night there late in November 1952. The Viet Minh mortar shells crumped among the barbed wire entanglements and trenches by the airfield. The answering guns of the French brought a trickle of dirt on the tables in the headquarters dugouts and the wine bottles rattled over dinner. There was confidence in positional warfare and contempt of *les jaunes* skulking in the hills. 'Let us catch them in a conventional battle', said a French captain, drawing his hand across his throat.

Giap launched his main attack on the night of 30 November–1 December, throwing in the full weight of the 308th Division. He lost a thousand killed, but he learned how to fight a set-piece battle, as the French were soon to discover.

Personally, these were difficult days. I saw no point in pretending that things were going well for the French, when so demonstrably they were not. A pessimistic article that I cabled from Hong Kong early in

December after spending a month in Tongking led to the decision to ban me. Since the French were now at least going through the motions of letting the Vietnamese run their own affairs, I used to arrange things though a Vietnamese friend in the French Embassy in Bangkok. My friend was a curious man. According to an official, and secret, American dossier he had been successively, or sometimes concurrently, a functionary in, or paid agent of, the Japanese *kempetai* (secret police) in Indo-China, the Viet Minh, the French intelligence service, the Thai police, and possibly the British intelligence service. He had also offered to perform intelligence work for an American he thought to be engaged in intelligence activities. In August 1945, when he was working with the *kempetai*, he foresaw the end of the war and won favour with the Viet Minh by furnishing them with stocks of Japanese weapons, an act that won him so much favour that he was put in charge of training guerrillas in the Hue area. Later, he accompanied Prince Souphanouvong to Laos under Ho Chi Minh's orders and helped to start the war there. According to Sisouk na Champassak, one-time Laotian defence minister, he was personally responsible for the execution of twenty-seven Frenchmen who died when he threw their trussed up bodies into a furnace. The American dossier was no less startling. In the summer of 1947, it said, he was working for Tran Van Giau, head of the North Vietnamese apparatus in Thailand and, according to this source, in one month alone furnished 5,000 Japanese rifles to the North Vietnamese. The Americans also accused him of arranging, or participating in, at least four murders, three of which were at the instigation of the North Vietnamese, and one of which was for personal gain.*

I knew little of the more shocking aspects of his career, although I was familiar, of course, with his early association with the Viet Minh. We were, nevertheless, quite close friends. He found it no problem to fix up a visa for Saigon.

These were the days before the secret police in Saigon, and elsewhere, had thought of establishing the 'black book' of undesirables at the airport, and to the despair of Monsieur Jean-Pierre Dannaud, who was in charge of such matters at the French High Commission in Saigon, I was no sooner asked to leave than I turned up again.

---

* He later became a senior representative of the Government of Vietnam in Washington, and then, with his infinite capacity to somersault, became a leading worker in the anti-war movement in the United States. I heard of him last when he sent me a postcard after attending the 1976 non-aligned conference in Sri Lanka. He said simply, 'I wish all we old-timers could get together again'.

Once again, when I had been told to leave the country immediately, I decided to plead my case with Monsieur Dannaud in his office in the palace. I arrived unannounced. Before his secretary told me that Monsieur Dannaud was out and unlikely to return, I caught a glimpse of him in the inner room. I knew that he had no alternative exit and that if I was patient enough I could sit him out. Noon and the long lunch break found me still sitting there in the outer office, and despite his secretary's entreaties, I refused to move. 'Having waited so long', I said, 'I would like to wait just a little longer'. Half an hour later, Monsieur Dannaud capitulated. We had our confrontation, and I made my plea that I had always and consistently reported the facts. I left uncertain of the outcome, but that afternoon as I was waiting to hear the judge's decision in my room at the Continental, a 'boy' arrived with a letter. It contained an invitation to dinner that night from High Commissioner Maurice de Jean, and his charming wife, Marie Claire. I had known her in Tokyo days when she served as official hostess for General Petchkoff, Maxim Gorky's illegitimate son, and at that time head of the French mission in Japan. Later, the de Jeans were to have an unhappy time in Moscow, when he was pursued by KGB 'swallows'. On this occasion, I sat on Marie Claire's right hand and enjoyed a splendid and entertaining dinner, full of cheerful reminiscences. At no time thereafter did I have any visa troubles with the French.

By the middle of 1953 Paris had replaced General Raoul Salan as commander-in-chief with General Henri Navarre, who had a background in intelligence but no previous experience in Indo-China. He was a brave man who made it his personal business to visit every part of his command, including Nasam. Here, he met Colonel Louis Berteil, commander of Mobile Group 7, who had drawn all the wrong conclusions from Giap's attack on the entrenched camp in November and December 1952. Instead of appreciating that to create further Nasams was to court total disaster, Colonel Berteil thought this was the way to defeat the Viet Minh. He went to Saigon as Navarre's deputy chief of operations, and it was on his advice that Navarre decided to repeat the Nasam experiment on a much larger scale, and to block the approaches to Laos, which the Viet Minh had already invaded, at Dien Bien Phu.

The French had a sentimental attachment to Laos and felt they had to defend it for political prestige. But Vientiane, the administrative capital, was inaccessible by road from Saigon and a month and a half away by boat up the Mekong River. Luang Prabang, the royal capital, was little more than a village. Among the million and a half inhabitants of the country, there was one engineer (the prime minister), one qualified doctor, one colonel in the army, and one graduate of St Cyr. Opium, grown by the Meo tribesmen on the mountain tops, was the only cash crop. The Lao were handsome, bronze-skinned and indolent. They caught fish in the rivers when they needed food, and ate fruit from the trees. Real work, the planting and harvesting of the rice crop, occupied no more than four months in the year.

Nearly all Lao were Buddhists and there were thousands of Buddhist monks. At the same time, the people were also profoundly animistic and superstitious. The French had established a protectorate over the country in 1893 and the Japanese gave it its independence during the Second World War. With support from Ho Chi Minh, the Lao had fought to prevent the return of the French. The resistance soon collapsed and most of the resistance leaders fled to Thailand. An exception was Prince Souphanouvong, Greek scholar and half-brother of Prince Souvanna Phouma, the prime minister, who had thrown in his lot with the Viet Minh and was now established in Sam Neua, thanks to two divisions of North Vietnamese forces, as the head of a rival government.

France had given Laos its independence in October 1953, and this was an added reason, French officers said, why every effort had to be made to defend the people who had no means of defending themselves. This sense of loyalty was to prove expensive, since in his preliminary feints before attacking Dien Bien Phu, Giap moved back into Laos with substantial forces, and the French were obliged to commit reserves in its defence that could have been used to much better advantage elsewhere.

On 20 November 1953, French paratroops landed without opposition in the vast amphitheatre at Dien Bien Phu, 150 miles away from Hanoi and capable of reinforcement and supply only by air. The initial task force consisted of only six battalions, but it was quickly and heavily reinforced. The immediate price was a rapid, and alarming, deterioration in the security of the Red River delta.

Thanks to my friend Bui Anh Tuan, I had been introduced to the Dai Viet fraternity that ran the civilian government in Tongking. In principle, the Dai Viet was a clandestine party, with its members sworn to absolute secrecy, on pain, literally, of death. When it got authority, however, the party, in common with political groupings everywhere, liked to have its own men running things. Nguyen Van Huong was Dai Viet, head of the Sûreté and a friend. He was a tiny man, very proud of his brilliant elder son.* He was dismayed by what was happening in Tongking. Navarre, he said, was wrong about Viet Minh intentions in Laos. They did not intend to capture either the royal capital of Luang Prabang, or Vientiane, the administrative capital. They had invaded Laos for psychological reasons and had left behind sufficient men in Sam Neua province only to establish a 'government'. But in Hanoi itself the Viet Minh had an underground army, with street committees already organized, regional guards and 5,000 police ready to surface at the appropriate moment. The delta was worse. The town of Thai Binh was held by the French but all the surrounding villages, without exception, were in Viet Minh hands. He lamented that his budget had been so heavily cut by the French that he could no longer pay two-thirds of his agents in Viet Minh areas. 'And at this time of all times', he said, 'when we have counts of guns and anti-aircraft guns coming in from China for Dien Bien Phu'. For the first time in the war, he said, the Viet Minh would have 105-millimetre artillery pieces. These were being drawn through the mountains by chains of coolies. On foot and on bicycle from across the border the greatest movement of men and supplies that the war had ever seen was under way.

What Huong had to say was sensational and unpublishable as long as I remained in Vietnam, or could not verify it from another source. The French deuxième bureau laughed at my inquiries and said the report was utterly false. British military intelligence in Far East Land Headquarters in Singapore scoffed when I returned home before Christmas. They had not heard a word of it. But a day or two later an Army friend phoned to tell me what I had to say had been confirmed. I wrote the story for the *Daily Telegraph* and next day found myself potentially in deep trouble again. The French had accused the British of leaking top secret information to me in Singapore. I replied that I had leaked it to the British, and the French seemed to accept my word. In any event, it was no secret in Hanoi that I had been briefed by someone early in December.

I paid a fleeting visit to Dien Bien Phu a week or two before the

---

* Twenty-two years later the son, Major-General Nguyen Van Hieu, was deputy commander of the Third Military Region in South Vietnam. The night before North Vietnam opened the battle for Saigon, he was shot and murdered at his desk in headquarters at Bien Hoa. Bui Anh Tuan borrowed General Tran Van Don's jeep and we went together to the chapel where his body lay in state to give an envelope containing some money, the custom of the country, to his widow. I spoke to Huong on the phone, but did not see him again.

battle began. With thoughts of all those 105-millimetre guns in mind, and shaken by what I saw and heard, I felt no professional pull to remain and to report the battle on the spot. The French press showed no greater fortitude, although with blind confidence General Navarre was not only waiting, but hoping, for the battle to begin.

Although none of the books about the battle have ever said so, that confidence was not shared by the admirable Tongking commander, Major-General René Cogny. I saw him to talk about the situation twice–each time on a Sunday evening–during the battle. I asked him on the first occasion how he felt about Dien Bien Phu. 'It is a crime against humanity', he said. When I saw him on the next occasion, I asked him how he felt then. 'It is a continuing crime against humanity', he said.

Like Huong, he was immensely concerned not only with the situation at Dien Bien Phu but also with the Red River Delta. He produced a revealing chart to explain his concern. It covered 6,492 villages in the delta. At the end of the third quarter of 1953 the Viet Minh held 2,902, the French 1,403 and 2,187 were in dispute. By the end of the year the Viet Minh had increased their hold to 3,266 and the French held only 1,266. Despite the great concentration of Viet Minh forces at Dien Bien Phu, they had nearly 100,000 men in the delta, including twelve to fourteen battalions along Route Coloniale 5, the essential road link between Hanoi and the sea. A year before trucks running supplies from Haiphong to Hanoi had been able to make the round trip in a day. Now, because of mines, the road was open only long enough each day for a single journey.

Richard Casey, then Australia's Foreign Minister, turned up on his way to attend the Geneva conference and I flew down to Saigon to talk to him. Apart from Wing-Commander Les Kroll, the Australian military attaché, those who briefed him had all been very optimistic. I read him my Cogny notes. 'That's just what Kroll says, too', he said. 'Why doesn't anyone else say so?' It was a good question.

The Americans were deeply involved. A u.s. Military Defence Assistance Advisory Group under Brigadier-General T. J. Trapnell, was there to provide technical information on the shiploads of supplies that continued to arrive. Senator Mike Mansfield, who had visited Indo-China in the middle of 1953, was an ardent interventionist. 'I'm sure you can't be right, I'm sure you can't be right', he repeated when I was invited to give him my views. He went back to Washington and wrote his report. It ought to be framed and kept as an international treasure. For here was Mansfield, the cooing dove of the 1960s and 1970s, wearing all the feathers of the hawk. He found the war situation much improved. 'The Communists may become more receptive to a cessation of hostilities once they are faced with the certainty of ultimate defeat', he wrote . . . 'They must be convinced, finally, that we are prepared to stay with the struggle until the liberty of this area is assured. And the need to stay with it is clear because the issue for us is not Indo-China alone. Nor is it just Asia. The issue in this war for so many people who would like to forget is the continued freedom of the non-Communist world, the containment of Communist aggression, and the welfare and security of our country.'

American Flying Box Cars now ran a shuttle service over Dien Bien Phu, and Brigadier Calder, of the u.s. Far East Air Force Bomber Command, arrived to investigate the feasibility of heavy bombing. Three wings of B29s–about a hundred planes–could deliver 450 tons of bombs on the Viet Minh around Dien Bien Phu within seventy-two hours, he said. General 'Iron Mike' O'Daniel appeared to advance his solution. 'You know what I'd do', he said. 'I'd send a task force barrelling up that road to Dien Bien Phu.' It would have been some barrel against a foe that had so brilliantly mastered the art of the divisional ambush and, in any event, there were no forces available to fill it.

Whatever one felt about the way the French had fought the war, or their broken promises to the Vietnamese, Dien Bien Phu became an agony that became difficult to bear. I wept as I wrote my report the day it fell–and immediately became embroiled with Sir Hubert Graves, the British Minister in Saigon, who thought he had found a way to have me removed from Indo-China for ever. It was all quite stupid. Because of the overload on the telegraph wires from Hanoi to Saigon, I had attempted with John Mecklin of *Time* and *Life* and Hank Lieberman of the *New York Times* to arrange to phone copy to Saigon, where we had hired the wife of a British functionary to act as our secretary, to take down the copy in shorthand, transcribe it, take it to the censor and then put it on the wire. Sir Hubert believed I was trying to evade censorship, and sent his second secretary to Hanoi to deliver an ultimatum: account for my actions in twenty-four hours, or he would initiate action with the Foreign Office, the *Daily Telegraph* and the French authorities to have me expelled immediately. I delivered a counter ultimatum: apologize, or I would write the account of his threat for publication.

Sir Hubert was on weak ground. During the battle I had advanced a suggestion for evacuating the wounded from Dien Bien Phu. The scheme failed, but the French had been grateful and willing to give it a go. They were not about to reward me by throwing me out again. Sir Hubert did not apologize, so I made good my own threat and in addition cabled Robert Menzies, then the prime minister, pleading, as an Australian, for his assistance in this plot.

The Geneva Agreement brought the first Indo-China War to an end on terms that seemed far less generous than the Viet Minh might have expected. The question remains why did they sign? Why did they settle for half of the country when all of it seemed ripe for the taking? Various explanations have been offered. One advanced by Robert F. Turner* was that the delegation from the People's Republic of China, headed by Chou En-lai, was motivated primarily by a desire to avoid war with the United States again. The Chinese were convinced that a strong and influential group in Washington, led by John Foster Dulles and the Joint Chiefs of Staff, were quite prepared to move against China if circumstances permitted. The Soviet Union, following the death of Stalin, did not want the Indo-China situation to get out of hand. And the North Vietnamese were so responsive to Soviet and Chinese advice and pressure–and so dependent on their assistance in whatever the future might hold–that temporary partition seemed a sensible expedient. One other point that should be noted is that the North Vietnamese also felt far from ready to accept a confrontation with the United States at this time. They had gone to the brink at Dien Bien Phu and were glad to be able to retreat from it while they firmed up their domestic base.

My own view at the time was that the Viet Minh felt Saigon was unlikely to stay the two-year course before elections were theoretically due to be held and would collapse. This was the view, also, of many of my friends in Hanoi. Nevertheless, most were determined to put off the day when they would live under the Communists and went South. A very large number of others went, also. They were encouraged by the c.i.a. and by people like my friend Tuan, who had got some of his own back for six years' maltreatment in prison by spreading black propaganda around the city. All means, including murder and torture, were used to prevent the exodus. The facts were known to the Canadian members of the International Control Commission set up under the Geneva Agreement, but proof in the face of Viet Minh resistance, Polish connivance and Indian disinterest was often hard to establish.

Tom Dooley, whose mission of mercy in Laos a few years later was abruptly terminated by cancer, was working as a u.s. naval doctor among the refugees. Their plight moved him to devote the little that was left of his life to helping the needy in Indo-China. He told me

---

* *Vietnamese Communism, Its Origins and Development.* Robert F. Turner, Hoover Institution Press, Stanford, California, 1975.

the story of a fourteen-year-old boy who had been caught by Viet Minh soldiers trying to join those going South. The soldiers beat him on the feet with their rifle butts until all the bones were broken. They then turned him loose, saying, 'Now walk to your freedom, if you can.' The boy crawled through the rice-fields and crossed the line, where a peasant found him and took him to Haiphong. 'I felt his feet', Dooley said. 'It was like feeling a couple of bags of finely broken sticks.' Dooley put him on the first plane and rushed him to Saigon, where the boy's legs were amputated.

Dooley's patients included men and women who had had chopsticks forced into their ears 'for listening to lies', two priests who were tied up by their thumbs and beaten on the testicles, and a boy with a bullet hole in his cheek. The great land reform campaign had already begun in the North, and hundreds of thousands of rich and middle peasants were in the process of being dragged before people's courts to account for their sins. The courts were now extended to include those responsible for inciting evacuation. According to the Liberation Radio, 'ten thousand angry peasants' attended the trial of a man named Lai Duc Linh, who was responsible for organizing petitions among the people of Nam Dinh. He was sentenced to four years' imprisonment by the court. He was lucky. Before Ho Chi Minh called a halt in 1956, many thousands of victims of people's justice had lost their lives.

I went back to Hanoi to watch the Viet Minh takeover in October 1954, with a sense of deep depression. Thanks to Tuan, I had found life agreeable there, though the war was all around. I had found friends among the Vietnamese and was beginning to learn of their way of life. I loved the flower market by the side of the Little Lake in the centre of the city, the flowers fresh with dew in the early morning. I hated the *crachin*, a sticky sort of Scotch mist and the hay fever I habitually developed when it settled in (I used to think it was caused at first by fear, since I always got it after moving out of Hanoi to look at the war). I didn't much care for the bitterly hot summer, either, but Hanoi had a character all of its own. There were excellent Vietnamese, French and Chinese restaurants and in those cheerful expense account days, money was no problem. The Hanoi I was going to now would, I knew, be very different.

I had booked a seat on the last Air Vietnam flight from Saigon, a Skymaster crowded with unspeaking passengers going from the South to throw in their lot with Ho Chi Minh. A German photographer, busy with his Leica, got shielded faces when he tried for close-ups. Across the aisle from me was a pretty girl in her early twenties, obviously well-to-do, with a diamond ring on her right hand and a smart leather vanity case. Throughout the flight she did not speak. When the hostess offered her a glass of beer and a ham sandwich, she merely shook her head and continued to stare out of the window.

It was a grim journey. No laughter, no smiles, no conversation. We might have been on the way to the executioner. Perhaps some were.

Uncollected garbage filled the streets in the French quarter of Hanoi. Outsized, menacing rats that held their ground when you walked by were having a fine time. The city was half abandoned but still teeming with people, a strange mixture of deserted shops, abandoned homes, empty streets, and milling excited crowds.

A huge picture of Ho Chi Minh, giving the appearance of having been painted on hessian, stared down with burning eyes from the wall of the visitors' room at Viet Minh headquarters, and the French who remained had abandoned the habit of referring to them as *les jaunes* and now talked about *l'Armée Populaire Vietnamienne*.

The steadily falling rain did nothing to relieve the gloom of the last few days of French rule. Brigadier-General Paul Masson, Cogny's deputy commander in Tongking, splashed across the water-logged and over-grown stadium outside the Citadel, for so many years French military headquarters, to take the salute at the final *descente des couleurs*. It was just before dusk on the eve of the Viet Minh entry into Hanoi proper and about twenty of us huddled together out of the rain to watch the ceremony. A clique of eight buglers sent the intolerably sad lament of the *descente* far across the empty stands of the stadium, the abandoned Citadel and the silent city. Moroccans, Legionnaires and troops from the *Garde Républicaine* stood in stiff salute as seventy years of French domination of Tongking came to its formal end.

The next day we watched the peasant army take over the city. Nearly four months earlier Lu Conein had made his reappearance on the Indo-China scene as the second in command of a clandestine military mission run by the legendary Colonel Ed Lansdale, who had played a major part in helping President Ramon Magsaysay beat the Hukbalahap insurgents in the Philippines. Conein's job was to create in a hurry a para-military underground force in the North to be ready to move into action when the Viet Minh took over.

Lansdale had been in touch with the Dai Viet leaders in Tongking, Do Dinh Dao and Tran Van Xuan, to help organize a black pro-paganda organization. They chose my friend Tuan for the job. Disguised as a Viet Minh official, he spread pamphlets in the suburbs of Hanoi, telling the people what taxes they would have to pay and how they would be required to behave when the Viet Minh took over.

99

The day after he had gone through the area masquerading as a Viet Minh officer, the flow of refugees doubled and the value of Viet Minh currency was cut in half. He also wrote a series of horoscopes, predicting disaster for the Viet Minh leaders and success for the Southerners. This was no less successful. But, in his third task, the destruction of Hanoi's biggest printing plant with high explosives, he failed.

Tuan, wisely, had left for Haiphong. Conein, who was unknown to him, was still around and about the only man in town with a car, which, for reasons of his own, he was glad to have us share. He appeared in the morning in the uniform of a full colonel, topped by an Australian slouch hat and carrying a 16-millimetre camera. To the collective dismay of his passengers, Conein halted the Viet Minh battalions as they moved into the city according to the prearranged plan and ordered them to display all their weapons and equipment. Incredibly, they did as they were commanded, and Conein went down the ranks with his camera, taking pictures of everything.

We complained that he would have us shot. 'Don't worry', he said. 'They think we're from the International Control Commission.' And so they did.

That night, precisely at 6 p.m., when the Viet Minh were due to close the city at the Pont Duomer, John Mecklin took over Conein's car, and we crossed the Red River, heading for Haiphong. Conein stayed behind to attend to whatever duties he had not yet concluded, contaminating the oil supply in the bus station so that it would destroy the engines (a trick from his French resistance days), arranging for the sabotage of the railway line between Hanoi and Haiphong, and making final plans for the infiltration of his agents who were being trained outside Vietnam. The French were bowing out, and the Americans bowing in. In the ashes of one war it was already possible to discern the sparks of the next.

The guilt was fairly evenly divided. If the North Vietnamese were all too ready to regard the Geneva Agreement as a scrap of paper to be produced as a sacred document, or to be contemptuously disregarded, as circumstances dictated, the Lansdale-Conein operations, obviously approved by John Foster Dulles in his almost religious campaign against Communism, provided an unfortunate justification for present and future violations by Hanoi.

Part two: The end of the beginning
1940 to 1975

2. The Americans bow in

Against this background of intrigue and defeat, an expatriate leader named Ngo Dinh Diem had emerged from retirement to take his place in the Vietnamese scene. 'We must continue the search for the Kingdom of God and Justice', Diem once wrote to his family from the Maryknoll Seminary, then at Lakewood, New Jersey. 'All else will come of itself.' The letter did not surprise his family. This deeply religious expression of faith was characteristic of their brother.

Even after all these years the legend persists that Diem was an American puppet, appointed at the insistence of John Foster Dulles. In fact, the State Department was much less enthusiastic about him than Justice William O. Douglas who, in a book published a year or two earlier, had described him as 'revered' by the Vietnamese people. Diem certainly had other American supporters, including Senators like Mike Mansfield and John F. Kennedy, but the ultimate choice was Bao Dai's. He had two candidates in mind. One was Diem and the other Dr Phan Quang Dan. Both had stood out as staunch opponents of the Viet Minh at the end of the Second World War. Dan had served briefly as a cabinet minister with Bao Dai, but broke with him in March 1949, because he did not feel that the agreement with the French promised anything like real independence for the Vietnamese people. Diem was no less strongly opposed to any compromise with France. In the full sense of the word, they were nationalists. Dan came from a family of leading Buddhists, Diem from perhaps the country's most important Catholic family. In the end, Bao Dai chose

Diem. 'Mr Diem's supporters proved more influential than Dr Dan's', the London *Economist* commented. What a difference to the history of our times it might have made if the choice had gone the other way.

On 7 June 1954, a month after the fall of Dien Bien Phu, Diem, who had always been certain that the day was coming for him 'to look after his country's fate', was entrusted with all the powers that had once been shared between Bao Dai and the prime minister. Few who saw him step from the plane at Tan Son Nhut eighteen days later felt that a new St Joan had come among them. He came slowly down the steps, paused to glance at the acres of barbed wire the French had rushed in to protect their aircraft from guerrilla raids, then shyly greeted some hundreds of well-wishers who had assembled to meet him. The day was hot, heavy and oppressive. The only touch of colour in this otherwise dismal scene was provided by an old gentleman in a red bandanna and sky-blue tunic. The news from the North was bad; from Geneva it was worse.

'Tell me about Diem', I said to a Vietnamese friend, as the squat, strangely youthful-looking figure–he was then fifty-two–who had stepped from the past, walked stiffly across the runway. My friend talked of Diem's early ambition to become a priest, of his subsequent and private pledge of celibacy, and of the hours he habitually spent in prayer each day. 'He sounds too much like a priest to drag Vietnam out of this mess', I said.

'Not a priest', was the reply. 'A priest at least learns of the world through the confessional. Diem is a monk living behind stone walls. He knows nothing.' That may have been an exaggeration, but Diem came singularly ill-equipped to face the tasks that lay ahead of him. Lee Kuan Yew in Singapore once called Vietnam 'pretty slippery ground' on which to make a stand. When Diem took over, there was no hard ground to be slippery, only quicksands.

Vietnam, soon to be truncated by the Geneva Agreement, was not functioning as a sovereign state. The Viet Minh were still in possession of vast areas in the South. The Hoa Hao and Cao Dai sects had carved out their own areas of authority in the Mekong Delta and around Tay Ninh, with their own armies and administrative organizations. The police were in the hands of the Binh Xuyen, led by the gangster Le Van Vien, who had bought the concession from Bao Dai. He ran the Grande Monde, a huge gambling slum in Cholon, the city's biggest department store, a hundred shops, a fleet of river-boats, and had installed sex on a barracks-square basis in Asia's biggest brothel, known, because of the unusual and spectacular motif of the cubicles, as the Hall of Mirrors. Twelve hundred girls serviced their patrons round the clock.

Le Van Vien, or Bay Vien, as he was usually known, lived close to the Y bridge behind a canal known as the Arroyo Chinois. In front of his living apartments were an auditorium and a group of offices. These were separated from his quarters by a muddy, unenclosed pool, perhaps thirty feet long. To reach this part of the building it was necessary to cross a narrow, unrailed wooden bridge. In the moat beneath were two crocodiles, only five-footers, but more than adequate to deliver a deterrent nip to any intruder. In the open space immediately behind, Le Van Vien used to eat his meals when the weather permitted. His sleeping quarters were on the right, protected by a tame, full-grown leopard, chained to allow maximum movement. On my one visit there, the beast was asleep on top of a large packing case.

Beyond the brown and sluggish waters of the Arroyo Chinois was the Binh Xuyen flagship, a heavily-armed river-boat, tied up at the wharf. Between the dining room and the canal was the rest of Bay Vien's menagerie—numerous monkeys, a great python curled up in its own cage, and a tigress. Bay Vien sometimes posed for photographers with the tigress, the animal obligingly throwing back its head to be scratched under the chin. About a hundred yards away from this unusual zoo was a small factory. It was also part of the Bay Vien empire. Its function was to convert raw opium from Laos into heroin.

Long before he returned to Saigon, Diem had regarded it with distaste. He saw it as a place of commerce made sordid by the French, and his senses, thoughts and feelings rebelled against coming to terms with the bizarre people who claimed to be its leaders. He survived from day to day, and sometimes from hour to hour. Once, just after Hanoi had passed into Communist hands, he was saved by a coup d'état only because Colonel Lansdale and his group had learned of the plot in advance and had spirited a couple of the leaders to the Philippines.

Lansdale's reputation had preceded him to Vietnam, and Diem turned to him as one man he could trust.

Once in the Philippines when Lansdale was out on a sweep with one of Magsaysay's forces, the Filipino soldiers lopped off the head of a captured Huk. Lansdale picked up the head by the hair and started to ask it questions about its organization. The Filipino soldiers, all devout Catholics, were shocked. They thought Lansdale had become insane.

Lansdale did, indeed, seem to have lost control of his senses. He began to shout at the head and to slap it on the face when it failed to answer.

'Colonel, Colonel, it is dead, it cannot talk to you', said an officer, clutching Lansdale by the arm.

'No, you stupid son of a bitch, of course it can't', said Lansdale, throwing the head on the ground. 'But it could have if you hadn't been so fornicating stupid as to sever the head from the body.'

It was this sort of approach that Lansdale and Conein now brought to bear on the task of preparing to save South Vietnam. Conein had not wasted a minute. While he was attending to the byplay in Hanoi, he had recruited and sent off for training his group of stay-behind commandos for underground work in North Vietnam after the Communists had completed the takeover. On the one hand, he was running refugees to the South, and on the other he was shipping supplies through Haiphong–radios, carbines, pistols, and ammunition–to lay the foundations for his own insurgency in the North after the Geneva Agreement closed the port of Haiphong on 16 May 1955.

In the South, Lansdale was equally busy. He provided funds for Diem to buy the support of one of the Cao Dai military leaders. He started to train Vietnamese guerrillas at Clark Field in the Philippines. He brought in some of his former Filipino associates to set up a security organization that would provide Diem with some protection.

But it was still all very much touch and go. On the night of 29 March 1955, I had dinner at a Chinese restaurant in Cholon, Saigon's Chinese twin, with Joe Alsop, the columnist, and Peggy and Till Durdin, of the *New York Times*. It was Till's birthday and we had dined magnificently on Szechwan duck.

I was no sooner back in bed at the Continental than a 'boy' began to hammer on my door, calling me to the telephone. In those days the Continental had only one phone, just behind the concierge's desk in the lobby. When I got to it, Till had already departed and Peggy was on the phone, talking to Joe Alsop. She handed the phone to me.

'My dear Denis', Alsop said. 'Let us go to the battle.'

'Battle? Battle? What the hell are you talking about?'

'You haven't heard? The mortars? Ever since we got home.'

An hour later we were lying on our stomachs along the road leading to Cholon while machine gun bullets whizzed by. Four or five mortar shells exploded in the grounds around Independence Palace, and almost simultaneously green-capped Binh Xuyen troops had attacked the headquarters of the Vietnamese National Army and a Police building on the boulevard leading to Cholon.

We were late, but not too late. The Binh Xuyen had been driven off in both attacks, but an occasional mortar shell came in with a resounding smack and every now and then a burst of machine-gun fire swept down the boulevard. The early minutes of the fighting had been hectic. Branches strewed the road in front of the Police building. Scattered heaps of small-arms shells littered the street and there was considerable evidence of damage among the buildings. A troop of Vietnamese National Army armoured cars, with their engines turning over, waited for the word to move. Past them, on either side of the street, and hugging the line of the walls, came red-bereted Vietnamese paratroopers, who had been held in the Saigon station yards for some days in anticipation of trouble.

A French general, accompanied by two enormous black Alsatian dogs, drove up in his Citroen and, after a few curt words with the Vietnamese captain in charge of the armoured cars, sped back toward Saigon. Some minutes later the results of his reconnaissance became apparent, and a line of French tanks trundled past. They swung off to the left between the Government and Binh Xuyen lines, effectively blocking Diem's forces in their contemplated counter attack across the Arroyo Chinois. Half an hour of violent fighting had been enough to satisfy the Binh Xuyen that they had had enough. They had sent out urgent signals to the French to stop the fighting, and the French had responded with the tanks.

The fighting of 29 March gave way to a brief and uneasy truce. General Lawton Collins, who had arrived at the beginning of November to take over the post of u.s. ambassador, had brought with him renewed assurances of American support for Diem. He had now reassessed the situation and become convinced that Diem was hopelessly unfitted for the task.

Bao Dai, the sects and the French, who detected in Diem dangerous opposition to the Geneva Agreement, were also united in their determination to get rid of him. Bao Dai ordered Diem to report to him in Cannes, and M. Edgar Faure, the French prime minister, followed this with a statement that the Diem government was no longer equal to its task.

Diem replied by cable that it would be damaging for the nation's interests for him to leave Saigon at that time. And, in Collins' absence, Randy Kidder, the u.s. chargé d'affaires (and Joe Alsop's cousin) stood firmly behind him. Also in the fight behind Diem were Lansdale and his team and the Australian minister, David McNicoll and Colonel Fergus Macadie, the Australian military attaché.

A revolutionary committee hastily put together by Diem's brother, Ngo Dinh Nhu, tore down Bao Dai's portrait in the Town Hall and trampled it underfoot. A general, under orders from Bao Dai to take over the army, was seized by the revolutionary committee and was lucky to escape with his life.

Spurred on by the news from Washington that Dulles had decided he should go–and encouraged by Lansdale–Diem now took the initiative, called on the French to take down the barricades and swept the wounded Le Van Vien back into his swamps and jungle lairs. Binh Xuyen headquarters was a shambles. The python died from the blast of a mortar shell. Another shell ripped a hole in the tigress' cage, and Tran Van Khiem, the palace spokesman, reported that human bones and the remains of a government soldier's uniform had been found there. The report got wide circulation. It was quite untrue.

Diem pursued the still dissident Hoa Hao sects in the south-western rice lands of the Mekong Delta, and by mid-July 1955, the armed, organized, non-Communist opposition to his regime in the South had been swept away. Only the real threat of the Viet Minh remained. Washington changed its mind again and, instead of working to remove Diem, decided to give him full support.

The events of his first ten months in office had soured Diem incurably. He had brought with him to Saigon the conviction that the Communists could have been defeated during the Indo-China War if only the French had given Vietnam full independence, or at least dominion status. As he saw it, or so he told me, those who had accepted office under the French were collaborators who, though they might be anti-Communists, had forfeited the right to be considered as genuine nationalists, worthy of inclusion in his government. By his standards now, he could trust almost no one, because with few exceptions all persons of experience were either opportunists or tainted. Instead of working for the Vietnamese people, they had worked for the French, who had drained Vietnam of everything they could get out of it. Many doors that were not closed to him, he deliberately closed himself.

Diem's style of government reflected his attitude. Lacking contact with the broad spectrum of Vietnamese society, he relied heavily on his family and a very small circle of acquaintances. Suspicious, watchful and devious, his real apparatus of government tended to become covert, almost Communist in its techniques, though not, of course, in goals.

His brother Nhu, an opium smoker, founded the Can Lao (Revolutionary Workers) Party, which was covert, tightly disciplined and Communist-like in its internal discipline. As in a Communist state, where the Party is more important than the government, Nhu was the most powerful single individual in the Republic of Vietnam. His wife, Madame Nhu, good looking, animated, intelligent and vain, was scarcely less important. Dr Tran Van Do, her uncle, once described her to me as 'a monster'. Do was foreign minister, and his elder brother Chief Justice. He confided to me years later that the office, which he had accepted in good faith, was devoid of any significance whatsoever. He was provided with neither a legal library, nor an assistant, and he was not expected to sit in judgement of anyone, or anything. Inevitably, he finally sat in judgement of the regime.

Another Ngo Dinh brother, Can, ran Central Vietnam like a provincial war-lord. An eccentric, unmarried recluse, he ruled with an iron hand. I have Madame Nhu's word for it that he was one of the most corrupt men in the country.

Archbishop Ngo Dinh Thuc, Diem's eldest brother, was the family, and state, ideologue, and with Nhu and Father Tran Huu Thanh, a Catholic priest, the creator of Personalism, a philosophy designed to persuade the people of South Vietnam that they should look beyond the Communists in their search for an ideology suited to their Vietnamese temperament. Another brother, Luyen, became ambassador in London. Tran Van Chuong, Madame Nhu's father, was ambassador in Washington, and her mother the Vietnamese observer to the United Nations. Tran Van Khiem, Madame Nhu's younger brother, was the palace spokesman. Tran Trung Dung, the defence secretary, was married to one of Diem's nieces.

Considering its almost comic opera–or true Graham Greene–beginnings, this family government did better than almost anyone had expected in the next two years. At first it controlled little more than the main cities and a few of the principal roads. By 1957 it had effectively resettled the 800,000 refugees who had fled from the North. The sects had been effectively brought under control, and the government writ extended to much of the countryside.

All of this was accompanied by very substantial quantities of American economic and military aid. A United States Operations Mission from 1956 to 1959 administered an economic aid programme totalling more than $1 billion. American military officers, operating through the Military Assistance and Advisory Group (MAAG), began to knock the army into some sort of shape, and large quantities of American military equipment arrived under a special military aid programme.

Curiously, the Americans had very little background knowledge of the country. There were a couple of Vietnamese linguists in the foreign service, but courses in Vietnamese language or history were not taught anywhere in the United States at this time. It was not until 1954 that the first American State Department officer was sent to Vietnam to study the language. One or two a year followed, until a training programme was begun which produced two specialists in 1957, two in 1958, two in 1959, two in 1960. In 1962, for reasons unknown, the course was ended for the time being.

Some of the Americans in Vietnam in the late 1950s did not bother to learn. The military were contemptuous of the French performance and showed no willingness to borrow from their experience. They simply did not believe that the Viet Minh had created an extremely significant military organization. They doubted even whether the French had ever really fought. Misled by their experience in Korea and the Pacific, they believed they had all the answers. People like Conein, who knew, were posted at this time to other parts of the globe.* By the time Conein, in particular, returned to set up the Special Forces it was too late.

The first chief of MAAG was Lieut-General Samuel T. ('Hanging Sam') Williams. ' "Hanging Sam" was a great conventional instructor, but he didn't know the first thing about guerrilla war', Conein told me. The French officer handling the intelligence organization embracing all the montagnard tribes in the High Plateau offered to turn it all over to Williams. He was not interested. He didn't even look through the files. 'When things got tough in the High Plateau, we didn't even know where to begin', Conein said. 'We had to start all over, right from the beginning.'

Most of the Americans in Vietnam, or at least all the more senior officials, having seen the Diem government begin to establish its authority, were wildly optimistic. Elbridge Durbrow, the American ambassador in Saigon, in 1959 summed up the situation:

The internal situation has been brought from chaos to basic stability; the Vietnamese armed forces have been built up from an ineffective, disorganized force, which is well on the road to becoming a cohesive, well-trained fighting force; rice production has increased substantially, so that the amount available for internal consumption and export has risen from 1.8 million tons in 1954 to 3 million tons in 1958; new rubber plantations have risen from a low of 325 acres in 1955 to 4,745 in 1958, the significant point being the evidence of growing confidence of foreign investors in Vietnam; a new highway from the coast to the interior, which has opened up new fertile lands for settlement, is practically completed; Vietnamese engineers are now beginning to build excellent roads on their own, using techniques and methods taught by American advisers; a jute mill adequate to meet the country's needs for burlap bagging has been equipped; a 200,000 spindle textile mill and a large glass factory are under construction, and scores of smaller industrial plants have been established or enlarged; for the first time large areas of hard fibre crops are under cultivation; fish production has reached the point that fish is being exported to Singapore and Hong Kong.

The military situation, it seemed, was even better. Major-General

---

* Conein was reassigned after his force was infiltrated into North Vietnam.

Samuel L. Myers, who had succeeded General Williams as chief of MAAG, reported in April 1959 that the 'Viet Minh guerrillas, although constantly reinforced by men and weapons from outside South Vietnam, were gradually nibbled away until they ceased to be a major menace to the government.

'In fact, estimates at the time of my departure (for Washington) indicated that there was a very limited number of hostile individuals under arms in the country. Two territorial regiments, reinforced occasionally by one or two regular army regiments, were able to cope with their depredations.' Speaking of the Vietnamese armed forces in general, he said, 'They are now able to maintain internal security and have reached the point where that responsibility could be turned over to the civilian agencies. If there should be renewed aggression from the North on the part of the Viet Minh, they can.give a really good account of themselves. There are many Vietnamese who are even more optimistic than that statement implies and feel they have the capability of counter-attack.' For another nine years this same sort of blind self-deception was to continue under a succession of generals of whom the kindest thing that can be said is that they were ignorant.

Ngo Dinh Diem was wiser. Under the terms of the Geneva Agreement in 1954 the Democratic Republic of Vietnam in Hanoi sent a delegation to the ceasefire committee in Saigon. Leader of the delegation was Pham Hung, who had worked directly under Le Duan and Le Duc Tho, who were, successively, the secretaries of the Central Office for South Vietnam during the war against the French. Hung was joined in Saigon by General Van Tien Dung, who had come South to head the North Vietnamese delegation to the liaison mission with the International Control Commission. Both used their privileged positions in Saigon to prepare the arms dumps which, a year or two later, were to make possible the outbreak of assassinations and ambushes that marked the early stages of the new war. Both were expelled from Saigon for having used their positions to engage in political activities. Twenty years later they were together again outside Saigon,. Dung as commander-in-chief, and Hung political commissar for the vast army that seized the city and won the war.

Well aware of their activities and that North Vietnam had left behind thousands of cadres and troops and had begun to infiltrate Southern cadres who had been taken North for training, Diem wanted to build roads into the mountains and to dig canals into the swamps, and to make the civil guard, for which the Americans had nothing but contempt, into a para-military force. 'On the U.S. side at that time they said my road and canal building programme in the remote areas was not spectacular enough', he told me. 'The Embassy and Aid told us it would be better to build roads to the cities where people could see them.' I said, 'If you don't have roads in remote areas how can you protect the population? And if you can't protect the population they will surely be lost to the Communists.'

He did not in any way share the optimism of his American advisers. 'When I complained that we lacked security, I would be told that there was security enough', he said. 'When I said that the North had started a war against us, I was accused of being obsessed with the security problem . . . You can build factories and mills, but if you don't have security you just build for the Communists.'

On 20 July 1955, Pham Van Dong, then Hanoi's foreign minister, addressed messages to Diem, to the International Control Commission, to Anthony Eden and to Molotov, the co-chairmen of the Geneva Agreement, demanding the opening of a conference between North and South Vietnam to pave the way for elections, as called for by the Geneva Agreement, on 20 July 1956. From Paris and London came pressure on Diem to agree to sit down and talk about the elections. Diem had not signed the Geneva Agreement, but he had undertaken not to upset it.

I was planning to leave South-East Asia and in September 1955, I asked for an appointment with him specifically to discuss the election issue. The appointment was set up for 10 o'clock one Friday morning, just two and a half hours before I was due to catch one of the then very infrequent planes to Singapore. Even in those days, before Diem had begun to ramble on for hour after hour, two hours was not much more than a curtain-raiser for one of his interviews.

It was long past eleven when we got round to the question of elections. Diem's interpretation of what the Geneva Agreement had actually called for differed substantially from the North Vietnamese concept. What the agreement had in mind, he believed, was a plebiscite to determine whether the Vietnamese people wanted reunification and not an election to unify the country. But the word that struck him most forcibly was 'free'. He spoke of the North Vietnamese violations of the agreement, and of the absolute impossibility of conducting free elections with the Communists. He declined to be drawn on whether he thought he could win a genuinely free election. My own feeling, and it was no more than that, was that he could not. It was still very difficult to see any real improvement in the countryside. Despite u.s. aid, very little went to agriculture. The much-vaunted rural help programme did not exist. Land reform was a joke.

Before the interview Diem had been equivocal about the election.

He was prepared now to make an absolute stand. He would not respond to British and French pressure to sit down with the North Vietnamese and talk. And, since there was no conceivable way in which such elections could be 'free', he would not participate.*

I looked at my watch and explained that I had a plane to catch, and that there would not be another one for days. Diem told an aide to phone the airport with instructions to hold the plane until I arrived. I was anything but popular with my fellow passengers when I went aboard the plane fifteen minutes late with what, on reflection, was certainly the most significant interview I have ever had. I wrote it as we flew to Singapore and filed it to London that night for publication next day. Diem had thrown down the gauntlet. Ho Chi Minh moved to pick it up.†

For a long time action and reaction were equal and opposite. As the Communists began their very skilful campaign of subversion and insurrection in the countryside, Diem hit back effectively but in a way that lost him non-Communist support. In 1956 he issued a president- ial ordinance authorizing the arrest and detention in 'political re-education centres' of all persons regarded as a danger to the safety of the state. This caused great damage to the Party apparatus, but it also helped to win new recruits for the Communist cause, and to drive others into opposition.

As soon as he became prime minister, Diem had cabled Dr Phan Quang Dan, offering him a cabinet post as secretary of social welfare. Still dissatisfied with the French colonial presence, Dan refused. He returned to Vietnam, however, put out his shingle in a slum area by the docks in Saigon and organized the first course in preventive medicine at the Saigon medical faculty. He also started to create a loyal opposition to Diem–to whom loyalty was soon to be equated only with unqualified support.

Fearful of Dan's influence among the medical students, Diem closed the course in preventive medicine. The newspaper *Thoi Luan*, of which Dan had become senior editor, was dynamited and banned. Then, on the eve of the legislative assembly elections in April 1956, police arrested Dan for criticizing the electoral laws.

---

* Subsequently, Washington urged Diem to force the North Vietnamese to refuse to allow supervision of free elections as they surely would have done. He rejected the advice.

† Among those who supported Diem in his stand was President John F. Kennedy who categorically rejected 'an election obviously stacked and subverted in advance, urged upon us by those who have already broken their own pledges under the agreement they now seek to enforce'.

Dan, who had now married his pretty young assistant, moved his medical practice from the dockside to a two-roomed house in the Ba Chieu market in Gia Dinh, just outside Saigon. The ground floor became his surgery. The room upstairs, partitioned with curtains, was both his office and the home where he was soon to raise his young family.

With degrees from the Sorbonne and Harvard, the practice of medicine could have offered Dan lucrative rewards in the middle-class suburbs of Saigon. He moved from the docks because he had to find a home but, characteristically, he elected to live and work among the poor.

It was a job just getting to his surgery. Outside his door each day it was usual to find heaps of vegetables and fruit, baskets of squealing pigs and trussed up ducks and chickens. Once I injured my ankle badly and hobbled into the surgery in mid-morning to take my place among the many peasant women from Tongking, recognizable by their betel-stained teeth and crowns of braided hair, sickly children and injured soldiers waiting with their few piastres for a consultation with Dr Dan. No one seemed surprised to see me. For Dan's following had grown with his practice, and all sorts of people were now coming to his door for medical attention or political talk.

In the 1958 elections for the National Assembly, in which Dan was running as an opposition candidate, the government moved eight thousand soldiers into his electorate to ensure the victory of the government candidate. To the unqualified dismay of Diem and his family, Dan polled 35,000 votes, the government candidate 5,000.

Despite protests by the American and British embassies, Diem decided that Dan, the first and only opposition candidate who ever polled enough votes to win a seat during his regime, should not be allowed to take his place in the Assembly. He feared that Dan might command such a following that he would become a 'demagogue', and thus endanger his own leadership.

On the morning that the new Assembly convened for the first time, Dr Dan dressed in a white sharkskin suit. He locked the doors of his surgery and set out for the Assembly. He did not get far. He was stopped by police and taken to the local station, where embarrassed officers, most of whom were his friends and patients, had orders to detain him during the Assembly session.

I went round to the clinic after the Assembly meeting and met Dan in his surgery half an hour after he had been released. It was the only time I remember seeing him angry. He was furious that he had been accused of giving free medical attention to the electors. 'If I were to offer free medical service', he said, 'I would be swamped with patients. We need a hundred times more doctors than we have now. You can understand the deluge I would get if the sick of Saigon thought that I offered free medical treatment. Sometimes it happens that if a person comes to you and is very sick and you treat him and he cannot pay, you forget about money. But to have charged me with having solicited votes through my medical practice is abominable. It means that there is no justice in this country. If I can be treated in this way, how do you think the ordinary citizen manages?'

Harassed now by Diem's secret police, who guarded his house by day and night and tried to follow him closely wherever he went, Dan ·became increasingly critical of the regime. In November 1960, when Vietnamese paratroopers staged an abortive coup and seized the radio station, Dan went on air in support of the rebels. Immediately thereafter the secret police raided his house and took away everything–his money, his medical equipment, his clothes, his books and his papers. Dan threw off his secret police shadow and hid in a friend's house but was arrested several days later with his friend, and all of his friend's family, including the family dog. Dan's new home became a 'tiger cage' under Saigon's botanical gardens.

Ngo Dinh Nhu visited Dan in prison. He was sure that Dan was involved in a generals' plot against the government and wanted the names of his fellow conspirators–of whom there was none. 'If you refuse, you will undergo water treatment', he said. 'If the water treatment fails to make you speak, you will get electric shock treatment. If this fails, you will be hung by your toes and, if this fails, there will be other things–more refined–to make you talk.'

These were not idle threats. Time after time Dan would be blindfolded and taken from his cage to be strapped to a table while water was forced into his mouth and nostrils. Sometimes electrical shocks were applied to more sensitive parts of his body. And sometimes both tortures were inflicted at the same time. Dan, who lost eleven teeth in prison, called it 'a terribly long nightmare with days and nights all alike, without a companion, without a book, with only harsh words and cruel treatment from torturers'. He kept his sanity by memorizing the characters for a book designed to simplify the teaching of Chinese.

Yet these repressive measures did have the effect of ensuring the detention of anyone suspected of having Communist sympathies, and made Hanoi's task of political penetration and subversion extremely difficult, just as the anti-Communists in the Indo-China states have found opposition and organization extremely difficult since the end of the war. Le Duan, who had gone to the South again in 1955, returned to Hanoi in 1957 with gloomy reports about the effects of

Diem's campaign on the Party apparatus. He had become convinced that it was no longer possible to win by political means, and that force would have to be used. During his stay in the South, he wrote and distributed what was in effect the first Order of the Day of the new war. He called it 'The Path of the Revolution in the South'. He made another visit to the South in 1958, returning to Hanoi early in 1959 to advise the Party 'to open a new stage of the struggle'.

The first, and eventually the last, shots of the war were fired in the Kingdom of Laos, a land of villages and graceful people who deserved a much better fate than the cruel years of war that lay ahead. When I first knew it, Vientiane, the administrative capital, was just another village. At dawn each day slender pirogues loaded with golden melons, long and spindly cabbages, papaya, frogs in buckets and suckling pigs and poultry in wicker baskets used to speed across the Mekong River from Thailand to sell their wares in Vientiane's market. It was an indolent, tranquil land, not at all the place for a war.

As a preliminary to activating the insurgency in South Vietnam, Hanoi needed to control northern Laos and, if possible, the Plain of Jars, an ancient burial ground in the north-east, which is also the junction point of all key roads in the north and north-east, and the source of all rivers running north and south. To protect the Ho Chi Minh 'trail', along which men and supplies would soon start moving into South Vietnam, Hanoi also had to control the eastern border areas. The first attacks came in July 1959, and immediately threatened the province of Sam Neua.

I flew to the provincial capital, also called Sam Neua, from the Plain of Jars and was in time to watch scattered groups of Royal Lao soldiers in soiled green uniforms straggling past Sam Neua's cottages of mud and thatch and the white-washed Roman Catholic mission church, fleeing from an enemy almost none had seen, but which, they all agreed, followed close behind. The cry was 'Viet Minh' and it sent the world to action stations. How extensively the North Vietnamese forces were actively engaged in the early attacks has never been satisfactorily established. My own view was that most were indigenous Pathet Lao. However, on 31 August the North Vietnamese settled the argument by invading from the north, the north-east and the south-east. For a time diplomatic interventions forced them back, but they soon returned and established themselves firmly in the positions they needed most to block any threat by the United States, or anyone else, and to protect the 'trail'.

Although they had used a series of tracks running through the Truong Son mountain range that runs almost the whole length of

Vietnam from north to south to infiltrate their forces into the High-lands during the Indo-China War, the real construction of the 'trail' did not begin until May 1959. The task force, known as Unit 559 (because it was set up in May 1959) was conceived as the essential means of fighting the war in the South, using North Vietnam as the secure rear and the border areas of Laos and Cambodia as forward supply depots and 'sanctuaries' for the Northern forces.

Its construction was one of the most remarkable achievements of the war. When the North Vietnamese engineers went to work, the terrain through which they planned to build the 'trail' was regarded as impassable by many South Vietnamese and American authorities. In 1962, when I was looking into the possibility of the 'trail' becoming a highway of some significance in the conduct of the war, I was told by an American military attaché in Laos, who had been through the area during the Second World War, that no motor vehicle would ever drive through the razor-backed ridges and needle-sharp mountain peaks.

He should be forgiven. The North Vietnamese engineers found themselves in some of the wildest country in the world. The French during their long period of overlordship had never set foot in many parts of the region. In most places there were no footpaths, a North Vietnamese historian has told us, or if any, they were narrow and slippery mountain tracks, where water-logged vegetable debris had become swamp. The most common means of transport, in areas where there was any transport, was small mules that walked shakily on bridges across turbulent mountain streams.

The engineers began by setting up a succession of stations about a day's march apart. The stations consisted of a few sentry sheds, built in the style of the montagnard huts. In the early 1960s the 'trail' was just a trail. 'Whoever passed in the 60s along this line cannot forget the image of the columns of combatants moving along the track, some of them carrying stretchers, climbing mountain passes roughly cut into thousands of steps, then across bridges dangling high above torrents and finally stopping over at some liaison station where they would take their frugal meals, sometimes consisting of nothing but salt and bamboo shoots', says a North Vietnamese writer. Fifteen years later the 'trail' had become a highway, or really a series of highways. The total length exceeded 12,000 miles, 'forming a thick network of strategic and operational roads, with 5,000 kilometres of oil pipelines crossing rivers, streams and mountain passes, many of them over 1,000 metres high'.

On 26 September 1959, less than a month after the North Vietnamese attack in Laos, two under-strength ARVN companies of the 23rd Division began a routine sweeping operation in the Plain of Reeds, west of Saigon. They were looking for a force of about forty Viet Cong. Instead of forty, they found themselves outnumbered by a force of about 150. The ARVN surrendered after about fifteen minutes. Twelve of their men had been killed and fourteen wounded. The rest surrendered all their weapons. The war had begun again.

This is not a history of the Vietnam War, and it would be pointless to record the detail of the decline in South Vietnam that followed its outbreak. There is abundant evidence that from the beginning it was directed from North Vietnam. The Southern recruits to the army fought under North Vietnamese control. Hanoi men staffed the Central Office for South Vietnam. The People's Revolutionary Party of South Vietnam was the Laodong Party of North Vietnam in another guise. The Provisional Revolutionary Government was a propaganda gimmick designed to deceive international opinion. It was held in so little account in Hanoi that North Vietnam did not bother even to accord it diplomatic recognition.

On the other hand, the National Liberation Front, although another Hanoi creation, did provide a framework within which the genuine Southern Communists could operate in the belief that they were helping to run, though not to lead, the revolution. In the end, it was these people, more than anyone else, who had reason to feel cheated by the speed of the North Vietnamese takeover and whose interests 'Nguyen Van Tri' so desperately tried to preserve when he was negotiating with Tran Van Don in the closing days of April 1975.

By the beginning of 1963 it was apparent that the war was going very badly indeed. The Strategic Hamlet programme, which planned to separate the villagers from the insurgents, as Templer had separated the two in Malaya during the Emergency, had been pushed too far and too fast. A small incident, ineptly handled, had the Buddhists throughout the country in an uproar. Men like Dr Phan Quang Dan, who had returned to found a loyal opposition, had been thrown in to gaol. Others like Dr Tran Van Do, closely related to the leading members of the regime, became disenchanted and quit. Madame Nhu's parents were among those who followed Do's example. In letters to his son, Tran Van Chuong said he regarded Nhu as completely evil and had broken off all association with him. He also said that he feared his daughter had become more Ngo Dinh than the Ngo Dinhs.

This was a curious period in the history of the Vietnam War. The consensus among a wide sweep of people living and working in the countryside was that the authority of the Viet Cong was greater than that of the central government, that it had more control over more people, was rapidly increasing the size and capability of its regular forces and, that far from being won, the war had scarcely begun.

This sort of reporting was anathema to the American Embassy, and it was in these days that the conflict between the Press and the official American line began. Hard working, able correspondents like Homer Bigart and François Sully had already come under bitter attack from the Vietnamese government and had left the country. Others, more recently come to the scene, like David Halberstam and Neil Sheehan, were soon to come under physical threat, and, at least in Halberstam's case, to get constant encouragement from James Reston and others on the *New York Times* to continue to expose the 'truth'. The implication was that neither the Vietnamese government nor the American Embassy could be relied on, and thus were planted the seeds that later were to flourish in the *New York Times*' often quite subjective reportage and analyses of the war.

Halberstam and Sheehan detested John Mecklin who, after John F. Kennedy was elected president in 1960, left his job with *Time* and volunteered for the toughest assignment he could think of–public affairs officer in Saigon. When Halberstam and Sheehan were threatened with physical violence, and worse, Mecklin invited them to use his guest quarters. They used to sit in his bar at night drinking his drinks (in his absence) and damning Mecklin along with everyone else. When I protested that if they distrusted him so much they ought to leave, I was told that it was his responsibility to protect the American Press.

Truth was always quite ephemeral in Vietnam. I flew to Hue to get what I believed to be an absolutely accurate account of the incident that had led to widespread Buddhist unrest. I published it in an edition of *The Last Confucian* in 1964, only to be told by the lawyer defending the deputy province chief before a military tribunal that I had done him a considerable injustice. In good faith, I corrected the 'error' in German, Japanese and Italian editions of the book, only to learn subsequently that my first version was probably correct. The reality was what people believed it to be. As early as 1962, the American Embassy had given orders that military advisers and others were in no circumstances to discuss reverses with the Press and, even more importantly, they were also under instruction to report positively in their own official assessments. The result was that both the American Embassy and the American military became the victims of their own propaganda.

Some Americans never did understand the nature of the war. In 1962 the Joint Chiefs of Staff in a memorandum to Defence Secretary McNamara had recommended increased participation in Vietnam, in a type of war in which they claimed to have a wealth of experience but in which the total of American knowledge, with the exception of odd characters like Conein, was very small indeed. To think of Vietnam in terms of Korea and the Pacific War was lunacy; but, Heaven help us all, this is how they thought.

The Americans in the field misled not only the Press, and themselves, they also misled Washington. After spending two hours with John Richardson, the C.I.A. station chief, he saw that I was obviously dubious about how things were going, despite his optimism. 'Have a look through these', he said, 'and you will see that what I've been telling you we've also been telling Washington'. I sat down on his sofa while he busied himself with affairs of state and found that, indeed, Washington had been given the same message that he had given me.

A long talk with Major-General Richard Stilwell, one of the United States' more eminent soldiers, followed similar lines. Stilwell said the only danger was that the Viet Cong would go underground, that they had no capability to move into mobile war, and that he had the capability with helicopters to move a division into action in any part of Vietnam within twenty-four hours. Since the helicopter had a radius of seventy-five miles, I asked him about petrol supplies. His answer was that the Viet Cong did not interfere with tankers carrying supplies on the roads. When I suggested that they certainly had the capability, and perhaps found it expedient not to interfere too much with the economic life until they were ready to take major action, he agreed that I had a point. But the most important point was that there were no reinforcements to spare, and no division in reserve to send anywhere. The reserves of ten battalions, or less than one-fifth the force in the French reserve in the Red River Delta in 1953, were all fully committed now.

Lodge and Bunker in their day were much more realistic and much better informed. They were also much more frank. But they couldn't beat the system. Once, after Defence Secretary Robert McNamara had whisked through Vietnam, and departed spreading euphoria in all directions, I asked Lodge how an able, intelligent man could have reached such conclusions. 'He was fed a tissue of lies by Harkins', (Westmoreland's predecessor) Lodge replied.

I had always been sceptical about the stories of corruption in the Diem family. Such stories are usually easily spread and almost impossible to check.

I decided to risk being bold enough to put it to Madame Nhu herself. 'Corruption?' she said, pursing her lips. 'You know my brother-in-law, Can?'

I didn't, but I knew who he was. 'You know he owns a shipping line and plantations and things to finance his secret party?'

I'd heard the tale but doubted its veracity.

'Well, of all things', she said. 'I've been accused of being corrupt because of Can's doings. I was furious.'

There was no doubt about her anger now. Though she stood less than five feet high and weighed, I guess, no more than eighty pounds, I was glad that it was Can who was catching it now and not I.

'I ordered an immediate investigation into his affairs', she continued. 'I told my agents to examine his ships a hundred times a day if necessary and within the law.'

From Can she turned her attention to the Minister of Finance, who had been accused by her brother, Tran Van Khiem,* of corruption. The minister had glib answers to her charges.

'You are wrong', Madame Nhu told her brother. 'There is no corruption in the finance ministry.'

'You are an innocent', said Khiem, 'a babe in the woods, I have dossiers and proof'.

Armed with fresh information, Madame Nhu said, she set to work once again. She searched for a descriptive phrase. 'How would you say it?' she asked. 'It was like kicking an ants' nest with my foot. I had them running in all directions.'

According to Khiem, Madame Nhu herself had no part in the corruption, but Nhu was up to his ears in it. Later, when Khiem spent long months in prison, he filled in much of his time writing me long, detailed letters, which his beautiful wife, Nguyet, smuggled out to me.

'The secret apparatus controlled everything', he said in one letter. 'It pulled all the strings. To find its money to finance its activities, the secret apparatus controlled a certain number of economic organizations, firms of all sorts. These firms in appearance only competed in the free enterprise economy. It was only theoretical, because, in fact, the firms were helped secretly by the official apparatus. The firms had a de facto monopoly.'

One of the people involved in this way was the stevedore boss, Le My, whose men were used by the secret police in 1960 to destroy the offices of a newspaper critical of Diem. In exchange for this service Nhu and Tran Kim Tuyen, then head of the secret apparatus, gave

---

* He was trained briefly by the Australian Security Intelligence Organization in Melbourne.

him the waterside monopoly. In addition to providing gangsters when the occasion arose, Le My also paid a large sum each month to the secret police. Again, to quote Khiem directly, Le My was employed in 'smashing, or even of liquidating opponents against the regime who sometimes disappeared mysteriously. This explained why so many bodies were found in the river of Saigon.'

At the height of the Buddhist crisis in 1963 I returned to Saigon after an absence of about a month and immediately checked in with Khiem. I phoned him about noon and he suggested lunch at his house around 1 o'clock. When I arrived there I was surprised to find a general's car waiting outside and Khiem in conference with a number of senior Army officers. When the gathering broke up, I asked him jokingly whether he was planning a coup. He surprised me by saying that he had had a reconciliation with the family, and was, in effect, combining the roles of head of the secret police, a position that had now fallen vacant because Dr Tran Kim Tuyen, who had filled the post with considerable skill, was not any longer regarded as loyal to the regime, and that of assistant secretary of defence, a post nominally filled by Nguyen Dinh Thuan, the senior member of Diem's Cabinet. During lunch Khiem accused these and others of treason and said they were marked for early liquidation. 'They will be kidnapped one night and never seen again', he said. One of those mentioned was Dang Duc Khoi, who had joined with Tuyen in writing a critique of the government for Nhu's consideration.

Khiem said that Dr Tuyen's position had been taken over by a man named Hieu, but that he, Khiem, had real authority. Hieu resented him and sent an agent with marked notes for 500,000 piastres, which he offered Khiem in return for family patronage. The payment was only the first of a series to be made each month.

Khiem turned down the bribe, explaining that he had adequate means of his own, a decision that he soon had reason to be glad about, since he discovered that the house had been surrounded by Hieu's men. It was at this moment, he said, he decided that he should influence his sister to give him full secret police powers. Then followed a bitter denunciation of Dr Tuyen, a tiny man. 'You know', said Khiem, 'we used to call him trente-neuf. Now we call him trente-huit. Do you know why?'

I confessed I was puzzled, and he explained that Tuyen had once weighed only thirty-nine kilos and now, because of his fear of death, was down to thirty-eight. 'For the past two months', he said, 'he has not slept twice in the same place, but he has been very shrewd and has placed in a sealed envelope in a Washington safe, with instructions that it should be handed over to Kennedy if anything happens to him, all the details of the Ngo family's evil doings'.

Passing now to Thuan, who was both assistant secretary of defence (Diem was his own defence secretary) and secretary to the presidency, Khiem said that while Tuyen was called trente-huit, Thuan, a much bigger man, was the fat in which trente-huit would be fried.

Since both Tuyen and Thuan had once been close friends of Ngo Dinh Nhu, I asked what had happened to the relationship. He replied that almost all of Nhu's friends had deserted him and with their departure had taken Nhu's power and security. The strongest and most important person in the government was his sister and he himself was now stronger and more powerful than Nhu. I asked him whether Diem was aware of this, and he replied that Diem was aware of very little and was not told much by Madame Nhu.

Khiem then said that he and Madame Nhu had decided that the chief of Vinh Long province, Colonel Le Van Phuoc, was to be brought to Saigon to take charge of its defence when it became necessary to suppress the Buddhists. A year earlier Khiem and I had accompanied Phuoc on a brutal mopping up operation in Vinh Long province, in which his force killed about thirty unarmed men and captured and tortured a similar number. Since Vinh Long was to have become the first 'white' province–that is, free from all Communist insurgents–and was now in apparently a worse state than ever, I readily agreed to accompany Khiem when he went to see Phuoc about the Saigon appointment.

The conversation moved naturally from the Buddhists to the possibility of a coup d'état, which Khiem said he took very seriously. I asked why, then, he had chosen this of all times to return to the family. He replied that he loved his sister, who was beautiful and enjoyed swimming, but now could swim in public no longer because of the burns she had received when pilots under American direction had bombed the palace. For no particular reason, except perhaps that Madame Nhu was a Catholic convert, and he was not, he explained that he always kept Imitations of Christ by his bedside. He also said he had found the best men were Catholics, and he named Phuoc and Le Quang Tung, head of the Special Forces, as men who could be trusted to perform any task set them, however bloody it might be.

During our visit to Vinh Long, we had about six hours to talk in his car (escorted by a full company of troops in armoured vehicles). He gave me in considerable detail the plan to suppress the Buddhists and said the task had been given to Hieu and Le Quang Tung. The Buddhists would be smashed completely. I attempted to persuade him that this was unwise. Though I succeeded in convincing him that the Viet Cong had had absolutely nothing to do with the troubles in Hue in May, when government forces killed eight Buddhists and wounded fourteen others, he replied that it was too late now to alter the plans. His sister was determined to go ahead. She wanted to make it another St Bartholomew's Eve.

I returned to Saigon where, at John Mecklin's invitation, I had installed myself in the guest cottage in his grounds. In my typewriter, when Khiem and I left to go to Vinh Long, was the second page of a long and pessimistic article intended for publication in the *Reporter* magazine in New York. I noticed that it was still in place when I returned. I had no reason to feel any less pessimistic, and continued the article where I had left off.

In 1961 there had been a couple of hundred badly-armed Viet Cong guerrillas in Vinh Long. In 1962 the numbers had increased to about a thousand. Now there were two thousand, apparently well-armed, and occupying no less than twenty-seven combat villages in the centre of the province. Phuoc had tried to turn the whole province into a sort of fortress by employing thousands of peasants on corvée labour to build walls, but this only wasted tens of thousands of man-hours and further alienated the people. In other provinces, closer to Saigon, the situation was worse.

Lu Conein was now back in Vietnam. His task initially was to set up a series of interlocking Special Forces camps, using American Green Berets to command local forces. I had gone with him some time previously on one of his tours of inspection. We travelled in a special STOL (short take off and landing) aircraft at a height of about ten feet above the paddy fields along the coastal valleys of Central Vietnam, with a Turkish pilot at the controls, and a terrified Australian in the rear seat.

Conein turned up for dinner at Mecklin's house the night after my return from the Delta. Mecklin had to leave during the course of the evening, but Conein stayed on. He was bitterly critical of the American Embassy, and late in the night urged on me under no circumstances to pass on anything I had told him or he had told me, or Mecklin had told us both, to anyone in the Embassy. 'If you do', he said, 'it will go straight to Nolting (the American ambassador) and straight to Diem'. He asked me to pass on this message to Mecklin before he left for the office in the morning.

Mecklin, naturally enough, was outraged at the suggestion that

Nolting and the Embassy could not be trusted. Conein's anger with Nolting was based, he said, on the fact that Nolting had informed Diem of the names of two c.i.a. agents who had been working with the Buddhists.

According to Brian Hill, the Australian Ambassador, Nolting at this time had become convinced that the Nhus were right in their belief that the Buddhists should be crushed. He thought the government had satisfied all their legitimate demands, and that they had become a political pressure group that would never be satisfied with concessions. In an interview with United Press-International, which was published in Saigon, Nolting said that he had seen no signs of religious persecution in Vietnam. This inflamed the Buddhists. If he was right in saying there had been no religious persecution, there certainly was religious discrimination. In any event, the interview was unnecessary and foolish.

I sought my own interview with Nolting. It could not be arranged. He was about to leave and to be replaced by Henry Cabot Lodge. He had also been involved in a strategic hamlet incident in which a helicopter opened fire, accidentally causing casualties, and one of Nolting's escorting jeeps knocked over and killed a child. He did not want to see the Press.

In the hope that some other outside advice might have more impact on Khiem, and through him, on his sister, I arranged a lunch for him with Brian Hill. Hill, who had spent four years at the United Nations, gave a brilliant and extremely convincing account of what would happen when the Buddhist countries took the issue of religious discrimination in Vietnam to the General Assembly. 'If you go ahead and crush the Buddhists, Mr Khiem', he said, 'you will not find a single country speaking in your defence. You will be totally isolated, and I fear that in the United States and elsewhere such public pressure will build up against your government that it may prove impossible to continue giving all the support necessary to win the struggle against the Communists.'

Khiem took copious notes and reported back to his sister. The talk only increased her determination to crush the Buddhists quickly. I saw her for two hours some days later and she spoke, though in less detail than Khiem, of quickly crushing the Buddhists and imposing martial law. 'That way', she said, 'we can minimize all this trouble. If we leave it for a month Sihanouk will take it to the General Assembly', and she then proceeded to tell me what might happen in the very terms Hill had used to Khiem. She confirmed everything that Khiem had told me about the relationship between the Nhus and Nolting.

She called him, among other things, a 'great patriot', and deplored his departure, describing him as 'most sympathetic', a feeling she obviously did not expect to have for Cabot Lodge, who had been named as his replacement. Nevertheless, despite her repeated statements that the Buddhists should be crushed, she left me in some doubt when she said that she 'was not sure whether this government [meaning Diem himself] has the courage to do it'.

Mecklin continued to assure me that there was no plan to crush the Buddhists, and that Nolting had in no way given any encouragement. But when I told Khiem my doubts he scoffed at them, repeating that the orders had been given and that there could be no turning back.

I went back to Mecklin, and asked him to submit a single question to Nolting: 'Is it true that you now support the Diem government in its plans to crush the Buddhists?'

Mecklin said he saw all messages and knew that Nolting had given no support to the Nhus, or to anyone else, and asked me to withdraw the question, which he regarded as gratuitously offensive to the departing ambassador. I agreed. Mecklin then went on to say that Nolting had firm assurances from both Diem and Nhu that Madame Nhu was speaking without any authority when she demanded the suppression of the Buddhists, and that both were in agreement that the existing policy of moderation was correct, and would continue.

Khiem at this time questioned me at length about Nolting's attitude to Diem and the Nhus. Since I was staying with Mecklin, a senior Embassy official, I suppose he felt that I was privy to all American attitudes. I replied that I didn't know what Nolting felt personally, but if other American attitudes counted for anything there remained much sympathy for Diem, despite his obstinate ways, but that the Nhus were cordially detested. The questioning about Nolting's attitude to the Nhus persisted over several days. I repeated that I couldn't believe Nolting had any respect for either.

'They don't believe it', he said, obviously having reported back what I had said. 'They are sure Nolting likes them and is in full agreement with them.'

'Even Nhu?' I asked.

'Nhu especially', he replied.

And so the plot went on as planned. In the early hours of 21 August the Nhus climbed into an army tank and were driven off to the Xa Loi pagoda, one of the hundreds to be attacked and seized by the Special Forces. While the Nhus watched, their police and Special Forces, armed with grenades and sub-machine guns, shot up the pagoda and finally took into custody most of the unarmed Buddhist monks who for weeks past had ridiculed Madame Nhu and her husband. In so doing they made all but inevitable the coup d'état of 3 November.

Refused a visa by Tran Van Lam, then Vietnamese ambassador in Canberra, I flew back to Saigon without one* to find that I had become a personal target for attack, and was in imminent danger of arrest. While they were cleaning up in the Xa Loi pagoda, the Special Forces had found thousands of xeroxed copies of the first pages of the *Reporter* article I had left in my typewriter the day I went with Khiem to Vinh Long province. At a press conference the morning I arrived General Ton That Dinh had produced the first two pages of the article as evidence of foreign instigation of the Buddhist affair. Dang Duc Khoi, who had fallen into disfavour along with Dr Tuyen, warned me that I was about to be arrested and in turn I was able to tell him that he was in danger of being killed. Khoi wisely fled across the Cambodian border; I tarried for a few days.

Khiem said he believed that Nhu was responsible for the appearance of my article, or parts of it, in the Xa Loi pagoda, and that he must have organized the raid on Mecklin's house to search my room when we were away in Vinh Long. It was a plausible, but incorrect, explanation.

Nhu accused Khiem of having passed anti-government material to me and also of working for the Buddhists. It was suggested that we should appear before a military tribunal of honour to clear ourselves. Khiem was exonerated by General Dinh and, having no wish to expose myself to Nhu's type of justice, or to 'explain' myself, as Madame Nhu suggested, I made plans to leave.

The tension, and the dramatics, of those days were hard to bear. My friend Bui Anh Tuan was deeply in trouble, also. He was writing at the time for the Philippine *Herald*. We were together in Mecklin's office one day when we learned that we were both to be named in the *Times of Vietnam* in an edition to be published at any moment. To avoid becoming more of an embarrassment to Mecklin than I was already, I had moved out of his house into the Caravelle Hotel. When we left Mecklin's office to walk the couple of hundred yards to the hotel we were not sure we would make it without being arrested.

My room at the hotel was ransacked twice. On one occasion, no doubt to make it appear that it was a matter of simple theft, my travellers cheques were stolen, together with the carbon copies of the articles I had written. Eventually, the travellers cheques came back, with my signature skilfully forged. They had been passed in Macao, Canada, and the United States.

---

* I went in as a tourist on a seven-day stopover.

I lunched with Conein and his wife one day at l'Amiral restaurant. For days the Special Forces, Conein's own creation, had been watching his house, presumably aware that he had become Washington's contact man with the generals planning the coup. Just as we were about to eat, Conein's wife, half Vietnamese-half French, had a premonition that something had gone wrong in their house where she had left their new born baby for the first time. 'I've got to go', she said and ran from the restaurant. At Conein's insistence, we did not follow, but waited, and waited, convincing ourselves that the premonition was correct. Nearly two hours later she returned. The premonition was only partly right. Another car load of Special Forces had put in an appearance outside the house.

I had a final dinner with Mecklin, who bet me $20 to $60 there would be a coup d'état before the end of September, and with a sizable escort of friends and a party from the Australian Embassy went to the airport and took off for Singapore. From there I arranged to have a note hand-delivered to Khiem by Garry Barker of the Melbourne *Herald* explaining why I had left in haste. I was glad to go. Madame Nhu was putting the final touches to an extraordinary article for the *Times of Vietnam* in which she accused the Americans not merely of planning a coup d'état, but also of intending to kill Archbishop Ngo Dinh Thuc. She even gave a German correspondent a list of names involved in the plot. Khiem confirmed it. At the head of the list was John Richardson, the C.I.A. chief, who had been a consistent supporter of the regime, but against whom the family had now turned.

The day after Barker arrived in Saigon the *Times of Vietnam*, which had now published a picture of the first page of my Xa Loi article on the front page, revealed that the xerox copy had found its way into the pagoda without my knowledge, that I was really an objective journalist, that I had been temporarily misled by a 'foreign adventurer'* from my own country. At the same time, Khiem cabled me a pressing invitation to return, with full assurances of protection. Through the Australian Commission in Singapore I received another message from Brian Hill, warning me not to return in any circumstances and to disregard any assurances of safe conduct that I had received.

Months later I learned the true story of how the copy of the *Reporter* article had turned up in the Xa Loi pagoda. It was even more bizarre than the notion that Nhu might have raided Mecklin's house. Returning home late one night with Paul Garvey of the *Voice of America*,

---

* One of the Australian military attachés was included in Madame Nhu's charges of plotting against the regime.

Mecklin heard a curious clanking noise coming from the guest quarters. He called for the Marine guard who forced their way through the door. There, busily printing pamphlets for the Buddhists, were two of his servants. They had seen my article when I was away, thought it would be useful for the Buddhist cause and had reproduced it generously. Mecklin dismissed them quietly and without fuss and kept his counsel.

I have given this personalized account of events leading up to the coup d'état in 1963 in some detail because it may help to explain the mood in Saigon at the time. There is much I have left out in discussing the Buddhists' campaign. They needled and goaded the Nhus into action. Since they could not trust the mails and the telegraph system, they were forced to co-ordinate their campaign by messenger, and the buses and planes were filled with monks, and monks in disguise, rushing messages from place to place about the next Buddhist monk to burn and where and how it should be done.

No organization had any better appreciation of the value of public relations, or the power of the foreign Press. Correspondents were summoned to the pagodas by telephone, or quietly tipped off to take the next plane out to Hue. Bonzes who planned to thrust daggers into their stomachs, or to go up in a blaze of gasoline, were freely produced.

One old lady of high social background, and the mother of a leading diplomat, told me she intended to burn herself to death. 'You may become a martyr here', I said, 'but I assure you that much of the rest of the world will think of you as a barbarian'.

It was difficult to convey the word barbarian, but when I eventually succeeded, she rose to her feet and, saying she felt ill, left the room.

On another occasion at the Xa Loi pagoda I had been singularly moved by the depth of feeling evident among the rows of kneeling and praying youths who were so numerous that they filled all the space in the temple and stretched far along the roadway. It was the final memorial service to the first of five monks who had burned themselves to death at this time. The heart had been removed from the charred body and was on exhibition in the flower-filled temple. It was impossible to doubt the sincerity of those who had come to pray.

Suddenly, however, I had an altogether different emotion when a monk came past with a can filled with petrol which he hid behind the flower decked altar.

It had all begun so simply, and stupidly.

The year 1963 was the twenty-fifth anniversary of Ngo Dinh Thuc's ordination as a bishop. The date almost coincided with the Gautama Buddha's birthday. Hue, Thuc's diocese, was decorated with pictures of him, crosses and flags. These celebrations came to an end on 5 May, only three days before the Buddhists were due to begin their ceremonies. While the Catholic decorations were still up, the Buddhists began to put up theirs.

On the night of 6 May from the presidency in Saigon came a telegram instructing that the order prohibiting the flying of all flags except the national flag should be enforced. This was regarded by the Buddhists as an act of religious discrimination, since they insisted that the Buddhist flag was essential to their own celebration.

Feelings ran high on 8 May among the Buddhists and that night a crowd of some 10,000 gathered in Hue. Orders were given for the crowd to disperse and when it failed to move practice grenades were thrown with unexpected, but lethal, effect.

Instead of making honourable amends and admitting the error, the family accused the Communists of having thrown the bombs, a story that was not accepted by a single Western embassy in Saigon and which, after all the available evidence had been sifted, appeared to be demonstrably false.

Even then wise leadership might have saved the situation. But the family, lacking any real contact with the people, was not wise, and South Vietnam took a giant step down the road to ultimate disaster.

Washington fell into step beside it. Cabot Lodge arrived to take over from Nolting furious about the raid on the pagodas and fully prepared to give a Roland for any of Madame Nhu's Olivers.

Into the scene, as if he was writing the outline for his own novel, stepped Morris West. He saw Nhu and gained the strong impression that he was willing to do a deal with the North, and the word spread. The generals were talking coup d'état. Conein was detailed off to act as liaison officer with the coup leaders. Without a thought for the future, without plans, without taking into consideration whether the generals would prove any better than the Diem regime, Washington gave the green light. The result was death for Diem and Nhu and disaster for South Vietnam, the United States and much besides.

There is little to add to the story of the coup that is not generally known. Three days before the coup, General Duong Van Minh decided to opt out and was reluctantly re-enlisted by Tran Van Don, who had been in constant communication with Conein.

Conein was in the Joint General Staff headquarters with the coup leaders during the whole operation. He had just called Okinawa to order a long-range aircraft to pick up Diem and Nhu when he heard they had been killed. The plan was to send them both to the first country to offer sanctuary.

Don had just spoken on the phone to Madame Nhu (who was

making a lecture tour of the United States) to reassure her that the two men were unhurt, when he was told. The initial order to kill the two brothers was given in a fit of pique by Big Minh when he went to the palace expecting to take their surrender and found they had fled. The order was transmitted through General Mai Huu Xuan, Minh's Chief of National Police, who accompanied by car the weapons carrier in which the two men were shot. The man who pulled the trigger was Major Nguyen Van Nhung, Minh's aide, who was subsequently assassinated during another coup. Among others to die on this day was Conein's bête noire, Le Quang Trung, head of the Special Forces. His death was an honorarium to Conein for services rendered.

Long before the coup, in the first edition of *The Last Confucian*, I had summed up my feelings and concerns about the situation in Vietnam at the beginning of 1963:

Nothing presents itself as an easy way out. Total military victory does not seem possible, and the restoration of order, if that is possible, will take years. Diem will not broaden his government. He will not change his advisers. He will not accept outside advice. Is the answer, then, that Diem must go? That the situation demands, and that the South Vietnamese people deserve, and need, something more effective and enlightened in the way of government is obvious, but though there are many men of talent and sophistication who have not been used, the opposition is scattered, disunited, in jail, or Communist. Nothing about the army suggests that it would provide a proper alternative. The probability is that the regime will go on, ever more isolated from the people, and that the Americans will meet the military challenge in whatever way it may develop until one day Diem abdicates his task (a real fear among some Americans in Vietnam) or is removed by an assassin, or a coup d'état. None of these possibilities is attractive; none holds a solution for South Vietnam, or South-East Asia.

3. And out

The coup d'état was as devastating to South Vietnam's chances of survival as the Nhus' decision to raid the Buddhist pagodas. Within weeks it was obvious that not just Diem and Nhu had been destroyed but almost the entire government apparatus. The intelligence organizations fell to pieces. The strategic hamlets collapsed. The new military leadership was untalented, untrained and incapable of performing the tasks that fell upon it. These inadequacies were apparent to all, including relatively junior officers in the armed forces, and there began a merry-go-round of coups d'état that would have been self-destructive in a country enjoying all the benefits of peace and not fighting for its life in war. The Viet Cong were taken by surprise. They could not react quickly enough, or strongly enough, to take full advantage of all the opportunities presented to them. As for corruption, it reached peaks undreamed of in Diem's day. In the pipeline to support the strategic hamlet programme were massive quantities of aid. With the villages the aid was intended for again under Communist control, or in dispute, there was nowhere for it to go but the black market in Saigon. Le My had been thrown into prison, but there were many others on the waterfront to take his place.

By early 1964 American strength in Vietnam had grown steadily to something over 20,000. General William C. Westmoreland arrived to take over from General Harkins, and the Military Aid and Advisory Group (MAAG) was soon to become the Military Assistance Command, Vietnam (MAC-V). After the first coup, General Tran Van Don had become commander-in-chief of the armed forces. He had some very definite ideas about how to capture, and to hold, the countryside. He briefed Westmoreland one day in January on the need to fight a small unit war and to hold the ground in populated rural areas. Westmoreland was interested enough to take notes. The next day a goateed, ambitious young general named Nguyen Khanh staged a coup d'état and Don found himself under arrest. Khanh had different ideas altogether. He wanted big units and big war.

In the months that followed, desperate efforts were made to recover the countryside. All failed. On 17 March 1964, a National Security Action Memorandum warned President Lyndon B. Johnson that unless the United States maintained an independent, non-Communist South Vietnam almost all of South-East Asia would probably fall under Communist influence, and the threat to India, Australia, New Zealand, Taiwan, Korea and Japan would be greatly increased. There were more sanguine voices. These were only partly heeded. With vivid recollections of the near disaster that had accompanied General Douglas MacArthur in his Home-for-Christmas-On-to-the-Yalu offensive in 1950, Johnson tried to follow the Kennedy policy of helping the South Vietnamese while hoping to avoid a heavy American involvment. When, despite himself, he became deeply involved, it became impossible to win within the parameters he laid down.

By the beginning of February 1965, the war in South Vietnam was all but lost, lost not merely in the sense that weak government in Saigon would one day want to negotiate a fictitious neutrality, but in the total sense of the word. What lay ahead for South Vietnam was absolute defeat.

'The National Liberation Front counts on a clear-cut victory over whatever u.s.-Saigon regime is in power at the time', wrote Wilfred Burchett. 'Pax Americana is unacceptable to the Viet Cong.' No foreigner knew the North Vietnamese better than Burchett. In conversations with International Control Commission officials, the North Vietnamese leaders now no longer expressed any interest in the resumption of the Geneva Conference, or in any negotiations that did not include the prior exclusion of all American military advisers and equipment from South Vietnam.

Opinions differed in Saigon about how long the final disaster might be averted. Some people spoke of a couple of months. The resilience of the Vietnamese people and the country's capacity to muddle along with ineffective government convinced the more optimistic that things might just go on getting worse for a long time. But few, if any, doubted the inevitability of defeat if the war continued to be fought on Viet

Cong ground rules, and the government remained corrupt and failed to govern.

Dr Phan Quang Dan had been released from prison after the fall of the Diem regime. Now it was Bui Anh Tuan's turn to be arrested. As publisher and editor of *Hanh Dong*, the leading Buddhist newspaper, he was arrested on a charge of criminal libel for exposing corruption in the government. He was detained for six months and then released to await trial. Every time the trial hearings were scheduled, Dr Dan would find that Tuan was too ill to attend, a stratagem that fought a delaying action until those accused by Tuan of corruption were thrown out by another of the many coups d'état.

The days when the Viet Cong depended on slingshots, home-made rifles and even captured American equipment had long passed. Main force units were now being equipped with ever more sophisticated weapons, including, for the first time, artillery. More and more North Vietnamese were joining the fighting in the South.

It was this change, and not just the question of retaliation against North Vietnam, that was the real challenge President Johnson faced on 7 February 1965. He could either opt out, or opt in.

There were many weaknesses in the thinking that led to the escalated bombing of the North and the massive intervention of American forces. Perhaps the gravest error was the appreciation that Ambassador Maxwell D. Taylor took with him to Vietnam when he replaced Henry Cabot Lodge: If only the United States could convince Hanoi, Moscow and Peking that it was in deadly earnest, that South-East Asia was really worth the risk of a major war, then a way could be found to terminate North Vietnamese intervention and to bring the insurgency to an end. For the plan to work, there could not be one ounce of bluff.

Assistant Ambassador Alexis Johnson spelled it out for me, drawing heavily on the Cuban experience in 1962 to justify the argument. What he could not understand was the difference between North Vietnam and Cuba and the relative importance of both to the security of the United States. The United States could risk a nuclear war to see Russian missiles pulled out of Cuba, since they were so demonstrably a direct threat. But what sort of direct threat was North Vietnam? And how on earth could the message be conveyed that Washington thought it was worth the risk of an all-out war, when, demonstrably, it was not?

The Tongking Gulf incident, and the bombing that followed, did not intimidate Hanoi. Instead of drawing its horns in after the American retaliation, it responded with a vastly increased volume of manpower, material and other aid to the Viet Cong. Attempts by aircraft of the u.s. 7th Fleet to close off the Ho Chi Minh trail in the general region of Tchepone in Laos were completely unsuccessful, more of a stimulant than a hazard. As Hanoi evaluated the situation, the United States had bluffed in the Gulf of Tongking, and its bluff had been effectively called.

'We shall always win if we know our enemy', said a National Liberation Front broadcast. 'We must neither overestimate the enemy nor underestimate him. We must not be subjective. We must assess the enemy's situation accurately.'

Until the tactical use of B52s began early in 1968, even American air power did not hold many terrors for the troops in the field. They devised ingenious listening devices to detect the approach of aircraft and helicopters, and worked out fire plans for anti-aircraft defence. The arrival of stocks of heavy machine guns put new heart into their ranks. Even the effect of napalm bombs, it was discovered, could be minimized by covering exposed trenches with damp cloth. Digging deeper, deploying more widely and moving quickly into attack at close quarters also helped to counter air power: these were also tactics identifiable with offensive planning.

'Digging', the French briefing officer in Hanoi habitually answered when he was asked what the Viet Minh were doing at Dien Bien Phu during the lulls between the brief and bloody main assaults there. It was an appropriate answer. By the time the battle ended, the Viet Minh trenches had spread from the hills, across the plains under the French wire, and into the last of their strongholds.

Much of the Viet Cong's extensive digging in South Vietnam went on underground and out of sight. Toward the middle of 1966, however, the North Vietnamese began surface digging in the six-mile-wide demilitarized zone along the 17th parallel. By October of that year they had burrowed for miles. There were long communications trenches leading to artillery positions and smaller trench systems with machine-gun emplacements. Trails just wide enough for a man, or a bicycle, grew overnight to accommodate jeeps or small trucks, and out of North Vietnam came troops to fill the newly-created position.

Not only was the digging reminiscent of Dien Bien Phu; there was evidence that it reflected Dien Bien Phu thinking.

In February 1964, the hard core of the Viet Cong forces numbered, by official American estimate, about 22,000 men. By the beginning of February 1965, despite heavy combat losses, their regular forces had grown to an estimated 35,000. With the active assistance of perhaps a hundred thousand part-time guerrillas and regional forces and the co-operation of some half million members of willing supporters of the National Liberation Front, the Viet Cong now had a substantially larger mobile attacking force than the 600,000 military and para-military troops of the government. With their responsibility for keeping roads, railways, rivers and canals open, and for ensuring that crops reached the markets, by far the larger proportion of the government's forces were tied down.

Tactically, helicopters had added a new element of surprise and mobility to the government's family of weapons. With this new strength, however, there were also weaknesses. While the helicopters often contributed to the success of government sorties against the Viet Cong, they also tended to give them the character of hunting parties, thus helping the Viet Cong to identify themselves with the peasants.

In December 1964, some inkling of the grave new turn in the war had become apparent when Viet Cong forces demonstrated in the Highlands that they now had the means to cut South Vietnam in two. The attacks against the American advisory teams' installations at Pleiku and Qui Nhon early in 1965, which led to the American air raids north of the 17th parallel, were premeditated and deliberate. For weeks the Viet Cong rehearsed the Pleiku attack. Few armies have ever given such attention to the planning of the most minute detail of small actions. From the sand table the Viet Cong moved to full-scale mockups, leaving little to chance, or luck–although by miscalculation, or inexperience, many of their rounds of mortar fire at Pleiku fell short. But for this, the u.s. casualties would have been heavy. The real significance of the Pleiku and Qui Nhon actions, however, was less the calculated selection of American targets than the threat this posed to the Highlands, to which Hanoi had always accorded high priority.

Despite the bombing, the North Vietnamese on a massive scale also planned to move South and to lure the Americans into major actions in the tangled mountains below the demilitarized zone.

At u.s. Marine headquarters in Danang a general hung on the wall some boldly printed extracts from the writings and speeches of the leaders of the National Liberation Front and the Hanoi government. Among them was the following: 'The National Liberation Front will entice the Americans close to the North Vietnamese border and will bleed them without mercy. In South Vietnam the pacification campaign will be destroyed.' It was signed by Nguyen Van Mai, National Liberation Front representative in Cambodia.

All the quotations were relevant but none more brutally so than this. For between the 1966 build-up and the 1968 Tet offensive the Marines were drawn into a series of bloody battles with North Vietnamese forces operating out of the demilitarized zone. The Americans came to search and destroy, and in principle, to block invasion routes to the South. Though they lost heavily themselves, it was worth the effort, it seemed, because they took such a heavy toll of the enemy. Yet with every succeeding campaign the nature of the war here began to change. Contrary to the Marines' natural inclination and training, they became involved in positional warfare. They built a whole series of frontier posts at Gio Linh, Con Thien, Khe Sanh and other places, all of them within artillery range of the North Vietnamese bases in the sanctuaries, and in the process they ceased to be the hunter and became the quarry. Far to the rear the guerrillas and cadres increased their hold on the hamlets and villages.

On the outskirts of Danang, just beyond the southern limits of the American airbase, was the village of Hoa Tho. Two of the hamlets within the village were only about a mile from the office that used to be the headquarters for the pacification centre in Quang Nam province, one of the five national priority areas in 1965 and 1966. By the beginning of 1967 the national pacification centre for the province had been withdrawn to a safer haven, the fences around the hamlets had been pushed down and a Viet Cong main force regiment was the dominant force in the area.

As early as 1950 General de Lattre de Tassigny had built a chain of concrete blockhouses here in a desperate effort to control the coastal plain. The interlocking forts were to provide co-ordinated fields of fire sufficient to keep the Communist cadres out of contact with the peasants. The scheme did not work. The Viet Minh simply infiltrated the countryside by night and knocked down the blockhouses one by one. Long abandoned, they still stood with their little moats overgrown and their barbed wire rusted. Tin cans that were meant to warn of the intruders' approach through the protecting minefields still rattled in the monsoon winds.

Ngo Dinh Diem tried to build strategic hamlets in the same area. His successors experimented with what were called 'New Life' villages, and operations designed to spread the government apparatus 'like an oil stain' through the hamlets and paddy fields. These attempts all had one common factor: a total lack of success.

At the height of one of the Buddhist political crises in the area the government forces simply moved out, leaving the hamlets and even abandoning their stock of 'Bouncing Bettys', one of the more lethal of the anti-personnel mines. The Viet Cong seized both the people and

135

the mines. Instead of becoming a cheerful and contented community, basking in the flow of a generous follow-up aid programme, Quang Nam became for a year or two an area of sullen, cold hostility.

Precious little of the economic aid intended to succour refugees and to provide a better life in the villages got through. I heard of one instance in which five hundred cases of cooking oil left the provincial capital but, according to the district chief, only a hundred arrived at his headquarters. In another district I found that all the village chiefs lived in the capital and some had never visited their villages.

I talked to a senior provincial official about it. 'Corruption! It is terrible', he said. 'It is almost impossible to get a district chief who is not corrupt. They expect graft as their right. They take risks and they expect rewards. It is very hard to fight this sort of corruption. Very few province or district chiefs are brought to court. The punishment is usually to let them go back to their military units. People like corruption. Everybody expects their share. They don't take everything. Perhaps half gets to where it is intended to go in the hamlets.'

Saigon importers reported that a fourth of all commodities entering the port were stolen there, often by the military who came at night with trucks and guns to intimidate the guards and load up. 'I think this is the only country in the world where you can be in an office negotiating the entry of goods and watch them being sold outside in the black market', said an American businessman. 'We've imported enough cement to cover this countryside a foot deep', complained an American official. 'Where do you think it has gone? Into new buildings in the towns and into Viet Cong bunkers.'

On both the government and American sides, officials deliberately tried to camouflage their reverses. I once asked the acting province chief in Quang Nam for an estimate of the number of totally secure hamlets in the province. He consulted his charts and awarded 155 to the government and 386 to the Viet Cong.

'How many do you think would be secure enough for you and me to spend a night there?' I inquired.

He paused for a moment and then pointed on the map to the island of Cu Lao Cham, about twelve miles off the coast. 'There's one hamlet on that island', he said. 'That's the only one in the province where it would be completely safe to spend the night.' As if to emphasize the point, a defector from the Viet Cong main force, who was visiting his wife in a village at the edge of the provincial capital, and just fifty yards from a large concentration of government troops, was murdered that night in his home by the Viet Cong.

I arrived back in Vietnam after an absence of several months in the middle of 1967 and dropped by the MAC-V information centre to seek an up-dating on the current military scene. A colonel welcomed me with a richly embroidered account of Viet Cong reverses. Among his more exaggerated claims was the statement that with the exception of one major highway all the main roads throughout the country were now secure.

'Do you mean I can drive from Saigon to Danang?' I asked.

'Why, certainly', the colonel replied.

'Now isn't that luck', I said, tongue in cheek. 'I've just hired a car, and I've always wanted to make that journey along. the coast.'

At this point, the briefing officer appreciated that he had overstepped the mark and qualified his statement with a reference to the need to check on local conditions from day to day. I went my way–which was not through the Viet Cong domains on the coast road to Danang.

One truly significant advance in 1967 was in the field of military intelligence. Yet to accept that the intelligence was accurate came close officially to admitting the inadmissible. At the same time that the MAC-V colonel was creating so cheerful and so positive a picture for the incoming correspondent, the same headquarters was wrestling with the problem of how to reveal that the combined strength of all enemy forces in-country was much closer to 392,000 than the figure of 292,000, which had been the official estimate earlier in the year.

Since the problem posed political questions of credibility and also military questions of an even more disturbing nature, it was resolved by relegation to the appropriate pigeon-hole. It was one matter to accept that Viet Cong armed strength jumped from 15,000 in 1961 to 45,000 in 1965. After all, this was the purely 'advisory' period of the war. But to reveal that the immense American build-up had been accompanied by a complementary increase in enemy strength, including a jump of 100,000 during the year of heaviest fighting, and heaviest enemy casualties, was also to reveal a lack of real progress that very few cared to admit.

The search-and-destroy operations with which General Westmoreland hoped to break up main-force enemy units of divisional and regimental size had been disruptive and richly rewarding in intelligence. But they did not succeed in their primary purpose. The enemy did not abandon his mobile and conventional war and fall back on purely guerrilla tactics. Hanoi was not only fighting a multi-fronted war but also a sophisticated multiplicity of wars, each with an interlocking purpose and design. The main-force efforts had a three-fold intent: to cause maximum American and allied casualties; to 'absorb' the expanding allied forces in defensive operations, thereby preventing the concentration of forces needed to protect and expand the pacified areas; and to permit intensified small-scale guerrilla actions against the pacification programme in particular and the allied rear and base areas in general.

To meet the threat from the demilitarized zone in April and May 1967, General Westmoreland had to strengthen his forces there by redeploying three brigades from II Corps to I Corps. Almost immediately a second threat began to develop in the Highlands, which necessitated moving the 173rd Airborne from around Saigon to plug the hole there.

Throughout 1967 Hanoi continued to make it clear that it had given up all thought of settling the war by negotiation. At an 'extraordinary' meeting the National Liberation Front brought out a new programme designed to meet the requirements of the new war-for-victory line. This was followed on 1 September (the day after the publication of the new programme) by a speech by Pham Van Dong, the North Vietnamese prime minister, in which he pledged to spurn all overtures and to fight on to final victory.

The death of Nguyen Chi Thanh, the COSVN secretary, in July was a serious blow in the preliminary build-up period to the Tet offensive, which was offset by the much larger supplies of military equipment now arriving from China by rail and from the Soviet Union by sea. While admitting the superiority of the allied forces in numbers, fire-power and equipment, Hanoi had concluded nevertheless that it possessed distinct military advantages. Among them were: better and more experienced leadership and training for this type of war; the advantages of fighting on one's own terrain among one's own people; mobility; morale; the too rapid rotation of U.S. forces and their lack of familiarity with local and tropical conditions; political and other problems encountered by the Americans in pouring large numbers of troops into Vietnam; the strain on the U.S. economy of supplying forces fighting thousands of miles from the home base; the unreliability of the South Vietnamese army; and the excessive proportion of rear-line U.S. troops.

As Hanoi evaluated the situation, the war had reached the stage of development that marked the beginning of the main Viet Minh offensive in the Indo-China War, that is, the period immediately preceding the battle for Dien Bien Phu, when General Giap launched a series of combined mobile-guerrilla operations that consumed the French reserves and destroyed all hopes for the Navarre Plan, which envisaged broad clear-and-hold operations.

Prisoners and defectors warned that the North meant what it said.

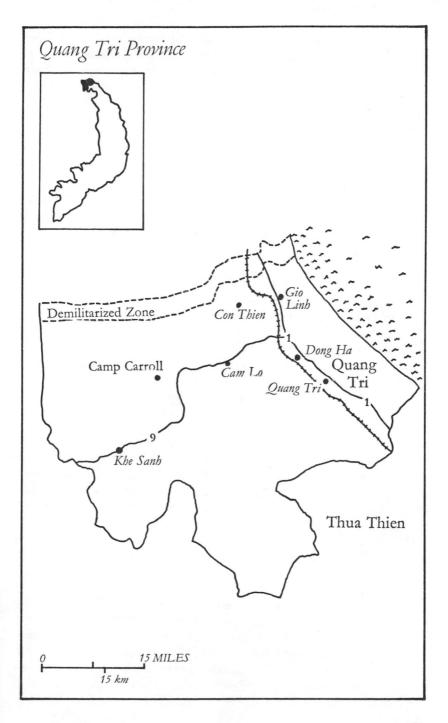

Quang Tri Province

Demilitarized Zone

Gio
Linh

Con Thien

Camp Carroll

Cam Lo

Dong Ha

Quang
Tri

Quang Tri

Khe Sanh

9

1

1

Thua Thien

0   15 MILES

15 km

One company commander said that the people's hatred of the Americans seemed to increase proportionately with the intensification of the u.s. air attacks in the North. Another Northern defector said that he did not know how long the war would last, but he believed the u.s. would tire of it first.

When and if they gain access to the documents from both sides, military historians are likely to find the trial and error tactics practised by the North Vietnamese in Central Vietnam through the long hot summer of 1967, the essential prelude to the Tet offensive, one of the most fascinating periods of the war.

Early in the year, with the Tet celebrations over and their stockpiles brimming–in the four-day stand down by South Vietnamese forces they moved enough supplies into South Vietnam to last one full division for a year–and with a monthly flow of 7,000 to 8,000 troops each month moving South along the Ho Chi Minh trail, the North Vietnamese tested both their tactics and their weapons on the toughest targets, the Americans and the South Koreans.

On 14 February they used flame throwers to attack a Korean position. Two weeks later they directed their first 140-millimetre rocket attack against Danang airfield. In a second attack on the same airfield on 15 March they fired fifteen rockets in fifteen seconds, setting alight a fuel line and damaging a number of aircraft.

The action now moved north into the critical area immediately south of the demilitarized zone. Early in March the monsoon rains ended here. The narrow coastal plain–South Vietnam is only forty-five miles wide from the South China Sea to the Lao border– had yellowed in the blazing sun. The rice was harvested and the west winds from Laos had turned the Marines' enclaves into dust bowls.

Dong Ha, forward headquarters for the 3rd u.s. Marine Division, was twelve miles south of the Ben Hai River, the dividing line between North and South Vietnam. It was at the road junction of Route 1, the old Mandarin Road, that leads to Hanoi, and Route 9, which went west through the Special Forces and Marine camp at Khe Sanh to Laos and the major staging point of Tchepone on the Ho Chi Minh trail.

Also due west of Dong Ha, and roughly in the centre of Quang Tri province, were the artillery platforms at Cam Lo and Camp Carroll. To the north, about six miles apart and just below the demilitarized zone, were the long-range artillery positions at Gio Linh and the Marine and Special Forces camp at Con Thien. These two positions were now in view of each other along the 'firebreak' which the Seabees had begun to bulldoze across the countryside.

Gio Linh's 175-millimetre guns, with a twenty-mile range, struck daily at positions in North Vietnam. Its 105s provided direct support for Con Thien, Dong Ha, and the other artillery positions at Cam Lo and Camp Carroll, which were in turn available to support isolated Khe Sanh, six miles from the Laotian border. Add to this total control of the air and naval support from ships offshore, and the u.s. Marine position, tripled in a couple of months to more than division strength, might have appeared to be beyond challenge. Instead, it was challenged, challenged and challenged again.

The opening round of this small, but highly significant, war of manoeuvre came at the end of the first week of March. The point platoon of a Marine battalion, moving west beyond Cam Lo, ran into the point of a Northern column, probably of battalion strength, moving south. The Marine commander died in the first phase of the action. Meanwhile, a second Northern column, moving south but further to the west, escaped detection and launched a 500-round mortar and rocket attack against the artillery platform at Camp Carroll. At the same time, a third column, with a much heavier supply of artillery, ran into a Marine patrol west of the Mandarin Road, between Dong Ha and Gio Linh. South Vietnamese reinforcements came in and were hit by 1,200 rounds of mortar fire.

From 15 March through to the first week in April there were widespread acts of terrorism through Quang Tri and Thua Thien provinces. A significant point about these activities was their lack of selectivity. The Viet Cong forgot about the hearts and minds of the local population. They made no effort to avoid hurting civilians. Where once they had been careful, for instance, to detonate their land mines electrically, they now used pressure switches. The roads became unusable not only for the military but for everyone.

On the night of 6 April, major attacks on a South Vietnamese regimental headquarters eleven miles north of Hue, and on Quang Tri city, the provincial capital of Quang Tri province, ended the military lull. Mortar shells landed on the Hue Citadel and there were reports that North Vietnamese troops had been seen in the centre of the city. Panic set in.

News that the South Vietnamese regimental headquarters north of the city had been over-run and the regimental commander killed coincided with Viet Cong action to close the road to Danang to all commercial traffic. Gasoline became so short that military supplies had to be made available just to keep the police on the roads.

Two divisions of North Vietnamese troops, the 341st and the 324th B, had now been committed to action in South Vietnam. Across the

Laotian border in Tchepone, where it had been waiting for six months, a third, the 325th, now prepared to move. Its targets were the Special Forces camp and Marine infantry company on either side of Khe Sanh, one of the more important listening posts close to the Ho Chi Minh trail and high in the mountains in the centre of a small coffee-growing area. The elephant grass here grew to a height of about twelve to fifteen feet and provided enough cover to conceal an army. The jungle cover was thick, with an especially heavy undergrowth. The French used to call the mountains north of Khe Sanh the Tiger's Teeth, an expression that conveyed some of the savagery of the country.

About mid-April the Marines noticed a sharp increase in the number of enemy troops passing through. On 24 April, two Marine patrols began to hunt for a series of caves which they thought the transients were using. Instead, they ran headlong into the invasion forces from Laos, the 18th and 9th Regiments of the 325th Division. The North Vietnamese came with one regiment forward, armed and ready for action, and with the second initially as porters but ready to take over the guns of the dead and wounded.

The first reaction back at company headquarters at Khe Sanh was that the patrols had tangled with local Viet Cong. But the Northerners tipped their hand. As the helicopters came in to evacuate the wounded, they ran into such concentrated small-arms fire that the Marines realized they were up against a major force, and the Northerners lost the advantage of surprise. An sos signal went out to Dong Ha, and in came the bulk of two Marine infantry battalions and two battalions of artillery.

On the three main hills dominating Khe Sanh, the Northerners covered their bunkers with up to six layers of logs hewn from the jungle with chain and cross-cut saws. Napalm, field artillery and the run-of-the-mill range of bombs had little effect on the bunkers. The 325th was there to stay—for months.

Individually courageous, disciplined, well-equipped and well-trained, but inflexible at this time in their command planning, the Northerners persisted far beyond the point of seeming reason with a whole series of co-ordinated attacks. The helicopter pad at Phu Bai, the Marine forward division headquarters at Dong Ha, and all the artillery positions, came under heavy and co-ordinated mortar, artillery, or rocket attack. At Dong Ha the bombardment knocked out the communications centre and put the vital radio net out of operation. At Phu Bai it damaged nineteen of the forty to forty-five helicopters on the field and five Army transport planes.

The Seabees under the protection of two companies of Marines had begun to extend the 'firebreak' west from Gio Linh to Con Thien. The operation met with much criticism from the Marines, who doubted the worth of an undefended line of this sort and scoffed at the suggestion that it could be pushed into the enemy-infested hills and mountains between Con Thien and the Lao border. The Northerners nevertheless reacted swiftly. They knocked out four of the five observation posts along the strip almost as soon as they were built, and on 8 May, three days after the fighting ended at Khe Sanh, threw two battalions against the small force of Vietnamese irregulars, about a hundred men in the Special Forces camp, and two Marine companies assigned to guard the Seabees at Con Thien.

Nine Northern battalions closed around Con Thien. For days on end they peppered its defences with recoilless rifle fire. When this failed to achieve its purpose, they tried multiple rocket attacks. On one occasion, some two hundred rounds fell within the perimeter in less than nine minutes. On another, sixty rockets landed on the helicopter pad in fifty-five seconds. The Marines and South Vietnamese forces counter-attacked into the demilitarized zone, but as soon as they moved out the North Vietnamese moved in again.

To the south, North Vietnamese engineers were building a road running through South Vietnam east from Laos, using bulldozers and other earth-moving equipment under the noses of the Americans. Opposite Pleiku and spread across the Cambodian border there were two other divisions of Northerners facing a significantly smaller American force.

In North Vietnam a massive recruiting campaign was in full swing. The campaign was built around a hero named Nguyen Van Be, who had been working in a transportation platoon in the Mekong Delta in May 1966. Be's group was attacked by a government force while it was moving ammunition and mines in three sampans along a canal in the Plain of Reeds, west of Saigon. The government forces killed all the Viet Cong except Be, who tried to escape by hiding underwater. When he was eventually discovered, he was beaten up by his captors who took him to the district capital of My An together with the booty from the sunken sampans. Here, according to Hanoi, American officers asked him if he knew how to operate some of the captured mines. He showed how one or two were armed, then, having pretended that a Claymore pressure mine was electrically detonated,

> Be sprang up and dashed to an armoured vehicle parked nearby. Hatred increased his strength tenfold. Raising the mine above his head, his eyes shining with a terrible fire, he shouted, 'Long Live the National Liberation Front. Down with the American imperial-

ists!' There was a general stampede. The terrified officers and soldiers tried to flee. But it was too late. Be smashed the detonator against the body of the armoured vehicle. A terrible explosion was heard. The mine caused the whole heap of mines and grenades to explode in a series of earth-shaking thunder claps. The men and vehicles around Be were submerged in a sea of flames . . . Sixty-nine enemy personnel were killed, among them twelve Americans (one captain), and twenty puppet officers. One M188 armoured car was destroyed, two M113s heavily damaged.

So great was the explosion, it was said, that the 9th ARVN Division opened fire on its own ranks, the garrison of a neighbouring post fled in terror and My An was put under martial law, which forbade the troops to talk about the incident to the civilian population.

With this magnificent material, Hanoi set out to elevate Be to something like sainthood. Day after day, *Nhan Dan* and *Tien Phong*, the leading newspapers in Hanoi, spread Be and his exploits across full pages. Sometimes they devoted more than half an issue to him. Poets, playwrights and composers went to work on the story. Stone masons and sculptors created statues in his image. A new natural fertilizer plant was named after him, and Nguyen Van Be sewing machines appeared on the North Vietnam market. Every youth and soldier learned the story of Nguyen Van Be until he knew it by rote.

'It is expected that all youth league chapters must satisfactorily organize the reading and exchange of ideas pertaining to the Nguyen Van Be story, so that all the four million members of our youth league will be permeated with the Nguyen Van Be spirit which consists of our resolution to resist against and defeat the U.S. aggressor and to be ready to make sacrifices for our fatherland and revolution', instructed a front page editorial in *Tien Phong*. 'Our youth league must uphold and promote the flag of revolutionary heroism: a will to fight, fight to the finish and be unafraid of making the supreme sacrifice', said an instruction to political cadres captured in Tay Ninh.

In Quang Tri province, cadres, party members and others were assigned an eight-hour period for the special study of Be based on two questions: 'How could he achieve such a great feat of arms while he was encircled by the enemy?' 'In his brave and heroic life and his glorious death, we could draw many precious lessons, but for you which lesson is the most precious and profound?'

The questions were not meant to be discussed merely in the abstract. All groups were ordered to create sections of young Nguyen Van Be commandos and to write collective 'letters of determination' to Ho Chi Minh.

The hamlet of My Hoa in the village of Kimson in the Mekong

Delta, where Be once lived, was good hero territory. It used to be an important Viet Minh centre during the war against the French. The story was still told of the Viet Minh flag with its yellow star on a red field that was tied so high to the top of a hamlet tree that the French had to chop down the tree to get rid of it. For years troops in a government outpost a mile away used to call for shellfire, or an air attack, on the hamlet, but otherwise avoided it like the plague.

The eldest son in a family of poor peasants, Be himself also had the sort of proper revolutionary background that the situation demanded. He was twenty years of age at the time of his deification and young enough, therefore, to be a symbol of youth. His Party background was flawless. He volunteered at sixteen to join the Viet Cong. Three years later he became a member of the People's Revolutionary Party youth movement. On the first anniversary of Be's 'death', Hanoi launched a fresh campaign of study into his heroism. It lasted until the great recruiting campaign in the North had ended.

While the youth of the land were pledging to turn themselves into Vietnamese *kamikazes*, Nguyen Van Be was moving, in fact, from detention centre to detention centre until he finally came to rest in My Tho prison not far from Saigon. Here, a government police officer, noticing the increased Nguyen Van Be propaganda in captured documents, compared the date of capture of the young prisoner bearing the same name and, scarcely believing what he was seeing, the pictures of Be appearing in Hanoi and Front publications. Even so, the heroism of Nguyen Van Be might have gone unchallenged but for the initiative of Donald Rochlen, who was running the American psychological warfare operation, and now found himself locked in combat with the entire Communist propaganda apparatus.

Hanoi bluffed it through. It silenced everyone who might have known the real story and attempted to drown out Rochlen by increasing the tempo of the hero emulation campaign. It denounced Rochlen for 'having resorted to the Hollywood technique of selecting actors and the medical art of changing facial traits as applied in Hong Kong and Japan'.

Be himself was horrified to find that he had become a hero. When Rochlen showed him the pictures and stories that were appearing about him, it was seconds before he could speak. A nerve in his throat began to pound. 'Why have they done this to me?' he asked Rochlen. 'This is a death sentence.'

Be's cousin, Nguyen Van Ba, a regimental political commissar, who defected now because he understood that Be was neither a hero nor dead and feared for his own life, knew why. His hair was of only moderate length; it had never seen a brush. His shirt was unpressed. But he understood very well what the Nguyen Van Be campaign was all about and was contemptuous because Saigon did not understand its real significance and could not differentiate between propaganda and genuine psychological warfare.

'The main factor in deciding victory will be the spirit of the soldier', he told me. He spoke of the 'soul of the truth'. The soul was what caused a man to accept that his life should be spent for the cause. 'The government regards this as a joke', he said. 'It isn't a joke. It is the most important thing in the world.'

It was the 'soul' of Nguyen Van Be that travelled down the Ho Chi Minh trail into the forests of the Highlands, the rubber plantations and the rice fields of the South. Morale was high as the base areas began to fill up and divisions were put in place to launch their co-ordinated attacks on Saigon and twenty-eight provincial capitals.

The effect of these potential threats was to drain off the American and South Vietnamese reserves and to pin down units that could have been profitably employed in the pacification programme. Before the Northern forces moved into offensive action in February 1967, that seemed likely to be the limit of Hanoi's intentions. With five divisions committed in the I Corps region and two others known to be within a day's march, it soon became clear from the level of command involved (three regular divisions operating under effective central direction), from the new weapons being tried out, and from the tactics of the assault troops, that Hanoi intended to maintain conventional military momentum along with complementary guerrilla action. 'The bigger war has just begun', I wrote in the *Reporter* on 29 June 1967.

It was not a popular, or generally held view, but it was gaining acceptance. Back in Saigon after some weeks in Central Vietnam, I was a guest at a dinner given by Major Peter Young, the Australian assistant military attaché, one of the most experienced and best intelligence officers in Vietnam. The other guests included Serong, the c.i.a. deputy station chief, the four American Corps level intelligence officers and the man from MI6 at the British Embassy. The topic for discussion over the dinner table, proposed by Peter Young, was 'we are losing the war'. If there was no unanimity on this point, it was agreed that a major push was coming.

Young's argument was that the North Vietnamese had to break the stalemate in which the u.s. controlled the open coastal areas with its firepower and mass, leaving the hinterland to the North Vietnamese because of the terrain. Morale had to suffer if forces kept pouring in and sacrifices continued to be made by the North Vietnamese population and nothing happened. The North Vietnamese could not take on the United States in an open battle, and they ran the risk of an eventual loss if they stayed put, with internal problems built-in at home. The answer lay, he contended, in a major military-political action.

Young's connection with intelligence in Vietnam began with his posting there in the first group of Australian advisers in 1962 when, after an initial training course in Singapore, he was sent to the c.i.a. station in Danang, where he and another Australian, wearing civilian clothes, not uniforms, accepted intelligence responsibility for the North Vietnam border area, Laos and I Corps region. Later, he had a roving assignment in Laos and Cambodia before returning to the desk in Australia in military intelligence.

Back in Vietnam again in 1965 Young was welcomed at mac-v in Saigon by the intelligence community who lacked his continuity of knowledge and experience. By the middle of 1966 he had full access to all American intelligence, the only Australian in Vietnam with this privilege. Instead of welcoming Young's access to the most highly classified American material, the Embassy regarded him with unconcealed distrust, a distrust unfortunately shared by his immediate senior who did not appreciate the level of Young's acceptance by the Americans.

On the basis of the information he was receiving from the Americans, Young, in July 1967, wrote a long report for the Embassy in which he concluded that Hanoi was within sight of achieving its military and political goals. On the assumption that the North Vietnamese might wait until they had completed a major reinforcement and internal reorganization around Saigon, he outlined a course of enemy action involving major attacks through I and II Corps and a possible special attack against Saigon. The period when the attack could be expected in these circumstances he listed as September to January. He not only tipped the Tet offensive, he tipped the time! It was, without doubt, one of the most brilliant pieces of intelligence assessment of the war. It should have been given the highest priority and read at the highest levels in Canberra. Instead, it was suppressed. The counsellor of the Embassy returned it to him with his own appended comments. These are worth noting.

The ambassador saw your paper in draft. He would have many comments. My own general comment is that it still contains many questionable assertions. I do not see what the enemy could seize and hold in order to force negotiations on his own terms. At points in your paper you seem to believe that the seizing of ground, even temporarily, is of importance to him. My guess–nothing more–

is that his intention is to inflict as many losses as possible while keeping his own as low as possible–for as long as possible–in the supposition that we will all get tired and settle. The build up of supply routes and effort in general is not inconsistent with this aim–and he realizes that his own losses in the long haul will be heavy. I'd like to keep this to read again in six months or a year's time–or two years.

He neither kept it nor sent it to Canberra. No one wanted to hear negative news.

And then came Tet!

It must surely rank as one of the most audacious campaigns in military history. It very nearly came off. Its flaw was the assumption that the Southern masses would rise as soon as the Viet Cong troops entered the towns to support their liberators. When this failed to occur, the North Vietnamese had only their psychological fallback position left: that by its sheer audacity the offensive would destroy American military credibility, anchor the troops to the cities, and so strengthen the anti-war movement in the United States that Washington would be forced to negotiate.

What they did not count on at all was the adverse reaction of the people. Those who had sat so long on the fence were suddenly forced to choose sides. In overwhelming numbers they chose the government side. Many people had not identified themselves with the government forces. Now they did. The South Vietnamese forces fought well under extremely difficult conditions. The population responded. In Quang Tri city the people were so pleased with the South Vietnamese soldiers' initial success that they showered them with flowers. Everywhere they did better than they had expected to do.

Having watched the government forces recross the Perfume River in Hue, I flew to Khe Sanh aboard a C-123 on Sunday 25 February 1968, almost fourteen years to the day after I had made a similar visit to Dien Bien Phu.

For several years the Special Forces camp at Lang Vei between Khe Sanh and the Lao border had provided a very useful intelligence base. Montagnards trained for the task sat along the Ho Chi Minh trail and listed what they saw, an undertaking that did not escape the attention of the North Vietnamese, who decided that the camp should be liquidated. From these small beginings the Khe Sanh garrison had grown. When the 325th Division moved from Tchepone in 1967, the Marines had reinforced their caretaker company, and fought grimly for hills 881 North and 881 South which dominated the camp site. Thereafter, to hold what they had in face of a constantly increasing threat, they needed heavy reinforcements. By the time the Tet campaign began the 26th u.s. Marine Regiment, one battalion of the 9th Marines and a Vietnamese Ranger battalion manned the entrenched camp. With the Special Forces camp overrun and long-range patrols abandoned, they could do no more than that.

Like Dien Bien Phu, Khe Sanh was a product of inadvertence and military frustration, of the urge to fight a set-piece battle, of dangerous underestimation of enemy capabilities, and of political imprudence. With the fall of the Special Forces camp it had only peripheral military importance and contrived political significance. To have won a battle there would have been useful and welcome for the Americans, but how to measure victory? To have lost would have been a relatively minor military reverse but a psychological and political disaster. Yet, as at Dien Bien Phu, to fight or not to fight were options that the North Vietnamese alone possessed. Despite all my resistance to the Dien Bien Phu analogy, the similarities proclaimed themselves from every green enemy-held hill overlooking the camp and every inadequately prepared trench and bunker. Because its water supply was outside the main camp area, Khe Sanh was, in one important way, in an even worse position than Dien Bien Phu.

My visit coincided with comparative enemy tranquility. Two or three days before, the main encampment, which was roughly two miles long and perhaps a mile wide, had been hit by 1300 rounds of mixed mortar and artillery fire, while the tally for 25 February was only three hundred rounds. It was, nevertheless, a useful introduction to the camp and its problems.

Because of the direction of the wind, we made a westerly approach that brought us over the North Vietnamese infantry positions at the end of the field–not once but twice. We failed to get down on the first run and had to come back for a second. The North Vietnamese marked the occasion with rifle and machine-gun fire in such volume that I might have been in Hong Kong on Chinese New Year's Eve. Safely down, we did not come to rest but spilled the few passengers and our cargo of artillery nose cones on the surface of the strip while the plane was still moving. An artillery piece that had received a direct hit was blazing on the edge of the strip, perhaps fifty yards from the plane. Next to it a dump of anti-tank mines was alight. It exploded ten minutes later. A sprinkling of incoming shells added piquancy to the scene.

The point about this experience is that it was not the exception but the norm. No plane or helicopter landed at Khe Sanh without running the risk of destruction by enemy mortar fire.

Care of the wounded within Khe Sanh and medical evacuation posed grave problem. It was an open secret that few of the bunkers were secure against shellfire. The hospital was not large enough to cope with the casualties that might have been expected from one major attack. And, though the anti-aircraft guns that were so effective at Dien Bien Phu had not yet put in an appearance, it was difficult to believe that they would not be on their way.

As at Dien Bien Phu, the North Vietnamese were digging their way in, zigzagging their way across the plateau. I watched bombs and napalm being used to destroy them, but since the trenches were empty, it was difficult to assess the effect, if any.

One of the lessons of positional warfare is that the best means of denying trenches to the enemy, especially empty trenches, is to occupy them with men. As ever, the Marines, magnificent assault troops, were ready to go, but they were restrained on orders from Saigon. Though this was subsequently denied at higher headquarters, the restraint curiously seemed to apply even to extensive patrolling within the few hundred yards (or even less) that separated the two forces.

I flew out late the same day on a helicopter with some wounded. We followed the course of the tumbling Cua Viet River, through the valley with the green and steep mountains rising sharply on either side of the road. I was holding plasma and whole blood for a terribly wounded Marine. He was dead when we landed at Dong Ha, the Marines' divisional headquarters, toward sundown.

I was convinced at the time that Khe Sanh would fall if the North Vietnamese wanted it badly enough. I had reckoned, however, without the tactical use of the B52s, which literally blew hills 881 North and 881 South to bits. I flew back to the hills months later. They were cratered like the surface of the moon. All the deep dug outs that had not been blown to bits had caved in. Perhaps there was some sense in trying to hold Khe Sanh, after all.

I was back in my hotel room in Saigon early in March, struggling to put together my impressions of the situation in Central Vietnam, without placing too much stress on Khe Sanh, which would only be significantly important if it fell, when the phone rang. Barry Zorthian, a much more high-powered John Mecklin, with a much bigger information role, was on the other end of the line. The following day was a Sunday and Zorthian had a light plane with which he planned to drop in on some of the Mekong Delta capitals that had been hit in the offensive.

I protested that I was involved in writing a long magazine article about Central Vietnam, not the Delta. 'I think you ought to come', he said. 'You and Carl Mydans [*Life* magazine's magnificent photographer] will be the only other passengers. You'll find it interesting.'

That was putting it mildly. Zorthian was heading for the Delta to play the role of district attorney determined to find out why provinces where the situation before Tet was reported to be so satisfactory had suddenly proved so bad. Our first call was at Rach Gia in Kien Giang province on the Gulf of Siam and adjoining the Cambodian border. Because the security situation was still so bad, we could not land at the airport, which was a couple of miles from the town, but were obliged to come down on the road, within a stone's throw of the town itself. The USIS headquarters was scarred with battle and no longer in use, and the official American community had retreated to the MAAG compound–in the centre of the town and on the sea. All the Americans were present for Zorthian's interrogation. Zorthian wanted to know how much ground was still held by government forces in the province. Around twenty per cent, was the answer.

'Show me on the map', Zorthian commanded.

Twenty per cent was a gross exaggeration.

'Is that by day or night?'

'Oh, by day, of course.'

'And how much by night?'

It came down to the compound we were in at the moment and half a dozen other enclaves, perhaps five per cent in all.

Then came the key questions about pre-Tet reporting. Why was there no warning of all this?

Embarrassed silence.

Zorthian then asked whether they had been required to report positively about the situation.

You could almost feel the relief. 'Yes, we were required to report positively.'

It was dusk when we approached Tan Son Nhut. Judging by the number of people who were defying the curfew outside the city, it was obvious that the Viet Cong and their colleagues from North Vietnam were still trying to get on with the fight. The offensive was not yet over.

'I think you should write a mood piece tonight', said Mydans.

Perhaps I should still write a mood piece. MAC-V's official report on military operations for 1968 begins: 'The year 1968 was unquestionably the most significant year of the war to date and may prove to have been the turning point. During the year, North Vietnamese Army and Viet Cong forces were severely beaten in their two major offensives and were pre-empted by Allied forces from carrying out a third offensive and probably a fourth.'

The year 1968 was unquestionably the most significant year of the war, and it was a turning point, but not at all in the way that MAC-V had in mind. After it was all over for Tet, and the North Vietnamese had pulled back, General Westmoreland, stiffly starched and letter-perfect, gave a briefing for a handful of selected American correspondents, in which I, because of my connections with the *Reporter* magazine, was included. It was a cool, detached, West Point-style lecture that ascribed plans to the North Vietnamese and Viet Cong, and tactical responses of his own; a lecture that seemed to me to be so far out of touch with reality that I wondered whether I was listening to a reading from *Don Quixote*. In his appreciation of the ideological and psychological motivation behind Hanoi's moves, and its expectation of a general uprising, there was no reaction to what must have been deep enemy surprise when the Viet Cong spearhead for the offensive, marching so bravely into the cities and towns of South Vietnam, failed to touch one off. His interpretation of the offensive was that Hanoi wanted to partition South Vietnam.

The Viet Cong cadre system took a beating at Tet from which it never recovered. The whole indigenous strength of the effort in South Vietnam was destroyed. The countryside, for which Saigon had battled so long and so unsuccessfully, was delivered into its hands at one stroke.

No attempt was made to take advantage of this situation. North Vietnam had drained itself of its reserves to mount the offensive. It was now totally vulnerable to a counter-offensive. General Weyand at Bien Hoa was ready and willing and anxious to go. Responding to pressure from General Wheeler, chairman of the Joint Chiefs of Staff, who was visiting Saigon, General Westmoreland asked for another 200,000 troops. When this appeared on the front page of the *New York Times*, and subsequently in papers across the country, it broke President Johnson's political back. It was one of the supreme ironies of the war that at the moment when it came closest to military defeat, Hanoi won its greatest psychological victory.

The 'report positively' policy was only marginally less disadvantageous for Australia than it was for the United States. In his book, *Australian Accent*, published in 1960, John Douglas Pringle noted that 'the Liberal Government's policy, which has never quite succeeded, was to lure the United States into committing itself to the defence, not only of Australia, but of the land-bridge of South-East Asia which is a necessary part of that defence'. Its efforts were crowned with full success in 1965 when President Johnson put his forces into Vietnam.

In continued pursuit of that policy, it was obviously in Australia's interest to show the flag in Vietnam and to become fully briefed on the facts. With commendable wisdom, it posted some of its first-rate military advisers, including Peter Young, to serve with the Central

Intelligence Agency in pure intelligence gathering and evaluation, and also in leading the Special Forces teams included in the formations originally set up by Conein. Under Serong, the Australians performed brilliantly. Says one of the men who served under him, 'Serong was a man out of his time. He manoeuvred a small third country "flag" into a major weapon which raised him to a major position within the U.S. councils. It was a combination of his use of the factual reporting by the people whom he was increasingly placing into "sensitive" C.I.A. run Special Forces areas and his own genius for analysis and presentation.'

One of the Australian coups was to detect the movement of the 325th Division into Laos long before anyone else was aware of it, or would accept it. A report in North Vietnam calling for handcarts to move baggage was the first hint that the 325th was on the move, first into Laos and then into Vietnam. It was picked up and followed by Australians on the ground who were fully aware of the significance of the move, since the first Australian battalion was about to be committed to Vietnam at this time. The clear message, as intelligence saw it, was that the Australian troops were not going to find themselves in an insurgency situation but in a major war.

When Peter Young left Vietnam, Brigadier-General Phillip B. Davidson, Assistant Chief of Staff, Intelligence, MAC-V, wrote to the commander of the Australian forces in Vietnam, and through him to Young, commending him for his contribution to military intelligence in Vietnam. 'You have strengthened the bonds of respect between the Australian and U.S. military establishments', he said. Young's reward was to be posted to a training battalion in Singleton. It was a cause for no surprise that he soon resigned his commission.

His problem was that he did not report positively, only objectively, to the anger of some of his immediate seniors and his Foreign Affairs colleagues. It is difficult to know what sort of leverage Canberra might have exerted on the United States if it had been forewarned six months in advance of the 1968 Tet offensive. Probably not very much. But at least it would have been useful for a country about to see its foreign policy take a body blow to have had some warning. That is what intelligence is all about.

4. South Vietnam's golden age

The years following the Tet offensive were good ones for South Vietnam. If the Republic of Vietnam ever had a golden age, this was it. The elections in 1967 were not without their flaws, but they did restore constitutional government, and they brought to an end the insane series of coups d'état that had plagued the country since 1963. In their determination to disengage, the Americans were only too willing to devote attention now to the long-neglected ARVN. There was still a lack of uniformity about the ARVN divisions, but the best, notably the 1st, had performed as well as any American division in the Tet offensive.

For the first, and only, time there was a spirit of relative optimism. The indigenous Southern Communists, pushed into the forefront of the Tet offensive for ideological reasons, had been shattered. Hanoi lost forty per cent of its political and propaganda cadres in the South during Tet and with them any chance of continuing the sort of quasi-military quasi-political war that the ideology required.

The much abused Phoenix programme, which targeted on the Communist infrastructure, prevented it from recovering its lost ground. From 1968 to May 1971, Phoenix claimed a total of nearly 70,000 members of the Communist infrastructure, of whom about 20,000 were killed, about 18,000 surrendered and the rest were captured. Although it had to abandon its ideology in the process, Hanoi was forced to rely now on conventional war, and its purely guerrilla activities, which had made life so uncomfortable in so many parts of the countryside for so long, tapered off, bringing to a virtual end the purely 'civil' component of the war. It became a pleasure to go out into the countryside and to see the peasants at work with new tractors and rotary hoes. The road from Saigon to the seaside town of Vung Tau was crowded every week-end with holidaymakers. When the Australian Task Force pulled out of Nui Dat, a single regional force company took over and was not hard pressed. The troops were gay and cheerful youths who really did not think that war would come their way.

Of vital importance during this period was the Land to the Tiller programme which, after March 1970, led to sweeping and successful land reform. More than two and a half million acres of rice were distributed to 837,000 peasant families, and billions of piastres were paid to landlords in compensation.

The free-spending Americans, though diminishing rapidly in number, were still about. Saigon, which had gone through an excessively squalid period, cleaned itself up. Saigon at peak hours became so filled with civilian motor traffic that the city seemed likely to suffocate in the smog. But it was all part of progress, part of the development of a consumer society. It was also a measure of American success. If the Communists had taken over in 1954, or 1956, perhaps a million or two might have found the system, at least to begin with, extremely painful. Now it was clear that many, many millions would find the Communist way of life intolerable. Just as in the two Koreas and the two Germanys, systems of government and life style and outlook had been created that repelled each other, so South Vietnam and North Vietnam had established altogether different values and had developed absolute incompatibilities. In North Vietnam society was hard. In South Vietnam it was soft.

South Vietnam underestimated the determination of Hanoi to win the war, however long it might take, and whatever sacrifice might be required. It could not comprehend, either, that the United States, having once been so deeply committed, could ever back completely away. It was also unready to make the absolute sacrifices that the war demanded. Above all, however, very few South Vietnamese understood the profound changes that were taking place in international relationships, that the reasons which had once taken the United States into the war, or the perceptions on which those reasons were based, had altered so much that a continuing American effort was no longer seen to be in the national interest and, on the contrary, was even inimical to the national interest.

The shock of the Tet offensive in 1968, and the mounting pressure of the anti-war movement in the United States, had persuaded President Johnson that the war had to be ended by negotiation. At the same time another change of major importance to South Vietnam was taking place in Chinese perceptions. The American decision to abandon its efforts to win the war came as a shock of major proportions to the Chinese leadership. In the Chinese view of things, it was scarcely credible that a great power like the United States could become so deeply involved and could give up so easily.

Peking was still digesting this unpredictable development when its own relations with its former ally, the Soviet Union, became strained, after the Russian invasion of Czechoslovakia, to the point where there were exchanges of fire along the Ussuri River and in Central Asia. If the United States was ready and willing to withdraw from Vietnam, it was clearly less of a risk to China's security than the Chinese leaders had hitherto believed.

In August 1969, the Central Committee of the Communist Party of the Soviet Union dispatched letters marked 'secret' to fraternal parties around the globe. The letters set out in great detail the alleged Chinese provocations and warned, in the bluntest of terms, that the Russians were prepared to use major military force to put an end to border incidents. To the embarrassment of the Central Committee of the Australian Communist Party, a copy of the letter passed into my hands a few days after its arrival in Melbourne. Of its authenticity there was no doubt, and I published it. Another copy found its way to Ted Hill, leader of the pro-Peking dissident faction of the Australian Communist Party. He immediately dashed to China to warn Chou En-lai. With the threat from the Soviet 'revisionists' now greater than it had ever been from the American 'imperialists', China started to move toward ping-pong diplomacy. The United States, seeking desperately to find a way out of its Indo-China quagmire, deftly returned the ball. By the time the game had been played to the point where President Nixon flew to Peking, no one in Washington was interested any longer in containing Chinese expansionism as manifest by the Vietnam war. The international Communist monolith was split asunder. It was now more important for the United States to get out of South Vietnam than it was to save it. That was not to prove easy, for the war, instead of dwindling away, had begun to spread.

One moment of truth came for the Nixon Administration in Washington, for the Lon Nol Government in Phnom Penh, and for the Thieu Government in Saigon when the pivotal Cambodian town of Krek fell to North Vietnamese forces early in April 1970. At one stroke, about a fifth of Cambodia, including most of its rubber plantations, a principal source of desperately needed foreign exchange, passed into Communist hands. Along the border areas everywhere the North Vietnamese forces began to turn their backs on South Vietnam and to move deeper into Cambodia. This short-term relief for South Vietnam caused the gravest long-term alarm in Saigon. With urgency, General Creighton W. Abrams, who had replaced General Westmoreland as U.S. commander in South Vietnam, reported to Washington that Cambodia's fall would destroy all chance for the Vietnamization programme and the solution President Nixon sought for the war.

Already black-clad Air Vice-Marshal Ky, still an ambitious vice-president, had led one raid across the Cambodian border, and South Vietnamese ground forces were poking and probing around the 'Parrot's Beak', an aptly named salient into Vietnamese territory, harassing, irritating but certainly not hurting their Communist enemies. Something far more effective was needed if the pressure was to be relieved on the unprofessional, untrained Cambodian Army, and the sanctuaries in the Cambodian border areas were to cease being a threat to South Vietnam.

There were days in Phnom Penh during the first weeks in April when Cambodia's collapse appeared imminent. The Yugoslav ambassador gave the country ten days. No one thought him excessively pessimistic—until U.S. forces crossed the border.

Cambodia had always been more the eye of the storm in Indo-China than the oasis of peace that Prince Norodom Sihanouk wanted it to be. But as late as 13 March 1970, only five days before they overthrew Sihanouk and destroyed the delicate balance that had for so long kept Cambodia out of the war, neither General Lon Nol nor Prince Sirik Matak, the new leaders, appeared to have entertained serious thoughts about removing him as Head of State. They wanted to restrain his activities, to turn him into something much closer to a constitutional monarch; but they still needed him as a symbol of Cambodian unity.

Sihanouk, the introspective, moody and sensitive Cambodian Hamlet was the instrument of his own destruction. For years he had referred to Lon Nol as a right-winger, but his was the decision that put the general into office as prime minister in August 1969 (with Prince Sirik Matak, a strong, clean broom as his deputy) at the head of a government of national salvation designed to pull Cambodia out of its mounting economic problems.

Sihanouk's idea was to make Cambodia the sort of state that more powerful Communist neighbours would tolerate. He was, of course, much more king than commissar, and his Cambodian Socialism was nothing like Communism. It was meant, like the boulevards Mao Tse-tung and ussr in Phnom Penh, to pay lip service to the Communist system.

The pity was that it did not work. Corruption, beginning in Sihanouk's own family, was widespread. Though Cambodia remained one of the most pleasant countries in South-East Asia, progress passed it by. The economy stagnated. At the same time, Sihanouk's accommodations with Hanoi and the National Liberation Front, another part of his planned survival, included military, territorial and economic agreements that were one day bound to become a source of discontent and friction.

Nevertheless, the coup that led to war had its origins not in anti-Communism but in the attempts to make government more effective. In time these efforts became overshadowed by rising anger with the Vietnamese Communists, but, until the final moments before the coup, this more dramatic aspect of the crisis was secondary. Sihanouk and the men who overthrew him agreed that the North Vietnamese should be inconspicuous while they were on Cambodian soil. They differed only in approach.

During the latter part of 1969, Lon Nol was away from Cambodia and Prince Sirik Matak ran the government. The prince, then fifty-seven and once ambassador in Peking, devalued the currency by almost fifty per cent, dismantled much of the apparatus of Cambodian Socialism, encouraged foreign investment and rejoined the Asian Development Bank and the World Bank from which Sihanouk had withdrawn. The National Assembly, which had long been feuding with Sihanouk over government monopolies, supported Sirik Matak.

Petulantly, but typically, Sihanouk forbade all National Assemblymen ever to appear at public or private functions at which he was present. Relations, naturally enough, became cooler, and when Sirik Matak's reforms began to erode Sihanouk's own unusual, but benevolent, dictatorship, the National Assembly applauded.

Sihanouk won when he over-ruled Sirik Matak's memorandum to all Cambodian embassies, instructing them to discontinue their private correspondence with the Head of State and to report only to the Foreign Ministry. He lost when he failed to cancel a similar order requiring the province chiefs, who had also reported to Sihanouk in the past, to communicate only with Sirik Matak in the Ministry of the Interior.

At any time Sihanouk could have changed the course of events by dismissing Lon Nol and Sirik Matak. Instead, he relied on his powers of persuasion. To his surprise, and anger, these failed when Sirik Matak presented his new economic policy to the National Congress at Phnom Penh in December 1969, and had it accepted. Four cabinet ministers, all of them close followers of Sihanouk, resigned. Sihanouk himself, in what appears to have been a spur-of-the-moment decision, left Phnom Penh in a huff to take a weight-reducing course at Grasse in France.

Late in January, Sirik Matak again attacked Sihanouk's authority when he closed the Phnom Penh gambling casino, the principal source of the private funds from which the palace had distributed its patronage. The name of the game had begun to change, however. What had been a domestic tiff over economic and administrative matters now began to impinge upon the more sensitive, and more dangerous, relationship between Phnom Penh and Hanoi.

After the Tet offensive in 1968, when the indigenous Viet Cong suffered heavily, the Communists fighting in South Vietnam had become increasingly dependent on Cambodia, not merely as a base area and as a sanctuary, but for the provision of pharmaceuticals, rice and other foodstuffs and as a funnel for military supplies.

Under an agreement with China, Peking supplied the Cambodian Army and the North Vietnamese and Viet Cong forces operating in the southern provinces of South Vietnam with almost all their munitions and other military material. To confuse American and South Vietnamese agents, all the supplies came through the port of Sihanoukville into the Royal Cambodian Army's storage depots outside Phnom Penh. There the consignments intended for the Communists were picked up by a trucking company, operated by Hak Ly, a Vietnamese-born Chinese with close relations with Peking's embassy in Phnom Penh.

Hak Ly was the middle man. He ran the supplies south along the Bassac River and across the Mekong ferries, at points close to the Vietnam border. There the North Vietnamese took delivery and carted them off to their own depots, or to the forces in the field.

From February through to November 1969, Cambodian rice had continued to flow to the Communist forces at the rate of about a thousand tons a month, but there had often been long delays in the delivery of military equipment from the Cambodian depots. The North Vietnamese had encroached more deeply into Cambodian territory than their agreements permitted, and Lon Nol, in the hope of applying some pressure that might lead to their withdrawal, not only rationed their supplies but published the text of his monthly report to Sihanouk on the whereabouts and numbers of North Vietnamese forces in Cambodia.

Having thus disposed of the fiction that the North Vietnamese were not making extensive use of Cambodian territory, Lon Nol flew to Peking for a meeting with the North Vietnamese and representatives of the National Liberation Front. The Chinese acted as mediators. They agreed that the North Vietnamese should eventually abandon the bases in Cambodia, but they also argued that winning the war in South Vietnam should have top priority. According to Sirik Matak, the Vietnamese 'reaffirmed the respect of the actual frontier of Cambodia'. They also paid hard cash for their temporary use of the Cambodian bases. In November 1969, the Hak Ly Trucking Company resumed round-the-clock operations from Phnom Penh to catch up on deliveries of Chinese military supplies to the North Vietnamese.

Every night lines of trucks waited at the ferries on their way to the border areas east of the Mekong River. 'Sometimes up to sixty trucks a night crossed the river here', the chief of the gendarmerie post at one of the ferries told me. I repeated this to Major Pok-Varon, who commanded the infantry battalion at Neak Luong on the opposite bank. 'Not always sixty', he said over a glass of Asahi beer, 'but sometimes'. At the ferry at Kompong Cham, far up river, residents had seen up to twenty trucks waiting for their turn to use the ferry.

'A hundred trucks were going out at a time with rice for Charlie' (the Viet Cong), Eu Ly In, chairman of the economic committee of the National Assembly, told me. 'Fifty trucks at a time made the military run.'

Instead of reducing friction, however, the new arrangements only added to the tensions. Twelve Cambodian battalions had been deployed in the extreme north-east, where they were fighting an indigenous Communist group armed and trained by the Viet Cong and the North Vietnamese. Since this area is malarious, remote and uncomfortable at the best of times, Cambodian officers began to grumble about the curious deal in which Phnom Penh was involved, helping to supply their enemies.

General Lon Nol began to share their concern. On 17 February 1970, an Air Liban jet arrived at Phnom Penh carrying 16.5 metric tons of pharmaceuticals. Princess Monique, Sihanouk's consort and then President of the Cambodian Red Cross, directed from Paris, where she had been having a face lift, that the cargo of pharmaceuticals should be handed over duty free to the North Vietnamese. Lon Nol refused to release it.

By this time, the commercial agreement with the North Vietnamese was ready to collapse. A sack of rice cost 550 to 600 riels, or $10 to $11 in Phnom Penh. The government price to the Communists at the more accessible delivery points was 1,500 riels, or about $27. In the more remote areas the price was more than $50 a sack.

The North Vietnamese usually paid in 500 riel notes, and they had such a copious supply that the Cambodians became suspicious. Investigations established that the North Vietnamese were heavy buyers of Cambodian currency in Hong Kong. The Cambodians discovered, also, a heavy increase in the circulation of counterfeit notes. 'The North Vietnamese use women as the currency porters', one Cambodian official told me, 'and they have a permanent team of three hundred on the job on the Ho Chi Minh trail, each carrying thirty kilos of counterfeit 500 and 200 piastre notes. Sometimes they even cart piastres to South Vietnam in truckloads. Now we found they were doing the same thing to us.'

On 23 February 1970, the Cambodian government withdrew the old 500 riel notes and limited the conversion to 10,000 riels per person. It also announced that diplomatic bags would be subject to inspection until after 7 March, when the new currency would be introduced. The government hoped to catch the North Vietnamese with millions of illicitly acquired riels in their hands, but the news leaked from agents in the Cambodian National Bank, and the Communists succeeded in converting a major part of their holdings.

Suspicion and tension heightened. On 8 March 1970, there were demonstrations against the Vietnamese in Svay Rieng, the 'Parrot's Beak' province, where the North Vietnamese had long found sanctuary. These were said to be spontaneous. There was nothing spontaneous, however, about the demonstrations in Phnom Penh three days later, when demonstrators wrecked the embassies of North Vietnam and the Provisional Revolutionary Government of South Vietnam, six years to the day after similar mobs had wrecked the American and British embassies.

Phnom Penh's diplomatic corps generally assumed that, according to the rules of the game, the Vietnamese were officially warned of the demonstrations in order to give them a chance to destroy important documents. The warning, if it was given, did not prepare the Vietnamese for the comprehensive sacking and looting, and a document, setting out a contingency plan for the occupation of all Cambodia by the North Vietnamese, found its way into the hands of the government.

Old Sim Var, a former prime minister around whom much of the National Assembly storm had centred in December, told me it was a detailed plan written in Vietnamese. His house in Phnom Penh had been turned into a fortress. The front door was bolted and barred by a platoon of troops camped on the doorstep to prevent assassination attempts threatened both by pro-Sihanouk and North Vietnamese groups. He was living in fear of his life, and what he had to say on such matters, therefore, might be reasonably questioned. But In Tam, governor of the critical province of Kompong Cham and another key figure in the National Assembly, repeated the allegation and the charge that Sihanouk would not listen when Lon Nol called by phone to tell him of the discovery.

A few months later a copy of the notebook containing the 'plan' came into my possession. Although it was difficult to decipher, its authenticity did not appear to be in doubt. It was written either by the Provisional Revolutionary Government ambassador, or his chief political commissar, and it clearly revealed the Communists' intention to create an insurgency with the object of overthrowing the Phnom Penh government.

Misunderstanding also had its part in the crisis involving Sihanouk and his government. Sihanouk, for so long the lion tamer, did not appreciate at the end of the telephone line in Paris how close the tame lions were to tearing the cage apart. If this was a critical error, it seems in retrospect only to have added speed to developments that now had a momentum of their own. Sihanouk was too much the embodiment of the state to have accepted any permanent limitation to his authority, and the causes for conflict had become numerous, deep and irrational.

He was not interested in Lon Nol's explanations, or in receiving the Foreign Minister and an emissary from the Queen Mother. So the gap between the Head of State and the government widened. On 18 March 1970, it finally became unbridgeable when the National Assembly, given the nod by the government, and more than willing to settle its past scores, unanimously voted Sihanouk out of office.

Both Sihanouk and the Lon Nol government miscalculated. When Sihanouk talked of the possibility of a coup d'état, he envisaged nothing more than a further attempt to prune his powers. Lon Nol and Sirik Matak, like the coup leaders in South Vietnam in 1963, had no conception of the forces that their actions would release and lacked all means to restrain them.

In the first two weeks after the coup they pushed on dangerously with the ultimatum to the North Vietnamese and the Viet Cong to quit Cambodian territory and with their plans to turn the Kingdom of Cambodia into a republic. Even after negotiations with the North

Vietnamese had collapsed, they failed at first to detect any real urgency in the situation.

Yet the once-secure Communist bases in the Cambodian border lands were now vulnerable to attack from South Vietnam. The Communists either had to move out of Cambodia, or move in. By moving out they would have gravely weakened their prospects in South Vietnam. By moving in they would be able to relocate their bases, secure urgently needed rice supplies and eventually force the reopening of Sihanoukville as the port of entry for military supplies going to their forces in the Mekong Delta.

By portraying Sihanouk as a traitor who had sold his country to the Viet Cong, and by whipping up race hatred against the Vietnamese, the government hoped to unify the people behind them. In the towns, and in some parts of the countryside, the effectiveness of this stimulated nationalism was widespread. But rarely has a country gone into a war with its eyes open and been less ready for it.

The thirteen Russian MIGS in the Cambodian Air Force had so little hydraulic fluid for their landing gear that when the war began the planes were flying only three hours each month. Of the six T28s, only five were serviceable. Green recruits, shovelled into uniforms, commandeered civilian buses and trucks and fanned out from Phnom Penh to meet every new threat. They had spirit on the way to the front, but they were like Boy Scouts when it came to war.

One day, south of Phnom Penh, I saw the road jammed for hundreds of yards with buses. Cambodian government troops, six battalions of them, were spread out along the road, making no attempt to guard their flanks. The head of the column had been halted and pushed back by mortar fire, and here the troops were following their natural and correct instincts to dig in. Over each foxhole they had erected shelters of banana fronds which they covered patiently with half an inch of earth—not to protect them from heat but from North Vietnamese mortars! At Kompong Cham the troops used park benches as barricades to block the road. Outside Phnom Penh they relied on earthenware jars filled with stones.

I went one day to Suong, twenty miles west of Krek, where the war had begun. When I arrived there the war, in ripples of fear, had come across the paddy fields, dry, hard and shimmering in the final burst of heat that precedes the life-giving rains of the wet season. Survivors of the Krek garrison, their guns, their wounded and their courage left behind, brought terror to Suong. For two days the town put its faith in the hope that the North Vietnamese, now that they had Krek, would come no further. Then the government detachments

163

guarding a road junction only seven miles to the east fell back beyond Suong. Nothing remained between the town and the war.

To run? Or to stay? The weak emissions from Radio Phnom Penh with the government's orders could scarcely be heard in Suong. But Radio Peking came in loud and clear. It urged collaboration with the hated North Vietnamese. The voice, no one doubted, was that of Prince Norodom Sihanouk, the god-king.

A French teacher in the town, it was really no more than a large village, had saved a picture of the prince when an official decree on 22 March had ordered that all pictures of Sihanouk were to be destroyed. Now the people came in large numbers and asked the teacher if just once more they could see the picture of the prince. When she produced it, they prostrated themselves on the ground, weeping and crying.

Many people closed their houses and went away–where, no one knew, or would say. A quarter of the approximately two thousand inhabitants of the town remained.

On the bougainvillea-covered patio of the house of the former district chief at the eastern edge of the town I found Suong's defence headquarters. The peeling yellow ochre walls of the house were grimy, and cobwebs hung in heavy veils from the rafters. An assortment of volunteers lay about on mattresses on the floor and beyond in a line of barracks-like rooms. A trench-digging machine had performed its task and now stood idle in the over-grown garden. Next to it stood one of the De Soto trucks of the Hak Ly Trucking Company, which only a month earlier had been the exclusive carrier of munitions and food for the North Vietnamese.

Five miles back along the road to the Mekong, on the fringes of a vast French rubber estate, a soon-to-be-annihilated Cambodian infantry battalion, supported by a battery of 105-millimetre guns, planned to react when the attack began at Suong. In front of the town there was nothing.

'You don't have patrols out?' I asked the lieutenant who commanded the forward position. He had survived when the relief column he was leading toward Krek was ambushed, and he had earned respect due to a veteran.

A black beret perched rakishly on the side of his head, and his jungle greens were soiled and stained. 'No patrols', he said. 'We do not have enough men for patrols.'

'Do you have enough men to hold?'

'We do not have enough weapons. Perhaps we do not have enough men.'

And then came the inevitable question, the question that continued to be asked until the Khmer Rouge broke through Phnom Penh's defences. 'Will the United States help us?'

I looked at the machine gun position so carefully prepared by the side of the road and wondered, as I was to wonder many times as I travelled from 'front' to 'front', whether all the weapons in the world would be of any use to these people who had so little knowledge of how to use them. With tender care, the gunner, without benefit of cement, had built a protective shield of thin red bricks around his gun, leaving just enough room for the barrel to poke through. A tennis ball would have been enough to demolish this 'pillbox'.

The country needed miracles as much as it needed guns, and when the miracles, and the guns, failed to materialize, the ugliness appeared. A few shots around an isolated town were enough to put the torch to Vietnamese homes in Cambodia. Frustration and fear kept company and, as is so often the case in war, led to blind savagery. Simply to be Vietnamese was to invite hideous retribution. And there was no worse example of this than the story I finally finished piecing together in the village of Tan Phong in South Vietnam in March 1971.

For a woman who had lived through such tragedy, Duong Thi Le, the 21-year-old widow of the bricklayer, Nguyen Van Muoi, showed few scars. Round-faced, stolid and unemotional, she sat on a chair in front of the altar in the not yet completed Roman Catholic church in the village to tell her story. An official with a pile of papers on his table was nearby, coping with the problems of administration, for in Ap Tan Phong, which was being built in the South Vietnamese district of Cu Chi for Vietnamese refugees from Cambodia, there were still no government buildings. The school, like the church, was under construction. Sixty widows had moved into their new homes with their families. A large number was still under canvas, a dozen or more families to a large military tent, on the other side of the road leading to Tay Ninh, about an hour's drive from Saigon.

'It was just before midnight on 11 April 1970', Duong Thi Le began. 'My husband and I and my mother-in-law were asleep in our room in our house on stilts overlooking the Tonle Sap at Phnom Penh. I awoke when I heard someone hammering at the front door. I was slow to open it, for there was a bar which we placed across it at night. While I was trying to move the bar, the men outside became impatient. They threw themselves against the door and knocked it down.'

On Monday 13 April, the front door of her house was still off its hinges. Nguyen Van Muoi and his two brothers, who had also been asleep in the house, and every other Vietnamese male in the community over the age of fourteen, had disappeared without trace. The women huddled out of sight in their homes and only Cambodian military police walked the single street between the two lines of houses on the banks of the Tonle Sap.

At the Soviet Embassy in Phnom Penh that morning, Khamidouline Rachid, the first secretary, sneered when I talked with him about what was going on in the countryside. 'You don't even know what is going on in Phnom Penh', he said. He helped himself to yet another cigarette from his packet of Benson and Hedges and with some accuracy, as I discovered later, described the events that had occurred across the Tonle Sap on Saturday night.

An hour or two after I had spoken to Rachid, I crossed what used to be known in Phnom Penh (until North Vietnamese sappers in 1972 blew it up and dropped it neatly into the river) as the Japanese bridge. It spanned the Tonle Sap not far from its meeting point with the Mekong, near the tip of a long spit of land between the two rivers which was called, because of its shape, *Chuoi Cong Bai*, or the Paddle. On the Mekong side of the Paddle there was a Cambodian naval depot. Facing Phnom Penh and stretched out for a couple of miles along the banks of the Tonle Sap was the Vietnamese community. It was said to be Viet Cong infiltrated, and no doubt it was but, like the rest of the perhaps 600,000 Vietnamese then living in Cambodia, it was primarily Roman Catholic. A large, solid Roman Catholic church stood back from the river and the two lines of mostly stilted, unpainted weatherboard houses. The church had once been white-washed, but now it was peeling and blackened by weather and time, though it was still a conspicuous landmark from the Phnom Penh side of the river. Next to the church was a rectangular, plaster-covered group of buildings, surrounded by high walls, where a group of Carmelite cloistered nuns, Vietnamese but led by a Belgian mother superior, who had been there for eighteen years, devoted themselves to teaching, care of the sick and charitable works.

In all of the Paddle I found there were no Vietnamese men, only women and young children, Cambodian military police, and Father Garad, the French priest. He knew no more than that the men and boys had been taken away late on Saturday night and early on Sunday morning. They had been loaded into naval ships which had beached near the church. Inquiries had proved fruitless, though it was known, of course, that all over Cambodia the frightened authorities had been rounding up the Vietnamese and concentrating them in school houses and other convenient places of detention. Not long after Sihanouk had been deposed a Cambodian soldier had been wounded near the church,

Father Garad said. This was a minor incident; the people were not for the Viet Cong.

After I left the priest's house and was walking back toward the Japanese bridge, where I had parked my car, the Cambodian guards tried to detain me until an officer arrived. They were unfriendly, but eventually let me go after I had produced my accreditation card and written down my name and address.

Two days laters I stood near the ferry at Neak Luong, about thirty miles down the river. I was with another French priest, Father Francois Chaudel, who was dressed, as is the French clerical custom, even in the tropics, in a long, flowing black smock. It was almost sundown, and as far as we could see up the river dead bodies, their hands tied behind their backs, were drifting downstream. 'Pas bon, pas bon', the priest repeated over and over again. Even then I did not connect this hideous and malodorous scene on the Mekong with the missing men from the Paddle. There had been some sharp fighting upstream. Prisoners, I thought, might have been shot and thrown into the river.

Later in the week I went back to the Paddle full of ugly, but unconfirmed, suspicion. With infinite caution, and absolute fear, the people were still trying to find their men. 'I cry a lot', said the 31-year-old mother of three, cradling her youngest in her arms. Her husband had sold fish, but now there were no fishermen and no fish to sell, and all that she had left in the world was forty riels, about seventy cents. I added a little to her sum and went my way without mentioning my own fears.

Until December 1971, I did not revisit Phnom Penh. Back at the Paddle when I returned, the scenery had not changed but there was a new cast of actors. I walked down the street behind lines of curious Cambodians, stopping every now and then to inquire of a householder how long he had lived there. 'Fifteen months'; 'three years'; 'five years' . . . No one, it seemed, was a newcomer. The church was bolted and the priest's house empty. As an afterthought, I rang the bell at the Carmelite mission, and was ushered in by a nun–a Vietnamese–to where the mother superior was sitting behind a grille. She received me graciously but cautiously. Yes, the entire Vietnamese community, with the exception of the nuns, had gone. The priest had gone, also, and not a single Roman Catholic remained outside her own compound. A Buddhist who worked for the nuns was the only man who ever attended Mass.

'And where can I find the men who used to live in the village?'

She became melancholy–and enigmatic. 'You will find the women and children in Vietnam.'

Four months later, and a hundred miles from Phnom Penh, I was to find the answer to the riddle of the missing men of the Paddle. The church in which we were sitting bore little resemblance to the solid building where Duong Thi Le had prayed in the past. It consisted of no more than the roof of shining tin, the still unenclosed uprights and the wooden altar with its cross. The floor was of dirt, pounded hard and smooth. As Duong Thi Le continued to talk, other women with children entered. All crowded around us, listening. Some sat on the dirt floor. Others stood behind our chairs.

'There were three men in the group that broke into the house', said Duong Thi Le. 'All were in military uniforms and wearing helmets. One soldier, with a rifle in one hand and a flashlight in the other, told me that everyone in the house must get out. There were seven of us altogether–two sisters of mine and two of my husband's brothers and my mother-in-law. All of us were held at rifle point by two of the men while the third went through the house with the flashlight. When he had finished, he told us that the women could return to the house and that the men would be taken away. They were to take nothing with them. Next morning I went to the Cambodian authorities and asked where they had taken my men. They had no information.'

While Duong Thi Le was talking someone brought another chair for an old man named Lieu Van Tam. He was sixty-nine. His face was withered and brown, with a wisp of hair hanging from his chin. A scar showed clearly through the thin grey hair on his head.

Around us now were perhaps forty women and children. Among them were a fresh-faced girl of twenty, patting the back of an infant boy clad in pink woollen trousers; a woman with a deeply lined face and three tiny children, the youngest perhaps twelve months old; and a tall, grey-haired woman with black teeth, a checked scarf around her neck and a gold wedding ring on her finger. Her name was Mrs Nguyen Thi Sach. It was she who suggested that the old man should speak.

He had been a fisherman on the Tonle Sap, he said, and had lived with seven members of his family in another of the stilted houses on the banks of the river. His story also began close to midnight on 11 April 1970.

'When I heard the knock on the door', he said, 'I went outside. Immediately the soldiers grabbed me and took me away. First they told me to lie on the ground with the other men they had taken. Then they told us to stand up with our hands over our heads. Anyone who didn't, the soldiers said, would be shot. After that they got us together on the road and made us lie down. I was there on my face with my arms outstretched for about half an hour, when the guards, about a hundred of them, marched us toward the church. A landing craft [the Cambodian navy had three] was waiting for us there. As I passed I heard the guard say that there were more than 1,800, but on the two landing craft that they used there were more than 3,000, all of us either men or boys.'

A carpenter had been hammering nails when the old man first spoke. Now there was absolute silence in the church as the workmen put down their tools and joined the throng around our chairs.

'As soon as everyone was aboard, the boats backed away from the shore and we sailed down the Mekong', said the old man. 'About dawn we came to a sand dune.'

'How far down the river?'

'I cannot say', he answered. 'But we sailed about 12.30 a.m. Before we left, the Cambodian soldiers took all our money, our watches, even our belts. They left us only with our clothing. I cannot tell you, therefore, exactly how far down the river, but it was coming close to daylight before we got there.'

'It was a place called Con Trung', said the grey-haired woman.

'Near the ferry at Neak Luong?'

'Yes, above the ferry', said the old man.

'After we got to the dune place, the landing boats stopped in the middle of the river and anchored', he continued. 'The officers sent sailors to get ropes and they tied all of us with our hands behind our backs. About nine o'clock they brought the landing boats to the shore, opened the gates in front and marched the men in batches along the sand dune where the soldiers were waiting with their rifles. At the sound of a whistle, the soldiers opened fire and shot them down.'

The grey-haired woman sobbed quietly. On the floor the mother of the three infants rocked backwards and forwards on her heels, holding her youngest baby with one hand and wiping away her tears with the other. All around the women cried. Pain showed itself on almost every face. Only the impassive Duong Thi Le showed no sign of emotion.

'They shot them in the back', the old man said. 'Those who tried to escape were shot from the side.'

Everyone, I suppose, had heard the story many times before. But, though a year had passed, the grief, and the horror, remained.

'They shot twelve members of my family', said the grey-haired woman. 'Twelve.'

Since there were only twenty men with rifles, the execution of the three thousand men and boys took a long time. When his turn came the old man decided that as soon as he heard the whistle he would fall to the ground. A bullet struck him on top of the head, creasing his scalp but causing no damage to his skull. He bent forward now to show with his fingers where it had ploughed its furrow. The women craned forward to see.

'I fell with two dead men on top of me', he said. 'I just lay there, not moving. I did not dare to move.'

As he lay, the firing went on and on. Late in the afternoon it stopped and some time after this he heard the engines of the two landing craft. He did not move until the noise was far away. Then cautiously, for guards might have been left behind to finish off those who moved, he looked up. There were no guards, and the boats were just dots on the river, far up stream, headed for Phnom Penh. Already, he noticed, the tide had begun to come in and the first of the bodies were drifting down the river.

Among the three thousand men and boys who walked from the landing craft to the sand dune, twenty-eight survived. They used their teeth to bite into the knotted ropes holding their comrades' hands, and then, independently, set off for home, begging for money or food at farmhouses on the way.

Most of the twenty-eight, including Lieu Van Tam, were arrested on the outskirts of Phnom Penh and placed in a concentration camp before being sent to South Vietnam. One got a message back to the Paddle.

Duong Thi Le went on with her story, 'When we heard what had happened we were very frightened. No one moved in the hamlet. It was quiet, deadly quiet. Everyone was afraid.'

Fearfully, the villagers ventured out for Mass the following Sunday. The priest was guarded in his sermon. 'He told us', said Duong Thi Le, 'that we must pray to God and that God will take care of us. He tried to give us hope. He told us that we must love each other and not listen to other people at this time. He asked us to give him photographs and the names of our men so that he could send them to the Cambodian authorities and demand that they should be released.'

The grey-haired woman spoke again. Her house at the Paddle had been next to the church. Among the twelve members of her family who lost their lives in the massacre were her husband, who was sixty-two, and her grandson, who was only twelve. She saw about a hundred Cambodian military police around the church. On Cambodian New Year's Day they broke into the houses to rape the Vietnamese girls.

'About two weeks later', she said, 'the Cambodian authorities came to tell us that if we wanted to go to Saigon we were free to go. We replied that we had no money. How would we get there? That evening they drove us out of our houses to the school yard. We were not allowed to take more than twenty kilos in weight, or any money. The Cambodian people were waiting to take over our houses. As we moved out, they moved in. At the school house we were given neither food nor water. The priest brought us food; for water we had to get what we could from a ditch, though the Tonle Sap ran past the school. We lived there for about a month and a half until a boat arrived from Saigon. At first the Cambodian soldiers tried to persuade us not to go. They said we would starve in Vietnam. When we said that we were going anyway, they grabbed our bags and took the few things we had managed to save from our homes.'

'And how did you get on when you got to Vietnam?' I asked.

'During the trip from Phnom Penh the ARVN troops gave us food and took good care of us', said the grey-haired woman. 'They took us first to My Tho [in the Mekong Delta], but there was no land for us there. Later they brought us here.'

'And what did they do for you then?'

'First they kept us in tents. Then they gave us each a house and a thousand metres of land. And, yes, for the first six months they gave each family half a kilo of rice each day for each person.'

'It was more than we needed to eat', said the twenty-year-old with the child in pink pants. 'We could save on the ration.'

There were no signs of undernourishment. The children looked well. And the Vietnamese Red Cross, and the church, had contributed mosquito nets, clothing, utensils and extra food.

Fear of the future ran high, however. Altogether the Vietnamese Government had resettled more than 200,000 Vietnamese refugees from Cambodia. Some villages had put down roots very quickly and were beginning to flourish. Ap Tan Phong was not one of the best. There were too few men and too many women and children. On the one hand, there was too much work to be done and, on the other, too little work that would produce money. And for the young women with children it was not easy to leave home.

'I was a seamstress in Phnom Penh', said Duong Thi Le. 'But here I have no sewing machine and no money to buy one.'

'The church gives us money to help with the building', said another woman. 'But what will we do when it is built?'

'If we had money we could buy and sell things', said the grey-haired woman. 'That way we could get by when the rice has gone.'

'What else do you think the government should give you?' I asked her.

'A gun', she replied, 'and I'll go back to Cambodia'.

The chances that Duong Thi Le, or anyone else, would go back to Cambodia receded with every passing month. The combined American-South Vietnamese invasion had succeeded only in driving the North Vietnamese deeper into the heartland of Cambodia and provided them with the opportunity to help the Khmer Rouge leaders recruit their peasant army, while they prepared for the next major offensive in the South.

This came at Easter 1972. Unlike the Tet offensive in 1968, this was a conventional main force invasion spearheaded by tanks, with the twin objectives of driving on Hue and Danang in Central Vietnam and Saigon in the South. It was the first major test of ARVN forces fighting without large-scale American forces in support on the ground. The Northern forces made many blunders and found difficulty in co-ordinating armour, artillery and infantry, but the South, despite some glaring errors, established that with sufficient continuing air support from the United States they had at least a chance of surviving anything the North could throw against them.

The offensive added another million homeless to the millions of others who had been driven from their farms and villages by the war. The obvious man to cope with the task of resettling these people was Dr Phan Quang Dan, who had now joined the Cabinet. His strongly expressed views about the ethics of some of his Cabinet colleagues who had sent their sons abroad to escape military service when his fighter pilot son was shot down and killed after making seven sorties in one day to try to halt the North Vietnamese tanks at Quang Tri in 1972, had resulted in his demotion. He retained his seat in the Cabinet, but lost responsibility for the refugees. His successor, Lieut-General Cao Hao Hon, had no interest in resettling refugees, and none was resettled in the nine months that Dan was cooling his heels.

Necessity, and American pressure, brought Dan back. With the slogan, 'Uncle Sam is going home, let's hurry back to Mother Earth', he went to work.

The refugee camps had become stews of demoralization and corruption. There were no reliable figures about the numbers in the camps, and thousands of refugees were drawing rations for non-existent family members. When Dr Dan took over he found 40,000 'ghosts' in the Danang camps alone.

Ideally, he wanted the refugees to return to their villages to resume the life they had led previously. But many villages were insecure, or lacked arable land, especially in the five northern-most provinces of Quang Tri, Thua Thien, Quang Nam, and Quang Ngai. Around the former base areas the withdrawal of the Americans had caused widespread unemployment. There was no point in sending people back to places where they would live in misery, and to which they did not want to go.

Dr Dan had only a tiny staff and no office in which to work. As a cabinet minister, he had moved out of his medical clinic in the marketplace in Gia Dinh into a modest house in Saigon, but his dining room table also had to serve as the office desk.

American funds bought an office building and helped to pay for a more adequate staff, but the administrative side of the operation was run on a shoe-string. Dan grabbed good men anywhere he could find them. Some he had known as political prisoners in the days when he was one of Ngo Dinh Diem's guests. Others came from the army, or civilian jobs. The requirements were dedication, absolute honesty and a willingness to work hard.

After eliminating the 'ghosts', Dan found that there were still 661,444 Easter offensive refugees in the camps when he began work. By the middle of October 1973, 505,554 had either been returned to their villages or settled on new lands. Three months later the camps were empty.

Return to village, where it was feasible, was relatively easy, but the task of moving hundreds of thousands of men, women and children hundreds of miles to virgin lands in the South was a highly complex task, made no easier when the Communists blew up the bridges on the highways and prevented, or delayed, the movement of convoys.

Temporary camps had to be set up to receive the refugees, food-stuffs laid in and water turned on. Even a small delay could destroy the timing of the operation on which so much depended. It was a race against time for the refugees to get the ground cultivated and the seeds planted. Wet weather held up cultivation, and prolonged dry weather killed newly planted crops.

'Charley' Brown, a field officer in Central Vietnam, reported to headquarters after a field trip with Dan that it was his view, without reservation, as he put it, 'that we Americans should support any plan, idea or programme that Dr Dan proposes'. He described him as wise, capable and dedicated, and added that no other Vietnamese came near to his stature when it came to getting a difficult job done, or presenting an untiring, unconcerned image to his people.

Dan played down his own role. 'I kept on telling the refugees that they represented the most important factor', he said. 'As long as they were not prepared to help themselves, no one else could.' What Dan did was to provide them with every means of self-help. Every hamlet office had handbooks showing the peasants how they should till the land and plant the seeds. Soil analyses and weather charts indicated the most favourable crops.

Dan's handbooks gave complete instructions for home building and for building wells, latrines and water tanks. Everything was set out in a simple, practical way. Each new hamlet had its market, a school and a medical clinic. Axes, hoes, saws and other implements came from a military factory. Everyone knew precisely what he was entitled to, the quantity of rice and seeds, the number of sheets of roofing iron, the quantity of timber. In case of doubt (and to prevent corruption), it was all painted in bold letters on a hoarding outside the administrative building in each hamlet.

Bulldozers cleared the building plots and farm lands to which the refugees were given title and also cut the roads. Contractors dug the wells and set up the administrative blocks. After that it was up to the people, though Dan paid about a dollar a day to the workers who helped build the marketplaces and schools.

If people were not willing to work, and to work hard, it was very difficult to plant the crops that would make them self-sufficient in food in six months–when the rice ration was cut off.

At one grievance session I attended, an old peasant with a wispy beard and a red band around his head asked that the bulldozers should do more. 'The trees that the bulldozers pushed down were very, very big, with many, many roots under the ground', he said. 'It would be simple for the bulldozer to come back and get rid of the roots.'

'Make a fire among the roots and burn them out', said Dan.

'Where will we get dry wood to make the fires?'

'Use bamboo', said Dan.

'It's hard to get the bamboo', said the peasant. 'They have many spikes and cut the hand.'

Another, younger peasant came to Dan's support. 'It would not be good to use the bulldozers', he said. 'They would cause erosion.'

In the end, everyone was more or less satisfied. Dan agreed to make available 5,000 piastres (about $10) to every family to buy saws and hatchets that he could provide.

A young woman still drawing rice rations complained that the supplies were inadequate. 'Write a report and send it to me personally', said Dan, while an assistant noted down her name.

An old woman said her name did not appear on the hamlet lists and that therefore she received no rations. Dan ordered the officials to investigate and report.

Because of the racial and religious divisions that had so long plagued

Vietnam, many of the hamlets consisted of transplanted communities, led by Roman Catholic priests or Buddhist monks. With dynamic leadership, the communities did well, whereas weak leadership almost always showed up in the people's discontent.

At Song My hamlet in Ninh Thuan province, not far from Cam Ranh Bay, the priest was a notable absentee the day I went there with Dr Dan. There were bitter complaints during Dan's meet-the-people session that the priest had distributed the best land to his friends instead of drawing lots by ballot.

I remarked later that it must have been difficult to work with such indifferent leadership. 'It's like marriage', Dan replied drily. 'You have to enjoy the best and put up with the worst or the marriage will fail.'

With all its half successes and some absolute failures, the refugee resettlement programme was one of the few significant achievements of the Saigon government. When he was forced out of office in the last weeks of the war because of his demand for real leadership, Dan had a million and a half applications from old and new war refugees, demobilized soldiers, the unemployed and needy city workers asking to be helped back to the land. A deputation of a hundred from one refugee camp invaded his office and waited for twenty-four hours, until he returned from a field trip, to present a petition asking for their resettlement. Dan had embarked on a humanitarian project that emptied the refugee camps, and gave a million war victims a second chance in life.

Another extraordinary, if controversial, humanitarian whose activities must not be overlooked during this period was an Australian-born social worker named Rosemary Taylor. Her work among the maimed, crippled, homeless, parentless and abandoned children made her name an inescapable byword in diplomatic circles in Saigon.

At the beginning of 1968 she was in Saigon, representing Terre des Hommes, the only international organization involved in any meaningful way at this time with the inter-country adoption of Vietnamese orphans.

The Tet offensive found her stranded away from her orphans by a seven-day curfew. As soon as she felt it safe to face the streets, she made her way to the American Embassy, where she asked the Marine guards for transport to take her to her home. They told her they dared not venture out because the area was unsafe. Crying from frustration, she continued on foot through the empty streets to the headquarters of the Sisters of St Paul des Chartres. There she found a car and a driver ready to take the risk of driving her back to her home.

Though there were still Communist forces in Saigon, she wasted no time in getting out to the countryside. She headed first for Vinh Long in the heart of the embattled Mekong Delta. What she found horrified her. Vinh Long had been all but destroyed. The orphanage itself had been badly shot up, and the walls were pock-marked by shell fragments. Many of the babies in the orphanage were dead from lack of milk and exhaustion caused by the noise of battle.

Some of the staff had fled and the mother superior in charge of the orphanage was more anxious than ever to see that the babies for whom inter-country adoption had been arranged should leave as soon as possible. Rosemary got a cyclo-pousse and, armed with as many babies as she could carry, headed for the airport to hitchhike a flight back to Saigon.

This was just the first of a series of journeys to snatch orphans quite literally out of the jaws of war. If the roads were closed because of the fighting, Rosemary inveigled herself aboard helicopters, aircraft and even the patrol boats in the canals and waterways of the Delta.

The Providence Orphanage in the central delta province of Sadec overflowed with orphans, but for much of the Tet offensive was virtually cut off from all outside contact. Once, when Viet Cong forces had closed all the roads, Rosemary found her way in and out of Sadec from Vinh Long by Vietnamese navy patrol boat, bringing out a child for adoption in Sweden and another for adoption in Germany.

No part of South Vietnam was too remote, or too dangerous, for Rosemary Taylor. She flew from Hoi An to Danang at tree-top level aboard a helicopter carrying several children, including a small girl in full typhoid crisis. On what she described as a 'memorable' trip, she got herself to a remote orphanage on the Cambodian border. It was cut off by water in the wet season, and she travelled by no less than twelve different means of transportation to get there.

There were many occasions when she arrived back in Saigon late at night from the provinces with what she called 'bundles of abandoned children', and had nowhere to put them. In these moments of crisis, the British military attaché came to the rescue and the babies were stacked away in the bedroom drawers of his house. 'We made temporary mattresses by crumpling up airmail copies of the London *Times*', she said. 'At least it was a respectable newspaper.'

A second crisis in Rosemary Taylor's work came with the North Vietnamese Easter offensive in 1972. A new flood of orphans inundated the institutions and, worse, an epidemic of measles threatened tens of thousands of infant lives. Rosemary's own orphanages were filled to overflowing. She could cope with no more. So she turned to others who could be trusted to care for the children. All through Saigon there sprang up Rosemary Taylor branch orphanages, where those with time and space to spare continued her work.

The British ambassador, Mr Brooks Richards, and his wife took four children, and in turn enlisted a 21-year-old bachelor on the Embassy staff. He was the eldest of nine children and had helped to bring up the rest. When he was recalled on compassionate leave to the United Kingdom (because one of his brothers had been killed in Northern Ireland), the head of chancery and his wife took care of the child. But not for long. The young man, Jerry McCrudden, soon returned to the Embassy to look after not only the first child but three others—and to marry an English girl who had been helping Rosemary Taylor.

A young girl secretary at the Australian Embassy took charge of a sick ten-day-old infant and restored it to health. Dr John Hodgkinson, an Australian eye specialist, was not too busy with his own private aid project to take four. His dinner guests learned not to be surprised when, eschewing the aid of a nurse, he would tuck one of the infants under his arm and feed it at the table.

The British residency became a semi-permanent annex for Rosemary Taylor. A year after the Easter offensive had spent its course the ambassador had forgotten the precise number of children he and his wife had taken in for temporary care. He thought it was about two dozen. Instead of the four in residence that he had a year previously, he now had six.

What should have been the crowning glory of Rosemary Taylor's mission to Vietnam was tragically shattered on 4 April 1975, when an American Air Force Galaxy took off from Saigon with 243 orphans aboard and crashed on its way back to the airport thirty-five minutes later, killing more than half the orphans. Among those who died in the crash was Margaret Moses, Rosemary Taylor's long-time associate in Vietnam, who had volunteered to help care for the orphans on the long flight to the United States.

Among those who saw the Galaxy crash was Margaret Moses' mother. She was helping to install another 212 Vietnamese waifs aboard a RAAF Hercules on the first stage of their journey to Sydney when the sound of the crash rocked the airport and the smoke from the funeral pyre of the Galaxy rose thousands of feet into the air.

Rosemary Taylor was an abrasive character, and not everyone approved of her work. Among those who did was Dr Dan, whose own work had planted a rare seed of hope in South Vietnam. Given a year or two of peace his grand scheme for draining the slums caused by repeated waves of refugees fleeing from the countryside could have transformed both urban and rural life. That was not to be.

Dr Henry Kissinger turned up in Saigon in October 1972, with the first draft of the treaty to end the war in his brief case and the news that Hanoi had capitulated on all major points. For twenty-four hours the euphoria persisted—until Thieu and his advisers saw the draft treaty for the first time.

They were shocked. The demilitarized zone between North and South Vietnam, which they wanted enlarged, was abandoned. No provision was made for the withdrawal of the North Vietnamese battle corps that had invaded the South in such massive force at Easter. The draft agreement also called for the establishment of a council of national reconciliation and concord, to which the English version of the draft assigned administrative functions to supervise elections, but which appeared in the Vietnamese version as coalition government.

Thieu dug in and refused to sign, forcing Dr Kissinger to cancel a scheduled flight to Hanoi and to abandon his hopes for a quick settlement before the U.S. presidential election. 'Peace with honor' would have to wait.

Negotiations began again in Paris on 20 November. Kissinger put forward Thieu's demands, softening them with Nixon's minimum demands. By 23 November the talks had reached the breaking point, with Le Duc Tho demanding the removal of the Thieu regime, the abolition of the demilitarized zone and the further partition of the South.

In the following days the United States called repeatedly for 'serious negotiations'. When a 72-hour Nixon ultimatum for the resumption of negotiations had passed without response from Hanoi, Nixon ordered the B52s to renew the bombing of the North, this time with a weight and sophistication that the North Vietnamese had not seen before. For twelve days the bombing continued before the signals came from Hanoi that it was willing to accept Nixon's minimum demands: the retention of the demilitarized zone, the retention of the Thieu government, and the clearing up of the misunderstanding about the functions of the national council of national reconciliation and concord to the satisfaction of Saigon. The North Vietnamese battle corps was to remain in the South. There would be a ceasefire in place. There were no restrictions on the amount of military support North Vietnam could receive from its Socialist friends. And no written assurances that Laos and Cambodia would not be used as springboards for future attacks on South Vietnam.

These were not terms to please Saigon. It had no choice. On 5 January, two days before Dr Kissinger returned to Paris to resume his negotiations with Le Duc Tho, Nixon in a letter to Thieu reiterated his promise to come to South Vietnam's aid 'with full force' if Hanoi violated the agreement. He added, 'I am convinced that your refusal to join us would be an invitation to disaster'.

Said Tran Van Lam bitterly, 'The signature was Nixon's but the words were Kissinger's'.

Part three

The end

1 April 1975 to 30 April 1975

1. 'The invisible star of the Milky Way'

I was at home in Australia on Easter Sunday when Danang fell. That night I went to Channel 7 in Melbourne, one of the local television stations, to make my usual, and contracted, weekly commentary on the week's foreign news. The programme, or at least my small section of it, was to be recorded about half an hour before it went on air. While I was sitting in the studio with the anchorman, waiting for the nod to begin, I noticed that the teleprompter from which he would read referred to the North Vietnamese troops at Danang as 'anti-government forces'. I suggested that it would be more correct to refer to them as North Vietnamese forces.

We had just begun when we were interrupted. The producer, an angry young woman, appeared on the floor. 'So now you're rewriting my script', she said to the anchorman. 'No', he replied. 'Denis just suggested that it would be more accurate to refer to the North Vietnamese.'

'Anti-government forces it is and anti-government forces it stays', she said.

'That's misleading', I said. 'You convey the impression that they are all indigenous South Vietnamese and they are not. There has been a very considerable invasion from the North.'

'I don't care whether you think it's misleading', she answered. 'I say they are anti-government forces.'

'Then if you insist, I shall have to correct it when I begin', I said.

She stared at me and then turned and stamped out of the studio.

The anchorman dutifully said anti-government forces had Danang in their grasp, and I said that there were also many North Vietnamese, and named the divisions.

The programme went on air as recorded. Although my contract required me to make one commentary a week when I was in Australia, I had seen the studio for the last time. For nearly a year, until my patience became exhausted, the station continued to pay me but to make no use whatever of my services. It was unwise, not to say unprofitable, to be closely identified with Vietnam, however objective one tried to be, or to correct, or to attempt to correct, the disinformation that others spread so well.

About the same time I received an anonymous letter on the letter-head of the Adelaide *Advertiser*. The writers identified themselves only as members of the editorial staff. They attacked me bitterly for having said in January 1975, that the North Vietnamese were planning to renew the war in the South. 'You won't be writing much longer for the *Advertiser*', they concluded. They were right. After twenty-six years, without even formal notification in writing–and with no severance pay, of course–I was told that the *Advertiser* no longer wanted my service. Many months later, John Bonython, chairman of directors of the *Advertiser*, apologized and said the decision had been made without any reference to the board. The first knowledge he and other directors had of my dismissal was the appearance of my articles in the *News*. They wanted to know why.

I recount these incidents not because they caused me great personal or professional harm, but simply to indicate the influence that could be, and was, brought to bear on those whose reporting and interpretation of events in Vietnam, and elsewhere, did not always conform to the 'conventional wisdom of the day. Even those strongly opposed to the war, who were nevertheless identified with it, suffered. Gerald Hickey, of the RAND Corporation, was a notable example of this. Hickey, whose important book, *A Village in Vietnam*, was followed by the most scholarly and important work ever attempted among the montagnards, found himself unable to get a billet in an American university simply because he was associated with Vietnam. After the Cambodian invasion in 1970, Henry Kissinger himself was warned by a group of his former Harvard associates that he might not be welcomed back if his answers and subsequent conduct were not satisfactory.

Americans did not want to hear the word Vietnam. Frank Devine, editor of the Australian edition of the *Reader's Digest*, commissioned me to write an article about the resettlement of refugees. He sent it off to New York, suggesting that the editors there might like to include it in the American edition. Back came the reply (while General Dung was preparing his forces for the invasion of the South) that Vietnam had receded into a remote little Asian country of little interest to anyone. New York counselled Devine against using the piece.

During the Korean War in the early 1950s a brilliant attempt was made to persuade the world at large that the United States was using bacteriological warfare against the North Koreans and Chinese. American prisoners of war made compelling confessions and appeared in print, over the radio, and on the screen to admit their crimes. The campaign failed primarily because those Westerners responsible for spreading the propaganda were themselves suspect. They learned their lesson. Although at least one of the principals in the germ warfare campaign in the 1950s was still working as a principal organizer of the Vietnam propaganda in the 1960s and 1970s, the technique this time was much more subtle. 'For nearly fifteen years the Vietnamese Communists have fashioned opinions throughout the world which dissolve if subjected to even casual inspection, yet this seldom happened', writes Douglas Pike. 'They created myths which defy elementary logic which yet endure and now threaten to become the orthodoxy of history. It has turned sceptical newsmen credulous, careful scholars indifferent to data, honourable men blind to immorality. No student of Vietnam can deny that American perception of Vietnam, both official and private (and therefore the policies which flowed from that perception) were to some degree consciously and deliberately shaped by the Vietnamese Communists' *action among the enemy* programme.'

Both Federal law enforcement agencies in the United States and American and foreign intelligence organizations say that the anti-war movement in the United States, and elsewhere, was financed from international Communist organizations. French intelligence specialists say that the Soviet Union supplied much of the money for North Vietnam as a form of economic aid, since Hanoi did not have the hard currency to do the job. About one million dollars in 'peace' contributions have been traced through disbursing Swiss and Swedish banks to the Soviet Union, China, Czechoslovakia, Cuba, and, until recently, Chile. For nearly ten years during the critical period of the war there was a numbered bank account (No. 5210-10-045-34) at the Skandinaviska Banken, Stockholm, to which anyone might send money (either cheques or cash) earmarked for any anti-war movement the sender wished to designate. Funds for the Stockholm Conference on Vietnam in 1970 and the War Crimes Trials by Bertrand Russell came from this source.

In Australia, Dr Cairns's Congress for International Disarmament and Co-operation, which has links with the World Peace Council and through it with the Communist Party of the Soviet Union, took the lead in guiding the anti-war movement. Similarly in the United States, the People's Coalition for Peace and Justice, which was greatly manipulated by the Communist Party of the United States, provided a lead that many non-Communists and anti-Communists were glad to follow. The importance of such organizations to the war effort was fully understood in Hanoi and in the field. A circular issued by the Central Office for South Vietnam* discussed the People's Committee for Peace and Justice in some detail. It said the committee maintained relations 'with the friendly side', and revealed that it was about to step up propaganda activity among u.s. servicemen, and that anti-war activity among American civilians was to be co-ordinated with the campaign among the military.

In the dark days of 1966, when the Americans had moved into the South in massive strength, Hanoi had come to the agonizing conclusion that it could still win the war but only if it fought so hard and for so long that pressures would build up within the United States to abandon the conflict. This was all spelled out by Nguyen Chi Thanh, writing in the *People's Army Review* in May 1967. The Americans, Thanh wrote, had been obliged to split and scatter their forces and to fight in areas where there were no clear-cut lines and no targets. Unable to organize battles that would bring their full combat efficiency into operation and produce results of a strategic effect, they had achieved only a low combat efficiency in terms of capability. They had not been able to gain control of the battlefield, or to shield the South Vietnamese in defence of the pacification programme. Nor had they been able to prevent the North Vietnamese from helping the Viet Cong. The result was that the scattered American mobile force was no longer in proportion to total u.s. strength.

On the other hand, Thanh believed that his own regular forces were capable of fighting in all tactical forms and with all combat methods on all scales and terrains. His plans did not call for exclusive reliance on conventional or mobile war, however, but for the maintenance of an offensive position by simultaneous attacks on many battlefields, using main-force units, regional units, guerrillas and also political forces. 'It is convincingly demonstrated', he wrote, 'that attacks on the enemy must be mounted simultaneously in three zones (the jungle, the rural, and the urban areas) in both the political and military fields in order to hold constantly the initiative on each battlefield in close co-ordination with all others'. By this tactic of hitting the Americans in

---

* cosvn Circular 06/tt-71, 16 July 1971.

many places while keeping sufficient forces in reserve to mass heavy fighting power in key areas, concentrating and dispersing quickly, fighting small battles and big battles, or combining the two, and avoiding at all costs the normal set-piece action, he believed that victory could be denied to the United States, however large the force it committed. He then added perhaps the most significant line of all. 'It is not yet known how much longer the u.s. expeditionary force will remain in Vietnam.'

Hanoi was confident at this stage of the war that the United States would not continue to accept indefinitely the casualties that Thanh's co-ordinated offensive had begun to produce. And in this, of course, it was absolutely right. It also believed that internationally all factors were in its favour. It saw the United States isolated from its old allies and subject to increasing pressure from the domestic anti-war movement which was developing rapidly and in desperate forms, such as self-immolation and the burning of draft cards. At all costs the anti-war movement had to be stimulated, not merely by propaganda in the United States and elsewhere but by actions in Vietnam which would contribute to the growth of the movement.

From the signing of the Paris Agreement until the beginning of General Dung's offensive, Hanoi and the Central Office for South Vietnam initiated actions for the specific purpose of feeding the anti-war and anti-Thieu movement. Even at the district level in South Vietnam, Party committees were watching the anti-war movement and seeking to find ways to help it along. The Baria district committee in Phuoc Tuy province on 23 July 1971, for example, issued a circular which stated: 'The anti-war movement in the United States has been widely intensified from Washington to New York and other states, and supported by most of Congress, former ambassadors, former secretaries, war veterans, troops returning from Vietnam, youths who oppose the draft, and workers. The anti-war movement is a spontaneous movement which has been guided and supported by our delegation at the Paris peace talks.'

Hanoi set up a Vietnam Committee for Solidarity with the American People to help the anti-war movement. 'We are deeply convinced that with the support and sympathy of the progressive people of the world . . . we will win glorious victory', wrote Professor Hoang Minh Giam, chairman of the committee, in a letter to the American people. 'We fight the aggressors fully aware that the American people are struggling vigorously in their demands for an immediate end to the war of aggression in Vietnam . . .' Deliberately, and effectively, the North Vietnamese ingratiated themselves into the anti-war movement.

Their representatives at the Paris talks spoke via a transatlantic telephone hookup to teach-ins at American universities. Their message was that the Vietnamese people were not the enemies but the friends of the American people. The enemy was the unjust person who wanted to pursue an unjust war.

The campaign went through the progressive stages–to stop the bombing of North Vietnam, to get the Americans out of the war and, finally, to stop further aid to South Vietnam at a time when Hanoi was readying itself, and committed to, the final push. In this campaign the international espousal of the Provisional Revolutionary Government and the fiction that the war was fought only by the indigenous Southerners against the tyranny of Thieu, were extremely important and, eventually, absolutely successful. By Easter 1975 the United States, and the world, had turned against South Vietnam.

The greatest nation in the world was not now prepared to raise even a hand in the defence of an ally that had been assured, on the authority of the President of the United States himself, that immediate and effective aid would be forthcoming in the event of any renewed Northern attack. That Nixon himself was discredited and at no time had the real authority to honour his commitments, and that South Vietnam under Thieu had failed dismally to take the political initiatives that might have made the Northern offensive impracticable politically, were important factors in the situation. But they do not detract from the most skilfully handled wartime propaganda campaign that the world has ever seen. The campaign made a mockery of the Paris Agreement, and was so successful that when the North, in total violation of the agreement, launched its massive invasion, none of the countries concerned asked Hanoi to stop.

I left Australia, heading for Vietnam again, on Easter Monday. Jim Robinson, an American networks reporter turned banker, was aboard the Air Vietnam flight that took us to Saigon from Hong Kong. He said he was going to 'assess' the situation. 'Do you really have to go there to assess?' I asked. The assessment had, in fact, already been made and his briefcase was packed with thousands of dollars to pay off his staff. It was not a question of how long but how soon. The Central Highlands had fallen. Hue and Danang were both in North Vietnamese hands. Along the jungle trails running from the Central Highlands to the coast and down the beaches and roads in Central Vietnam, in trucks and buses, on motor cycles and on foot, on boats and barges, with or without sails or engines, a million refugees were on the move. In this awful story of human suffering the crash of the C5 Galaxy on the evening of 4 April with its 243 orphans aboard was scarcely more than another incident.

I checked into the Continental just before curfew on 2 April and made two phone calls, one to Dr Phan Quang Dan. He sounded very tired. 'Be at my house at 6.30 tomorrow morning', he said. 'I'm going on a long flight and it will give us time to talk.'

The second call was to Bui Anh Tuan, a mutual friend. 'It's the finish', he said.

I was at Dr Dan's house at the appointed hour next morning. As we drove to the airport, he was still looking for signs of good cheer. 'See, the policemen are still on duty', he said. 'That's a good sign. That means morale isn't bad, doesn't it?' And, indeed, in the first light of day, Saigon did appear to be going about its business in the usual way.

Dr Dan was heading south for Phu Quoc, an island off the south coast, renowned for its *nuoc mam*, or fish sauce. With town after town falling to the advancing North Vietnamese forces along the central coast, refugees were finding each new haven unsafe. Some refugees had been moved three or four times. With more than could be handled at the port of Vung Tau, Dr Dan had decided only at 3.30 p.m. the previous day to divert as many as possible to Phu Quoc, and now, together with his own technicians and representatives of the International Red Cross, the German Red Cross, the Vietnamese Red Cross and international voluntary agencies in Saigon, was leading an advance guard to make rushed preparations to receive the first 6,000 refugees that night. The Royal Australian Air Force had made a Hercules available to take Dr Dan and the team to Phu Quoc. We would be in the air at 7 a.m. We were not in the air at 7.30 a.m. Or 8 a.m. Or 8.30 a.m. Then an embarrassed American aid official arrived to inform Dan, his assembled staff, and the various international voluntary agencies with him, that the Australian government had withdrawn permission to use the aircraft. The Embassy had received a message during the night that senior Vietnamese government officials, or any officials for that matter, and Australian correspondents were not to be transported by the RAAF. Hanoi objected to this sort of use of Australian aircraft, and Canberra ordered Geoffrey Price, to his great embarrassment, to deny the use of the aircraft to all Vietnamese government officials, military or civilian, and all members of the Press, of whatever nationality.

Hours later, on a much slower (American) plane, we were airborne. It was no thanks to the Whitlam government that the refugees when they arrived at night found arrangements were in hand to receive them.

Dan filled me in. He was, of course, preoccupied with the refugees and their plight. But he was bitter over Thieu's lack of leadership. 'We can still save the situation if we fight', he said.

On the plane with us, attached to Dan's staff because there was nothing else for him to do, was Colonel Dong, my old friend from Danang, who had been sent by General Truong to brief Thieu on the situation on 27 March and, mercifully (or so I thought at the time), had not been able to get a plane back.

He was much less optimistic than Dan. 'We must have a long talk', he said. 'I've got to tell you what happened in Central Vietnam. It has to be recorded.'

He saw the current situation in the gloomiest light. 'It is just a matter of time before we lose the rest', he said. 'If we are able to reorganize, we can hold the rest of the South for six months, or even for several years, depending on how quickly the enemy is able to deploy all his resources from Military Region 1 and Military Region 2. If we don't find real leadership, Saigon will fall in two weeks to a month. If we can hold a defensive line in Nha Trang, we can hold on for some time. But sooner or later the enemy will take over. Everything is penetrated here, from the Cabinet Ministers down. The enemy hasn't just prepared this attack. He's been preparing for twenty years.'*

Two days later an Air America plane flying over apparently deserted Nha Trang took small arms fire. So much for Colonel Dong's hope there.

It was not at Nha Trang but at Phan Rang, south of Cam Ranh Bay, that Thieu hoped to hold the line. General Fred Weyand, the U.S. Army Chief of Staff, and the most able American general who ever served in Vietnam, had been sent by President Ford to make a personal on-the-spot appraisal of the situation on 26 March. He had reported back that if an additional $722 million worth of urgently needed spare parts and military equipment were made available, the South Vietnamese had a good chance of holding out until the wet season. Phan Rang, he believed, was a good place to start holding.

Weyand believed that at all costs the North Vietnamese had to be prevented from concentrating in strength around Saigon. In 1967, when most of his peers were still having difficulty in differentiating between the apparent withering away of the Viet Cong and its tactically expedient breakdown into company-sized and smaller units, Weyand, whose Second Field Force Command in Vietnam included the Capital Military District of Saigon and eleven surrounding provinces, had made a highly professional military appreciation of the rapidly changing situation. 'Until last November (1967) the enemy had

---

* For four years General Hoang Xuan Lam, then I Corps commander, was blackmailed into allowing his sister-in-law to stay in his house, though he knew she was an agent for Hanoi.

fragmented his units down to twenty to thirty men to avoid our sweeps and B52 strikes', he told an interviewer three weeks before the Tet offensive. 'Two months ago, on orders from COSVN, they began merging in mass formations. A word-of-mouth campaign is under way telling people that any coalition government which includes the Viet Cong will be Viet Cong-controlled. Viet Cong prisoners around Saigon are saying that the Viet Cong battalions are getting North Vietnamese replacements to puff them up. They're getting a lot of new weapons.'

To Weyand, an intelligence specialist, who served in the Burma-China-India theatre during the Second World War, all the indicators pointed to an attack on Saigon. 'You could make a case for putting companies in eighty or so critical areas around the city', he said at the time. His pre-Tet redeployment stopped short of this, but fortunately for the security of all concerned, he moved a brigade from the border back closer to the Saigon area, pulled out two Australian battalions from their base in Phuoc Tuy Province to form a reconnaissance screen in front of the Bien Hoa air base, and put artillery into Saigon in defence of South Vietnamese and U.S. units. His foresight played a considerable part in saving Saigon at the time.

At first glance, the apparently open terrain around Saigon seems relatively easy to defend. It is, on the contrary, extremely difficult. Only forty roads lead into the city, but there are myriad minor waterways that were not policed and could not be. Although Saigon is about thirty miles in a direct line from the sea and much farther by river or road, the Saigon River is tidal for many miles above the city. At times the rise and fall is as much as six feet. The salt water coming in from the sea backs up the fresh water around Saigon, which explains not only the magnificent irrigation systems in the orchards and vegetable gardens that draw their water from the serpentine coils and tributaries of the river around the city, but also much of the Viet Cong's covert success in the region before the 1968 Tet offensive. It is possible to move from the sea to Saigon by unpatrolled canals without appearing on the main river itself, except to cross it. From the north, the approach by land and water offers even better opportunities for concealment. The Viet Cong's main route from the Maquis D, north-east of the city, led through the Michelin rubber plantations to the Iron Triangle and the Hobo Woods and from there along the west bank of the Saigon River through a lacework of canals and irrigation ditches.

When the tide is in, the Saigon River rises and fresh water flows through dykes about eight feet wide and is reticulated into smaller channels that irrigate rows of papaya and banana and dense crops of sugar cane. The soil is rich, the water abundant, the sun hot and, since Saigon is close by, fertilizers are, or used to be, abundant. The result is one of the richest and most closely cultivated pieces of farmland in the world.

Before the Tet offensive, the Viet Cong came by sampan with their guns and rockets, fortified the sides of the innumerable dykes, and set up a rocket-control headquarters in a Buddhist temple long used as a meeting place for dissident monks in their contacts with the National Liberation Front. Until Tet, there was little to disturb these activities. The Vietnamese Navy maintained routine patrols in heavily armoured craft along the main waterways but made little contact in the general Saigon area. What happened in the smaller canals and irrigation channels no one knew. These were navigable only by the smallest boats, which could not pack enough men to deal even with local-force Viet Cong ambushes. What they could not cope with, they did not trouble.

Against the relatively small forces available to Hanoi for the attack on Saigon during the Tet offensive–approximately seventeen battalions, both main force and regional troops–General Weyand reckoned that a force of three divisions was necessary, and this excluded the area under command of the Capital Military District and the rest of the all-important enveloping province of Gia Dinh.

Now, in 1975, with the Americans all gone, without the support of the B52s, and with much of the Vietnamese Air Force grounded because of lack of spare parts, it was clear that a very much larger force would be needed for Saigon's defence if the vast North Vietnamese forces now available in the Highlands and Central Vietnam could be thrown into the battle. General Dung had under his immediate command, and earmarked for the battle, 153 main force battalions, all at full strength, or nine times the force committed by the North Vietnamese and local forces against the combined u.s. and South Vietnamese forces during the Tet offensive in 1968. Five full Army corps, each consisting of three full-strength infantry divisions, plus supporting arms, and with two divisions in reserve, were Dung's to command–and for Saigon alone. Seventeen battalions during Tet: no less than 153 battalions in divisional formations and many others in independent regiments made up the force now.

What no one had reckoned on yet was the Politburo's decision to throw everything into the battle for Saigon at the earliest possible moment. Hanoi was worried about the approaching wet season. It was even more worried that military action might be forestalled by political manoeuvre for another negotiated settlement, involving either a coalition government, or partition.

As early as 20 March the Politburo in Hanoi, its armed forces massively strengthened by enormous quantities of Russian military aid, had decided that nothing should be allowed to stand in the way of a military solution to the war. 'The enemy', wrote General Dung, 'was planning to carry out a large-scale strategic retreat in order to concentrate forces in the Saigon area and part of the Mekong Delta, and perhaps also in Danang and Cam Ranh, with a view to establishing a relatively strong position to seek a political solution–forming a coalition government, or agreeing to a partition of South Vietnam. It was, therefore, necessary for us to lose no time in using the factor of great surprise in matters of timing, direction of the attacks, strength and boldness while ensuring certain victory. Accordingly, the Politburo weighed pros and cons and drew up a plan to liberate Saigon earlier than had been anticipated.'

At the end of the first week in April, I met 'Nguyen Van Tri', General Tran Van Don's contact with the National Liberation Front, at the house of a mutual friend. We began by discussing who might be acceptable in a new government, assuming that Thieu bowed to the Front's demand and resigned. 'Nguyen Van Tri' insisted that Thieu had to go and that the Front would accept no other anti-Communist nationalist as leader. A leftist from the Third Force had to take over, he said. Most ministers in the Cabinet would be from the Third Force, but not all. Their responsibility would be to ensure the absolute execution of the Paris Agreement. In effect, he said, it would be Third Force government under the guidelines (and, he implied, the supervision) of the Front–Independence, Liberty, Democracy and Self-sufficiency. There would be respect for private ownership. Houses left vacant by evacuees would remain vacant. No one would have the right to take them over. On the contrary, refugees would be invited to return to regain possession of their houses and farms.

The Provisional Revolutionary Government would organize the government on democratic lines, very much leftist inclined but including non-Communists and religious groups.

Obviously alerted to the Politburo's intentions to press for a quick military victory, he said that there would be very quick reunification of North and South Vietnam if Saigon collapsed. If, however, a political solution could be organized quickly unification would be delayed for a long time, even years.

There would be no reprisals except against those who had 'done lots of harm to national reconciliation'. Those people would be tried by the courts. He expected that many Vietnamese would want to leave the country if they had opposed the Front. Others would be re-educated to become good citizens.

I asked him about the liquidation of tens of thousands of people in

North Vietnam after 1954. He replied that there had to be a land reform campaign in the North after 1954 because of the fear of a threat from the South. The threat had now decreased, although there was some concern about the continuing u.s. presence in other countries. Thailand, for example, would be asked to order the withdrawal of the u.s. troops.

'In terms of global strategy', he continued, 'the North Vietnamese will have the leading role in South-East Asia. Only India, which is a sub-continent, will be more important in the region. We Vietnamese are more disciplined [than the Indians] and we will advance more quickly in technology. In the past we were kept back by religious superstitions. That will change now, but we won't make South Vietnam a Communist State because if we do the technicians will be afraid to return. If we want to strengthen the political system, we will need to strengthen the economy, and to do this we need the technicians who are abroad.'

'Nguyen Van Tri' ended by saying that the United States underestimated the suffering and the fighting will of the Vietnamese people, but he believed that in the proposals he had outlined there would be good prospects for co-operation between the American people and the Vietnamese. But now there was no time to lose if Saigon was not to fall by force.

Indeed, there was not. The I Army Corps in North Vietnam started moving south on 25 March and after an amazing 1,000-mile forced march arrived in time to take their place along with the other four corps in the battle line up outside Saigon. The II Army Corps, consisting of the 2nd, 304th and 325th divisions, after capturing Hue and Danang, headed south and made the journey to the Saigon front in eighteen days, fighting as it advanced.

Dung took risks that no North Vietnamese commander had ever taken before. He set the air force in motion to ferry supplies from North Vietnam to Pleiku, Kontum and Danang. A flotilla of ships carried both men and supplies into the South Vietnamese ports as they were liberated. North Vietnam was stripped almost bare of its defences, and the eight million people in the newly-liberated territories, together with all the captured armed forces, were left to local Viet Cong troops, stiffened with North Vietnamese, to disarm and guard.

Here is General Dung's description:

From the North various types of vehicles sped bumper to bumper southward to move troops and supplies to the front line. In Dong Ha, the convoys broke into two columns, one turning to cut down east and west of the Truong Son mountain chain and the other taking Route 1 directly South, passing through Hue, Danang,

Quang Ngai and Qui Nhon in the wake of the advancing units. On the red earth Truong Son route (part of the road network built by the North Vietnamese after the Paris Agreement to replace the Ho Chi Minh trail), swirling dust could now be seen at the southern end. The stream of traffic flowed further and further south . . . and then split to enter the various rubber forests in Dau Tieng and the Maquis D, and to move along the banks of the Saigon, Dong Nai, Song Be and Vam Co Dong rivers.

Watching for the first time the endless flow of revolutionary troops passing through their native land, seeing our young, healthy and cheerful troops, and gazing at the big artillery pieces, anti-aircraft missile launchers and long columns of tanks, armoured cars, anti-aircraft guns and engineering units, the Central Highlands people living in the newly-liberated areas along Route 14 were filled with joy and could not hide their surprise . . . Seeing trucks loaded with missiles pass by, they pointed at the missiles and called them wingless airplanes.

Hundreds of thousands of vehicles sped southward, bumper to bumper, day and night. On some sections of the road, where the dust churned up by their wheels decreased visibility, our vehicles turned on their headlights and blared their horns repeatedly. The long trail of dust did not settle. It snaked through the dense jungles of the Central Highlands, passed through the green pastures of Bu Prang and entered the bamboo forests in Bu Giap Map.

Yet another deputy chief of Hanoi's General Staff, Major-General Phung The Tai, had set up his command post at the point where the two main routes from the North converged. Above his desk was a large poster which read, 'Lightning Speed. More Lightning Speed. Boldness. More Boldness'. He performed an extraordinary task. For in addition to the fifteen divisions earmarked for the attack on Saigon, General Dung also wanted two in reserve, close enough to the front to be on ready call when the fighting began.

General Tai used not only the North Vietnamese Army's own complement of vehicles, but also vehicles captured from the South Vietnamese, passenger buses, cargo trucks and motor cars seized from the 'liberated' population, and driven by prisoners of war. Helicopters, transport planes and captured Air Vietnam planes were loaded with newly-printed maps of Saigon and rushed South.

Also rushing South was Le Duc Tho, the peacemaker, who won–and declined–the Nobel Prize for his part in negotiating the Paris Agreement. He left Hanoi by plane on 28 March, and on his arrival in the South found time to write a poem to Le Duan, who was still back in Hanoi.

Brother, you told me to go and return with victory.
At that touching moment, I could not speak.
Your words are truly the call of our country,

Which fills me with vigour to cross the Truong Son mountains.
The way to the front line is enlivened by good news.
Victories are scored everywhere.
As I hurry on my long trip,
Favourable opportunity has been given us.

Le Duc Tho and Le Duan had been closely associated since 1949. Ho
Chi Minh appointed Duan as the first secretary-general of the Central
Office for South Vietnam and made Tho his deputy. In late 1952, or
early 1953, Tho succeeded Duan. The two men did not agree on
tactics, and the differences between them were said to have been very
bitter. If so, these were soon forgotten. For many years in Hanoi they
shared adjoining offices.

Until he appeared in Paris to negotiate an end to the war with
Henry Kissinger, Tho had been very much a backroom boy. He was
born in North Vietnam in 1910 and became a founder member of the
Indo-China Communist Party in 1930. According to some reports, he
was arrested in 1940, and escaped to China, returning in time to take
part in the early days of the resistance. He was at Ho's side when the
Viet Minh marched into Hanoi in 1945.

The Americans believed during the war that Tho was the only
civilian member of the Central Military Party Committee. The evidence
now suggests that both he and Le Duan were members and that
responsibility for the military-political co-ordination of the 1975
offensive was jointly theirs. Since Hanoi had decided to abandon the
fiction of the Provisional Revolutionary Government–it had, in fact,
never diplomatically recognized its existence–and to end the war
with a clear-cut military victory for the North, the situation now clearly
called for one of the men to remain in Hanoi while the other supervised
all operations, political as well as military, in the South. Dung ran
the war, but Tho was the senior man in the field.

On 31 March, Tho was making his way south along the mountain
route in the Highlands toward Ban Me Thuot, where Dung still had
his headquarters. A general meeting of all the top North Vietnamese
political and military leaders in the South had been planned for
Ban Me Thuot. As part of the plan to expedite the offensive against
Saigon, Duan telegraphed all the principals, told them to cancel the
meeting and to head for the Saigon front.

Dung began his drive south from Ban Me Thuot on 2 April, just
ahead of the 316th Division and an advance party from the III Corps.
His destination was Loc Ninh, about eighty miles from Saigon. He
arrived late in the afternoon and went immediately to the Central
Office for South Vietnam, where Pham Hung, the secretary-general,
also a senior member of the Politburo of the Laodong Party, was at

work with his shirt unbuttoned and cooling himself with a fan made of parachute material.

Like Dung and Tho, Hung was a founder member of the Indo-China Communist Party, and an old friend of Dung. Arrested by the French in My Tho, near Saigon, on May Day 1931, for complicity in the death of a French official killed by a crowd which he was said to have led, his death sentence was later commuted to life imprisonment. He was released in 1945, and quickly began to rise both in the Party and the government apparatus. During the Indo-China War, he worked directly under Le Duan and Tho and became a member of the Laodong Party's first Central Committee in 1951. After his expulsion from Saigon with General Dung for misusing his diplomatic functions for political subversion in 1955, he returned to Hanoi. He became deputy prime minister in 1958 and served as acting prime minister for a brief period in 1961. Following the death of Nguyen Chi Thanh, who had been running COSVN before the 1968 offensive, Hung had taken over and had been in charge ever since. Now, reunited again on the outskirts of Saigon, the two men hugged each other and sat down to talk about the victories already won and those that lay ahead.

Workmen were busy putting the final touches to the new and enlarged headquarters that were to serve as the nerve centre for the vast army heading south. A number of wooden houses with thatched roofs had been built and provided with shelters and trenches, just in case the South Vietnamese Air Force became active or, small chance, the B52s appeared again.

From all parts of the country the top North Vietnamese military leaders had begun to gather for the kill. Giap, who had been undergoing treatment for cancer in a Moscow hospital, was the only notable absentee. Cadaverous looking Tran Van Tra, who had once led a squad of assassins in Saigon, and emerged from the jungle after the Paris Agreement as Hanoi's top military man in the South, was there. So was Le Ngoc Hien, one of the deputy chiefs of the General Staff, now the battle planner for the Saigon offensive, and Dinh Duc Thien, one of Dung's principal lieutenants.

On the afternoon of 7 April, while the military leaders were in conference, a motor cycle came to a stop in the courtyard and off stepped a tall man wearing a light blue shirt, khaki trousers and the traditional Viet Minh sun helmet. Le Duc Tho had arrived.

He brought news of the most recent Politburo meeting and its decisions and announced the command leaders for the Saigon operation: General Dung to be commander-in-chief; Pham Hung political commissar; Tran Van Tra and Le Duc Anh to be deputy commanders. Le Trong Tan, who had commanded the North Vietnamese operation against Danang, and had already moved into action east of Saigon, was subsequently appointed deputy commander-in-chief and had overall command of II Corps and IV Corps on the eastern approaches.

While the North Vietnamese planners went about their tasks at Loc Ninh in absolute confidence of early victory, the Saigon government was falling to pieces. The Senate met in an emergency session on 2 April and called for a change of leadership, without specifically mentioning Thieu or Khiem, the prime minister. After the session was over, Tran Van Lam called on Thieu to present him with the resolution. Thieu reacted violently and abusively, ranting at Lam and accusing his former supporters of having deserted him. He refused to consider either resigning or handing over real power to a new government. He was not even prepared to discuss the military situation with Lam or the rest of the Senate.

Next day Thieu called a meeting of his closest advisers, including his nephew, Hoang Duc Nha, a former minister for information and open arms. The outcome was the decision to go part of the way in meeting the Senate's demands. Thieu would force Prime Minister Khiem to resign.

In his address to the nation on 4 April announcing the resignation of Khiem, Thieu satisfied neither the doves nor the hawks. Former vice president and prime minister, Nguyen Cao Ky, had flown from his farm not far from Ban Me Thuot to the sanctuary of his house on the Tan Son Nhut air base and had there begun to plot. On 27 March he had announced the formation of a National Salvation Committee. His friends openly talked coup d'état, and on 4 April the ministry of the interior announced that a number of arrests had been made among the coup plotters.

Outside the National Assembly building other nationalists, including Tran Van Tuyen, demonstrated for the dismissal of Thieu. Father Tran Huu Thanh, an activist Catholic priest who had been campaigning vigorously against the corruption in the government, threw in his lot with Ky.

Others, deeply conscious of the dangers of tampering with the Constitution in any way and fearful of the shattering consequences of a coup d'état, wanted Thieu to continue in office as a constitutional president, thus preserving the legitimacy of the regime, while handing over all powers to a fighting Cabinet. Among the strongest advocates of this was Dr Phan Quang Dan, a man of absolute integrity and an infinite capacity for hard work. The Third Force and the National Liberation Front wanted Thieu's resignation and the appointment of a caretaker president who would quickly bring the war to an end by negotiation.

Thieu accepted none of these alternatives. He retained full powers and in the place of Khiem, who had been weak, and corrupt, but well meaning,* appointed Nguyen Ba Can, chairman of the House of Assembly, a lightweight, whose efforts to attract moderate opposition figures into a 'war cabinet', or a 'cabinet of resistance', failed dismally. Dr Dan paid the penalty for his criticism of Thieu and was thrown out, for which I, as a friend, was grateful, since it meant that he was free to leave the country when the end came. His success in resettling a million wartime refugees on the land had not only been effective, it had contributed enormously to the erosion of Communist influence in the countryside. He was, I knew from Front contacts, a marked man. For the next two weeks there were repeated rumours of a coup. Late one night I was phoned in my room at the Continental by a staff officer on the Joint General Staff who told me that the coup was in process and that I could safely write that Ky would take over before morning. My contact was so absolutely reliable that I got out of bed and started to write the story. Then, after second thoughts (or a cowardly unwillingness to face the troops in the streets without a curfew pass), I tore it up and went back to bed. Which was just as well.

Ky had, indeed, made plans for a coup, using the air force, para-troops, and special forces. He held his hand at the last minute only because he believed Ambassador Martin had agreed to put pressure on Thieu to resign. Whether General Hieu, the deputy commander of Military Region 3 (the Saigon front) was involved in the coup plans I do not know, but on the evening of 7 April he was shot and killed at his desk in Bien Hoa. According to General Dung, his murderer was the Thieu loyalist and Hieu's immediate superior, the commander of Military Region 3, General Nguyen Van Toan.

Precisely at 8.22 a.m. the following morning, when the rue Catinat was full of bustle, an arrow-like F5E fighter, piloted by Lieutenant Nguyen Thanh Trung, of the South Vietnamese Air Force, streaked over the city and down toward the presidential palace.

In the Australian residence on rue Pasteur, less than a mile from the

---

* He had not shown himself to be very well meaning in his days as a divisional commander in the Army. In July 1961, I had accompanied an operation in Vinh Binh Province in the Mekong Delta led by Khiem. He used his artillery to blaze away at villages ahead of the line of advance and from which not a single shot was being fired. When I complained, he replied, 'The villagers have asked us to use artillery because it gives them an opportunity to run away from the Viet Cong'. In all my years of covering wars I think that was the most cynical remark I ever heard.

palace, Geoffrey Price, the ambassador, was having breakfast with Father Hoan, a Vietnamese priest, whose village of orphans, a hundred miles north-east of Saigon, had been adopted by the Australian women's group in Vietnam.

'Don't be alarmed', said Price, in jest, as the sound of the diving plane shook the windows in the residence. 'It is just someone about to bomb the palace.' As he finished speaking, the first bombs landed in the palace grounds.

From the Australian Embassy in the Hotel Caravelle, where I was delivering a letter to the ambassador's secretary from an Australian girl married to a Vietnamese, I, too, had heard the plane and was at the window to see the bombs as they sped for the palace.

The first run took the palace defences by absolute surprise. When the plane came in for the second pass, however, there was a stuttering of anti-aircraft and small arms fire, and a helicopter took off from the palace grounds and headed down river. The Saigon traffic flowed on. In Catinat there did not even seem to be any curiosity.

My own reaction was that I was watching the end of the Vietnam tragedy. In the next three weeks the curtain went up several times, for there were certain rituals to be performed and bouquets to be bestowed, but the attack on the palace by a Viet Cong 'sleeper', who had for years waited for a chance like this, marked the end. No playwright, and no recorder of the facts, either, could ignore the symbolism of the performance. The continued lack of national unity, despite the peril, the frustration of the political scene and the fears of so many people of what was about to happen, were all reflected in this startling act.

Of more immediate importance to me at this moment was the real significance of the attack. It was now mid-morning in eastern Australia and around midnight in London, and in both places I had obligations to move news like this with the utmost dispatch. I waited at the window for two or three minutes to see whether more planes returned to the attack. No other plane appeared and the firing stopped.

As I ran downstairs and along the street to the United Press-International office, where I could write and transmit my story, I considered and rejected the possibility that this was Ky's coup. It seemed more like a farewell gesture of contempt for Thieu by a departing pilot. Two hours later the story, in roughly these terms, was the lead article in the *Daily Telegraph* in London.

The story, as told since by General Dung and *Vietnam Courier*, is that the pilot, Nguyen Thanh Trung, was the son of a Viet Cong Party secretary in the Mekong Delta, who was killed in a government operation in 1963. Trung wanted to join the Viet Cong (his mother and sister had been arrested), but was advised to change his name, get on with his education and bide his time. Toward the end of May 1969, Trung, who was now in his second year at the Faculty of Science at the Saigon University, was admitted to the Vietnamese Air Force flying officer training school. He did so well that he was sent to the ' United States for two years' training there, returning to Vietnam to become, with the full support of the Party, first a bomber pilot 'and then a fighter-bomber pilot, but always waiting for the main chance.

On 8 April he volunteered to fly on a mission to Nha Trang. Pleading a slight technical difficulty in his plane, he waited at takeoff until the other planes were on their way to Nha Trang, and then headed for Saigon, where Thieu was in conference with Vu Quang Chiem, chief of his military cabinet. His bombs discharged, without much accuracy or effect, Trung sped north to land on a liberated airfield and to prepare his colleagues in the North Vietnamese air force for an even more spectacular finale just twenty days later. Thereafter, Hanoi called him 'the invisible star of the milky way'.

Part three: The end
1 April 1975 to 30 April 1975

2. The battle for Saigon begins

On the morning of 9 April, the day after the bombing attack on the palace, I had breakfast early at the Continental with Bob Miller of United Press-International, a friend of more than thirty years in countless places and numerous wars. We had flown into Phnom Penh together at the beginning of the war in Cambodia, the only passengers that day on Air Cambodge's Caravelle. Miller stayed on after I left and was captured by North Vietnamese troops one night with Kyotchi Sawada,* the brilliant Japanese war photographer. Incredibly–or, knowing Miller, perhaps not so incredibly–they talked the officer in charge of the unit that captured them into allowing them to go free. It was after midnight and the officer suggested that they should wait until the following morning when crossing the lines might prove less hazardous.

Afraid that a higher headquarters might have a change of mind during the night, they elected to go immediately. They also decided that it would be wise to make as much noise as possible. But what sort of a noise can a Japanese and an American make together so that no one shoots them in a Cambodian no man's land?

They settled for 'Waltzing Matilda'. At the top of their voices they sang of billabongs, jumbucks, coolibah trees, swagmen and squatters. They made it, too.

I cabled Miller my congratulations on his escape. Back came the

---

* He was subsequently killed.

reply, 'As grandfather used to say, it doesn't matter if you have sawdust for brains as long as you have luck'. This, the luck, or the judgement, he always had. In 1958, during a lull in the Chinese Communist bombardment of Quemoy, I flew with Richard Hughes from Taipeh at wave-top height to land on the airfield tucked away behind the sand dunes, out of sight of the mainland gunners but not out of range. We were among the first correspondents to get to Quemoy, we thought. We were wrong. An hour or so later we were walking down the main street of Kinmen town when a man surrounded by a flock of laughing children appeared coming from the other direction. Miller, of course.

'When did you get here?' we asked.

'A month ago', he replied. It was, I had discovered over the years, typical of Miller.

Miller was the first correspondent to ride into Paris in 1944–on the handlebars of a bicycle. And, one day just before Phnom Penh fell, he flew three times into the airfield at Pochentong, under fire each time, sitting on a sack of rice. When I remonstrated with him, he reminded me that we had occupied the entire Air Cambodge jet when we flew into Phnom Penh at the beginning of the war. He saw the war begin and he had seen it end. 'Besides', he said, 'the crew had to fly into Phnom Penh three times and I had joined them for the day. How do you think they would have felt if I had said it was too hot after the first shelling?'

The Vietnam War threw up more impostors and charlatans in the name of war correspondents than I can remember in all the other wars I have covered put together. There were many notable exceptions to this. Reporters like Michael Richardson of the *Age*, Robert Shaplen of the *New Yorker*, George McArthur of the *Los Angeles Times*, Don Oberdorfer of the *Washington Post*, Daniel Southerland of the *Christian Science Monitor*, Kate Webb of United Press-International, photographers like Horst Faas, Neil Davis, and others like Miller were courageous, hard-working, knowledgeable and informed. There were some who invented, distorted and lied, like the TV reporter who went down the Mekong Delta on one occasion and drummed up his own crowd to make a demonstration, and turned a crowd of hundreds in Danang into thousands of demonstrators.

Their publications were no less culpable than the reporters. I had just left Vietnam on one occasion when I received a letter from *Look* enclosing a number of clippings about the damage caused by defoliation on Route 1, running north from Saigon through Xuan Loc. The magazine wanted an article describing the crime. 'Don't bother to go back to Vietnam, of course', I was told, 'but just use the clips and your own knowledge'.

As it happened, I had just driven along this section of Route 1 and was astonished to note that in the defoliated areas on either side of the road, once primary or secondary jungle, the defoliation had opened up new land for cultivation and that crops of bananas and papaya were flourishing. I told New York. It was not the sort of article the magazine had in mind.

We had by this time become accustomed in Saigon to the appearance of friends and friends of friends and Vietnamese we hadn't seen for years, all looking desperately for a way out. It was easy enough to transfer money. I sent the life savings of one senior official to Hong Kong for deposit in my account in Australia. It wouldn't have bought a good second-hand motor-car. So much for his corruption! Doing anything helpful for people who wanted to get out was much more difficult and, for an Australian, almost impossible.

As Miller and I were eating our papaya at the Continental, two doctors, husband and wife, called on us. I had helped a brother-in-law and sister in Australia with their problems with the immigration authorities a year earlier. Could I please, please help them now?

The Australian government, already unsympathetic, had been told by Hanoi that evacuation plans were not humanitarian and did not help the South Vietnamese people, or friendly relations with the North. When Mr Whitlam, the Australian prime minister, was informed of a large increase in the number of nominations of Vietnamese for permanent residence in Australia within the normal guidelines of Australian immigration policy, he simply ordered the Department of Labour and Immigration to suspend the processing of these applications. That was one way to deal with the problem.

Canberra was well aware of my friendship with Dr Dan and apparently thought I would make an effort to obtain permission for him and his family to enter Australia. He had for years been closely associated with Australians in Vietnam, and it was on his initiative that a war memorial to Australian troops who died in Vietnam had been erected outside Baria in Phuoc Tuy province. 'If you want Dr Dan to come to Australia, don't under any circumstances nominate him yourself', said a message from a friendly official in Canberra. 'Your association with him is well known to the government, which is waiting for your application only to turn it down.'

I passed on the names of the two Vietnamese doctors to the Australian consular officials. They did not come within Mr Whitlam's new ground rules. For two *hoi chanh* (Viet Cong or North Vietnamese defectors) to whom I was immensely indebted for assistance, and whose lives seemed certain to be forfeited if they were still in Saigon when it fell, I pleaded all the way to the highest levels in the American Embassy. I was assured that Ambassador Martin had personally approved their evacuation, but along with many others they were destined to remain–and to die. For the *hoi chanh* the North Vietnamese had special care. They sent them back to the units from which they had defected and brought them to trial before special courts. There were more than 200,000 of them in South Vietnam when Saigon fell, and every file, every dossier, fell into the victors' hands.

Miller and I sat too long over our coffee that morning, depressing each other with our own helplessness. 'Let's get out of town', said Miller. 'At least we can see what's happening in the countryside.' We picked up a hire car outside the Continental, planning to head for Xuan Loc, about forty miles to the east and not much more than a comfortable hour's drive. Both of us, in the words of a Korean photographer with whom I had once worked, liked to test the bridge by tapping the stone. We stopped to look once again at the memorial to the Unknown Soldier on Route 1. It was the most moving piece of statuary in Vietnam. The statue in front of the National Assembly building in Saigon was hideous, but the Unknown Soldier, sitting wearily and helmeted by the roadside at Thu Duc, a picture of utter fatigue, was the embodiment of the tragedy and the suffering of the war. Having depressed ourselves again, we decided to tap the stone at Bien Hoa

The Miller luck was working again. News agencies like to be first with the news, and this day Miller was hours ahead with the report of the first North Vietnamese attack on Xuan Loc, headquarters of the 18th ARVN Division. After an intensive bombardment with rockets, mortars and 130-millimetre artillery, infantry battalions of the 6th North Vietnamese Division had broken into the town. No less significantly, the North Vietnamese had brought their 130-millimetre guns within range of the Bien Hoa airfield, putting the field virtually out of commission to coincide with the ground attack on Xuan Loc. The battle for Saigon had begun.

Saigon knew the importance of Xuan Loc. The headquarters of Military Region 3 at Long Binh were twenty miles to the east, and twenty miles closer to Saigon. If Xuan Loc was to fall, this last major defensive position before Saigon, and the air base at Bien Hoa, would come under direct threat.

With three divisions, the 7th, the 341st and the 6th, concentrated for the attack on Xuan Loc, General Dung believed that the town

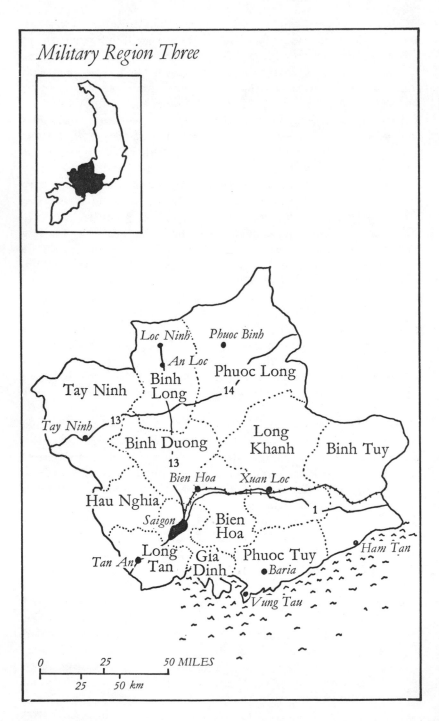

Military Region Three

Loc Ninh   Phuoc Binh

An Loc

Binh
Long   Phuoc Long

Tay Ninh   14

Tay Ninh   13

Binh Duong   Long
Khanh   Binh Tuy

13

Bien Hoa   Xuan Loc

Hau Nghia

Saigon   Bien
Hoa   1

Long   Gia   Phuoc Tuy   Ham Tan
Tan An   Tan   Dinh   Baria

Vung Tau

0   25   50 MILES

25   50 km

would fall easily and quickly. He was mistaken. The 18th Division had never been regarded as one of ARVN's best. On the contrary, it had once been considered one of the worst. In these closing days of the Vietnam War, however, it fought with courage and determination, not only holding its ground but counter-attacking day after day.

Any lingering doubts that the persistent Northern attacks on Xuan Loc represented the beginning of the offensive against Saigon were erased on the third day of the battle when we learned that the 341st Division had been committed to the fight. Part of North Vietnam's strategic reserve, it arrived in Quang Tri province from North Vietnam in January and, without being committed to action, moved all the way to Military Region 3 along the new highways that had been built by the North Vietnamese in the Annamite Chain. It had last been reported, about a week earlier, forty miles to the north of Saigon. 'This is not only a remarkable and speedy tactical manoeuvre, but an indication, also, of the formidable nature of the challenge to Saigon building up east of the Dong Nai River', I wrote that night.

The sound of the battle did not yet reach the city. It did not need to. Unlike Phnom Penh, which was suffering from melancholia, Saigon was experiencing both fear and a deep sense of betrayal. Betrayal by Thieu, who had failed to give the country the leadership it needed when the crisis came, betrayal by those who had failed to take the war seriously, betrayal by some who had grown rich on corruption, but beyond all, betrayal by the United States and the world.

'This is the only war ever lost in the columns of the *New York Times*', said an intellectual who detested the Communists, but saw no possible means of escape, as we discussed ways and means over a Coca Cola in my room at the Continental. He was not exaggerating very much. For the *New York Times*, and many others, had succeeded in creating an image of South Vietnam that was so distant from the truth as not even to be good caricature.

From those early days in 1963, when Reston cheered David Halberstam on to further revelations as the source of truth (in contradistinction to the u.s. Embassy, which was the purveyor of falsehood), the *New York Times*, whether consciously or unconsciously, had played the role of opposition. Some of its more senior staff members, notably Anthony Lewis, whose first-hand knowledge of South Vietnam was negligible, wanted the North to win. In terms of propaganda value, nothing was more significant than Harrison Salisbury's visit to North Vietnam at Christmas 1966, under the care of Wilfred Burchett, who devoted many years of his life to the propagation of the North Vietnamese Communist faith. Salisbury's despatches, making no reference to his constant association in Vietnam with Burchett, marked a turning point in the anti-war movement.

'Never have so many lies been written about so small a country', said Dr Dan. 'There are very few countries in Asia today that live under less dictatorial circumstances than we do.' Coming from almost any Vietnamese other than Dan this sort of remark might have seemed irrelevant. But Dan over the years, in and out of government, had established a reputation for himself of absolute frankness and honesty. There was simply no comparison between Vietnam under Diem and Vietnam under Thieu. Years before Dan had bitterly attacked the United States for its blind support of Diem and the injustices his family committed. 'The only message the Americans bring is anti-Communism', he said. 'They criticize the Communists for the very things they countenance here . . . The sad result is that many South Vietnamese believe that the United States is just a bigger South Vietnam, with more corruption, more nepotism, and bigger concentration camps. The Americans intervene when they want to. Why don't they intervene when moral issues are at stake? They accept military and economic responsibilities. They must also accept a moral responsibility.'

Seventeen years had passed since Dan made those remarks. In the interim, he had spent three and a half years in prison and had re-emerged to help shape a society that, with all its faults, permitted more freedom of expression and action than I have seen in any country, including my own, in time of war.

On 18 April the Saigon *Post* published a long open letter to the people of Vietnam and America. It was apparently written by an American who had been in the Army in Vietnam in 1966, married a Vietnamese and settled down. He wrote:

A few days ago while riding to Bien Hoa in the back of a small bus with my wife, there were two very small children sitting all alone crying because their young mother had gone in search of her husband who had fled from the Highlands, so they had to return alone. Another woman was crying because her son had just been buried. A man was crying because he had lost his whole family in Hue. Another woman showed us the picture of her husband and five children who were still trapped in Danang when it fell to the Communists, and as she talked the same tears and choking sobs started. I had to turn away. I could not look at her face. All I could do was hang my head and stare at the floor in my shame. I felt her pain and sorrow choking me as I sat with tears running from my eyes and dropping to the floor. This is the Vietnam of today. All sorrow, all pain, all blood and bones and endless, endless tears. This is the Vietnam that you, the great humanitarian people of America have created. The Vietnam that you now refuse to take responsibility for and traitorously turn your back on.

Anti-Americanism increased in Saigon as the full weight of the North Vietnamese attack at Xuan Loc became apparent and Nixon's pledges were seen to have been some sort of confidence trick. President Ford's speech to Congress on 12 April was made without consultation with the Government of Vietnam, which viewed with dismay his decision to put a 19 April deadline on emergency military aid. I wrote that night:

> If Congress rejects the President's appeal on or before 19 April, it must be expected that the decision will be as catastrophic as President Thieu's ill-fated strategic withdrawal from the Highlands. If the South Vietnamese government had been consulted, it would have advised strongly against it. The incoming news from Washington suggests that Congress is most unlikely to accede to President Ford's request. If it is rejected out of hand, senior Vietnamese officials fear that it may precipitate a collapse. If it is postponed indefinitely, the regrouped South Vietnamese forces will lack the weapons with which to fight. After the tragic events in Danang, no one can predict what would happen here.

What was predictable immediately after the President's speech was the imminent fall of Phnom Penh. In August 1973, when the Nixon Administration believed that it was on the point of making a breakthrough in negotiations to end the war in Cambodia, Congress ordered the cessation of American bombing and, according to Philip C. Habib, Assistant Secretary of State for East Asian and Pacific Affairs, effectively thwarted the negotiations. 'Beginning in early 1973 and going through mid-1973', he told a U.S. Senate Committee on International Relations, 'there was a series of contacts and discussions which we characterized as extremely promising. Just as they appeared to be approaching a serious stage, there is no doubt about that, that was when the bombing halt was legislated.'

At the beginning of March 1975, Habib was back in the committee appealing for approval for emergency aid just to keep the ammunition up to the Cambodian forces, now fighting so desperately for their lives around Phnom Penh. But Congress had given Cambodia away.

By 6 April Cambodia's stocks of ammunition had declined to the point where it had only fifteen days of supply left. By 11 April funds had run out to make any further air drops to enclaves of government forces. In Phnom Penh there was enough ammunition left to last another two weeks.

On 12 April the U.S. Ambassador in Phnom Penh, Mr John Gunther Dean, sent a letter to Prince Sirik Matak implying that the Americans had to leave and that he should go with them. An hour and a half before Dean took off, he received the following reply:

Phnom Penh
12 April 1975

Dear Excellency and Friend,

I thank you sincerely for your letter and for your offer to transport me towards freedom. I cannot, alas, leave in such a cowardly fashion.

As for you and in particular for your great country, I never believed for a moment that you would have this sentiment of abandoning a people which has chosen liberty. You have refused us your protection and we can do nothing about it. You leave and my wish is that you and your country will find happiness under the sky.

But mark it well that, if I shall die here on the spot and in my country that I love, it is too bad because we all are born and must die one day. I have only committed this mistake of believing in you, the Americans.

Please accept, Excellency, my dear friend, my faithful and friendly sentiments.

Sirik Matak

Sirik Matak was executed at the Cercle Sportif some days after the Khmer Rouge took over.

On 16 April Pochentong airport fell and the following morning the Khmer Rouge over-ran Phnom Penh. Useless and corrupt Lon Nol, who had fled the country on 1 April with the promise of a million dollars to provide for his retirement, was in Hawaii.* The no less corrupt Sihanouk was in Peking. Long Boret, who had seen Lon Nol off, flew back under fire to Phnom Penh, while the airport was still open, to what he must have known was certain death. Chang Song, the minister of information, who had sworn to remain 'to do what he could', was also executed.

Watching the ease with which Cambodia could be disposed of by Congress, the South Vietnamese realized at last that there would be no miracles to save Saigon. People clung to each other for security. You saw it at the front, where the villagers stayed with the troops close to the line, despite the rockets, and shells and the constant presence of death, until the position collapsed.

Then they fled with the troops, taking what they could, blocking the roads and tracks, terribly afraid, terribly confused. It used to be said by those who favoured the Communists that the peasants ran to the government side, or to the American side, because they knew they would be safe from shelling and bombing there. There was no way of proving whether this was true or false until the last offensive.

In Saigon fear did strange things to people. Naturally enough, business had all but ceased in the French restaurants, but the Vietnamese

---

* The money was to have been paid in instalments. It is possible that he received only the first $200,000.

restaurants were as crowded as they usually were during the festivities before the lunar new year. 'People think they will never have a chance to enjoy a good meal again', said Bui Anh Tuan. 'We want to enjoy things, but food doesn't taste the same any more.'

Nothing was the same any more. Day and night there was the same nagging fear. When I was at my hotel people rang me at all hours of the night during the curfew to find out if I knew anything.

There was a charming telephonist at the Australian Embassy who was married to an air force officer. Every day I called there she asked me about the situation. I told her I didn't think the war would last very long. She closed her eyes and clasped her hands together in prayer. 'Thank God', she said. By Canberra's instruction she was left to her fate.

Not always, but often, the Europeans distinguished themselves by their duplicity. They simply walked out, caught a plane and never returned. Yet the loyalty to their firms persisted among the Vietnamese. The foreign banks, for instance, continued to do business with a smile long after the managers had gone, often without a hint that they were off.

Even among the Vietnamese there was always the expectation that the individual fears would become collective and infectious and totally destructive. I was sure it wouldn't happen. And it didn't. For behind the fear there was also dignity.

Almost imperceptibly at first, and then very quickly, the city began to wither away. You noticed it first in small ways. The cyclos, for so long such an essential part of the city life, had been found to be carrying plastic high explosives instead of people and were put out of business. But instead of a shortage of taxis, there were never so many seeking passengers.

The number of beggars in the streets increased sharply. The wharves were suddenly almost empty, because ships did not dare to come up the river. Airlines began to shun Tan Son Nhut airport as if it had the plague, though not a single rocket or shell had fallen there at this time.

It was a city full of plans–plans to escape, plans to fight on, plans to negotiate, plans to form a government in exile, plans to commit suicide. A brilliant youth of twenty-two–I had known him since he was born–told me he had a grenade. But not to tell his father. The adults preferred barbiturates,* although one morning outside the Continental a man plunged a knife deep into his heart and died, with the hilt sticking in the air, on the grass by the monument in front of the National Assembly building. The city went on around him.

---

* General Phu, who led the disastrous retreat from the Highlands, was among those who took his life in this way after the fall of Saigon. He was offered, and rejected, the chance to go to the United States.

'I don't hate the Americans as I used to hate the French', one of my friends said to me years before. He paused for a moment, then added, 'But I expect to'. I asked him if he remembered. 'I don't hate', he said. 'I'm just disillusioned.' Non-American Westerners began to display their national flags prominently on their homes and cars, and even to wear small flags in their lapels. The run on the banks went on and on, as people raced against time to turn piastres into gold, or travellers' cheques, or diamond rings, or anything else that might be carried easily.

On the night of 11 April Dr Henry Kissinger apparently briefed the home offices of the *New York Times*, the *Washington Post*, *Time* and *Newsweek* about the real situation and the difficulties in arranging a secure evacuation. It resulted in some abrupt departures to join the 7th Fleet. About the same time, a member of a Congressional investigation committee in Saigon phoned Dan Southerland, the *Christian Science Monitor's* excellent correspondent. 'Don't leave your departure too late', he said. 'You can't trust the Embassy's evacuation plan. It won't work.' Southerland decided to stay.

The day after President Ford delivered his speech I called on Tran Van Lam in his office in the Senate. He ran through the situation and the poor chances of getting more aid. He regarded the letters from Nixon to Thieu as of great significance. They were either binding on the United States to act or were one of the shabbiest confidence tricks in the history of allied relationships. One, dated 14 November 1972, when Saigon had rejected the first Kissinger-Tho plan and Nixon was trying to come up with a formula that might satisfy Thieu, said, in part, 'But far more important than what we say in the agreement is what we do in the event the enemy renews its aggression. You have my absolute assurance that if Hanoi fails to abide by the terms of the agreement, it is my intention to take swift and retaliatory action.' In the same letter, Nixon repeated the pledge, saying, 'I repeat my personal assurances to you that the United States will react very strongly and rapidly to any violation of the agreement.'

A second letter, dated 5 January 1973, read:

Dear Mr President,
This will acknowledge your letter of 20 December 1972. There is nothing substantial that I can add to my many previous messages, including my 17 December letter, which clearly stated my opinions and intentions. With respect to the question of North Vietnamese troops, we will again present your views to the Communists as we have done vigorously at every other opportunity in the negotiations. The result is certain to be once more the rejection of our position.

We have explained to you repeatedly why we believe the problem of North Vietnamese troops is manageable under the agreement, and I see no reason to repeat all the arguments.

We will proceed next week in Paris along the lines that General Haig explained to you. Accordingly, if the North Vietnamese meet our concerns on the two outstanding substantive issues in the agreement, concerning the DMZ (demilitarized zone) and the method of signing, and if we can arrange acceptable supervisory machinery, we will proceed to conclude the settlement. The gravest consequences would then ensue if your Government chose to reject the agreement and split off from the United States. As I said in my 17 December letter, 'I am convinced that your refusal to join us would be an invitation to disaster–to the loss of all that we have together fought for over the past decade. It would be inexcusable above all because we will have lost a just and honourable alternative.'

As we enter this new round of talks, I hope that our countries will now show a united front. It is imperative for our common objectives that your Government take no further actions that complicate our task and would make more difficult the acceptance of the settlement by all parties. We will keep you informed of the negotiations in Paris through daily briefings of Ambassador Lam.

I can only repeat what I have so often said: the best guarantee for the survival of South Vietnam is the unity of our two countries which would be gravely jeopardized if you persist in your present course. The actions of our Congress since its return have clearly borne out the many warnings we have made.

Should you decide, as I trust you will, to go with us, you may have my assurance of continued assistance in the post settlement period and that we will respond with full force should the settlement be violated by North Vietnam. So once more I conclude with an appeal to you to close ranks with us.

Sincerely,

Richard Nixon

His Excellency Nguyen Van Thieu,
President of the Republic of Vietnam,
SAIGON.

These letters, at this moment in Vietnam's history, were obviously news. But Lam didn't know whether to give them to me for publication or not. As a newspaperman, my first reaction was to publish and be damned. My second was more cautious. I really did not have any right to offer advice that might lead to a Congressional backlash while there was still any chance that Vietnam might get the additional military aid it obviously needed. I promised to sound out others more qualified than myself.

The response among other Western diplomats was so mixed that I had the American Embassy toss it up to Ambassador Martin. He was unable to make up his mind whether it would be helpful or unhelpful, and I was asked whether I would delay for twenty-four hours while the question was put in Washington. Thirty-six hours later, the reply came back, 'It wouldn't be helpful at this time'. The Embassy implied that the response came from the White House.

I phoned Tran Van Lam, who was just taking off for a lightning visit to Taipeh, and told him. He held the letters until Congress had turned thumbs down, and then, before returning to Vietnam, released the text, or part of the text, to the Associated Press.

Over a period of several days Thieu conducted a number of meetings with political and religious leaders in the bomb-proof shelter under the palace, which he had now begun to use after the bombing attack. It was totally self-contained, with a communications system that enabled him to be in constant touch with all generals, all military units, province chiefs and district chiefs. Thieu was concerned that the response to the call for a new cabinet had been so meagre, and he continued to regard Ky with the gravest suspicion. Although Thieu was well aware by this time that Ky had nothing to do with the attack on the palace, he planned to resurrect the incident, if necessary, as a basis for Ky's arrest.

It was not easy to arrest Ky, however, while he remained within the security of the air base. According to Ky, plans were then made by General Dang Van Quang, Thieu's special adviser on security, and up to his ears in every type of corruption, including the drug traffic, to arrange for Ky's assassination. Ky's guards caught one of the would-be assassins, who said that fifteen special passes normally issued to the security forces had been given to the men assigned to kill him. 'We were told to wait for orders', the would-be assassin told Ky, 'but I beg you to remain in the house. If you go out, you could be killed.'

While Saigon waited for Congress to make up its mind on aid, and the ARVN continued to resist at Xuan Loc and Phan Rang, a new factor had to be taken into consideration. The French had offered their good offices to arrange a ceasefire, and the word spread that if only Thieu would step down Hanoi would negotiate. Over the years the U.S. and the South Vietnamese had succeeded in penetrating Hanoi's Central Office for South Vietnam, just as Hanoi had penetrated high levels of government in Saigon. Late in March the agents in COSVN reported the Politburo decision to go for an all-out military victory. Thomas Polgar, the C.I.A. station chief in Saigon, who was well aware of the accuracy of other reports from the same sources in earlier years, did not believe it. According to Ambassador Martin, 'At that time the report was not given that much credibility by the C.I.A. station chief.

It was not sent back [i.e. to Washington] by the C.I.A. station chief in the normal reporting channels. It was not until he was pressed by the officer who was in direct contact with this particular penetration to do so that this man was allowed to send it back through operational channels.'

Martin gave the report a much higher level of credibility than Polgar had been prepared to concede it. Polgar was not alone in his thinking, however. For months Washington had been toying with the idea of a political accommodation, the creation of an interim government, perhaps under General Duong Van Minh, the enlistment of some members of the Third Force, and an ultimately peaceful process of reunification.

The Hungarian delegation to the ICCS in Saigon was only too willing to further this concept, and Polgar was in frequent contact with the delegation to discuss the possibility of a political settlement and orderly withdrawal. On the one hand, the C.I.A. and the Defence Attaché's Office in Saigon were well aware of the vast movement of men and materials that was now targeting on Saigon, and of the utter incapacity of the government forces to meet the threat. On the other, they saw the tantalizing prospect of a halt to hostilities, a retreat with some semblance of honour–if only Thieu would go and make way for Big Minh.

On 13 April the Foreign Ministry in Hanoi issued a statement condemning President Ford's request to Congress for additional aid, but holding out what appeared to be several straws. It said that the Vietnamese people had no interest in maltreating their fellow country-men who had been led astray 'but now sincerely wish to redeem their past mistakes'. If they really wanted an honest life, those Vietnamese who had collaborated with the Americans would be 'well treated in the spirit of reconciliation and national concord'. It added, 'So long as the Ford administration is bent on keeping the Nguyen Van Thieu clique in the saddle to prolong the war and sabotage the Paris Agreement, it can only invite upon itself still heavier defeats'. In other words, if only Thieu would go, all would be well.

That all should not be well in the sense that a ceasefire or a political settlement ought not be allowed to stand in the way of the absolute military victory now so clearly in their grasp was very much in the minds of Le Duc Tho and General Dung. There were clearly advantages to be gained, however, from maintaining political pressure in Saigon. At all costs Saigon had to be prevented from organizing a last ditch stand.

Under pressure from Hanoi to launch the final offensive against

Saigon in the last ten days of April, General Dung was dismayed with the resistance put up by the 18th Division at Xuan Loc. 'Right at the outset', he conceded, 'the fight in Xuan Loc became fierce'. The 6th and the 341st North Vietnamese divisions were reinforced by the 7th Division, but still Xuan Loc held on. The artillery expended much more ammunition than Dung had expected and losses in tanks and armoured cars were also high. Dung wrote: 'At the outset, the IV Corps plan to attack Xuan Loc did not fully take into account the complex development of the situation, nor did it fully assess the enemy's stubbornness and the see-saw nature and fierceness of this battle, which was caused neither by the enemy's 18th Division nor the scope of the Xuan Loc-Long Khanh province battle itself, but by the fact that the Xuan Loc battle would determine the collapse or survival of the Saigon puppet administration and the prolongation of the Thieu regime's agony. It was, therefore, impossible for us to organize, command and conduct the fight as initially planned, so we had to change our fighting method according to the situation.'

The United States had provided the South Vietnamese with a handful of massive CBU-55B asphyxiation bombs that destroyed the oxygen over an area of two acres. These were intended to be a weapon of last resort against large formations of troops. When the target presented itself outside Xuan Loc, the Vietnamese Air Force dropped one of the bombs with stunning effect. Terrified North Vietnamese troops, who had seen the bomb drop but had been far enough away from the target area to survive, spread the rumour that the South Vietnamese were using tactical nuclear weapons.

General Dung decided that Bien Hoa had to be taken out, despite the expenditure this would involve in 130-millimetre artillery rounds. 'Don't waste your ammunition', said Nguyen Thanh Trung, who had defected after bombing Thieu's palace. 'You need to pump in only one shell every thirty minutes, because the pilots go to their planes from their shelters only half an hour after the last shell has landed.' Trung also advised that the South Vietnamese Air Force had been reduced in numbers to 120 A-37s and 70 F5Es, that only two-thirds of these were airworthy at any one time, and that, at most, they could make 120 sorties a day.

Much impressed with this intelligence, General Dung requested the High Command's authorization to send Trung to Danang to instruct the North Vietnamese MIG fighter pilots how to fly the A37s, which had fallen into their hands, and to form an A37 squadron for use if the need arose.

Disturbed by the failure of the repeated, and costly, frontal assaults against Xuan Loc, now heavily reinforced from Saigon's dwindling strategic reserve, General Dung decided to change his tactics, to concentrate overwhelming force against outlying government positions and against forces moving in to counter-attack. With the divisions now available to him, the tactic could not fail.

A steeply-increased flow of refugees along Route 1 to Bien Hoa told us that the tactic was working. In the early days of the fighting it was possible to drive along Route 1 to within a few miles of Xuan Loc and to watch the distant exchange of fire from villages where life was almost normal.

After pounding the district capital of Gia Kiem, about seven and a half miles north-west of Xuan Loc, with a thousand rounds of heavy artillery fire on the night of 15 April, Dung threw in a full division of North Vietnamese troops to attack the 18th Division's 52nd Regiment. The first ground attack came at 1 a.m. on the 16th and was driven off.

I drove that morning without difficulty to the intersection of Route 1 and a small road leading to Gia Kiem. The Vietnamese Air Force was bombing positions close to Gia Kiem and a bored looking couple of gunners were firing some harassing rounds to the south. It looked as if all was well within control, but for the refugees.

The columns of people pouring out from the by-road in an endless living stream were a reminder of the realities. They came on Hondas, or pushing carts, or on bicycles, with everything they could carry. They told us that Gia Kiem had fallen at four o'clock.

'Why did you run away?' one of my companions asked a woman who had been directed with thousands of others to make camp in a rubber plantation. 'I wanted to find peace', she said.

She would be lucky to find it where she was going. Ahead was the Bien Hoa airbase, which was now taking incoming fire round the clock, but neatly spaced to keep the pilots in their dugouts. Fourteen rounds of 130-millimetre artillery fire fell on the north-south runway during the night, badly damaging the surface. Other rounds destroyed the principal generator on the field.

The effect of Gia Kiem's fall was to make the 18th Division's position in Xuan Loc extremely vulnerable. It was now outflanked and unless it pulled back some miles was in real danger of being cut off. The ARVN had now identified the 325th North Vietnamese Division in the area, and the 316th, which had been plotted in Darlac Province on 11 April, was also known to be heading for Saigon.

'The very grave danger now', I cabled that night, 'is that Xuan Loc may have been a diversion, intended to tie down as many government forces as possible, while bolder plans were hatching for an attempted coup de grâce. This is the impression that the Poles and the Hungarians on the International Commission for Control and Supervision, perhaps the most ill-named of all supervisory bodies ever created, have been trying to spread. This may be propaganda, but the red flags on the map are moving so fast at the moment that a direct assault on Saigon in days cannot now be entirely discounted.'

The following day I teamed up with Keyes Beech to go back toward Xuan Loc. Beech likes to be where the action is. He does not tap on stone to test the bridge, and despite our driver's protestations, we drove through the village of Trang Bom, midway between Bien Hoa and Xuan Loc, without stopping. One moment we were in a roadway full of people, the next we were on our own. I suggested that it was becoming lonely, that perhaps we had gone far enough. 'There must be troops ahead', said Beech.

The sense of loneliness grew more oppressive, but ahead was a bend in the road. Once we turned we would be in full view of Xuan Loc.

On the slope of a hill to our left, and in front of a much damaged building, a soldier appeared and fired several warning shots with his rifle. Our driver responded as if he had received an electric shock and jammed his foot on the accelerator.

'I think he is anxious for us to stop', I said, trying to speak in a way that would not add to the driver's terror.

The soldier fired again and signalled us vigorously to turn back. By this time the driver had the message and we sped back to Trang Bom.

'You're lucky you didn't get any further', said a Vietnamese officer. 'The NVA (North Vietnamese) have got the road zeroed in.'

Trang Bom was not zeroed in, but rockets fell intermittently. Refugees were still dribbling out from over the hills. One family had two huge pigs in the back of a small three-wheeled bus. Others were driving their cattle along the road toward Bien Hoa, where every spare inch was crowded with refugees soon to be refugees again.

At the extremity of the ARVN line we found a woman sitting in her shack nursing a two-year-old girl. She had nine children, she said, and would not leave while there were still troops around. I assumed that she was a farmer's wife and that her husband was away in the fields. 'No', she said. 'He's a barber.' She pointed round the corner.

We found him busy at his trade. His name, he said, was Huynh Lo. He was fifty years of age and had fled from Danang after the Communists' 1972 Easter offensive, hoping to get away from the war.

His house was right in the rocket range now and the highway outside was littered with debris. No military vehicle ventured beyond this point.

216

'How many customers do you get each day?' I asked.

'Three or four', he replied.

'But before the fighting came here, how many?'

'Always the same', he replied. 'About three or four.'

And the price? A hundred and fifty piastres, or about twenty cents.

'Why do you stay?'

'If the Army stays, I will stay', he said. 'Where else do I earn my living? If the Army goes, I must go too.'

He did not stay much longer. That afternoon, to avoid being cut off, the 18th Division began to fall back closer to Bien Hoa.

We called at the American Consulate-General in Bien Hoa on the way back to Saigon. The car park was sprinkled with the ash of burnt documents, and there was no little agitation among the Americans there. In an arc around the Bien Hoa airbase they had plotted six North Vietnamese infantry divisions, a tank division, an armoured division and an anti-aircraft division.

Beech had a c.i.a. friend in the consulate and we dropped by for his assessment. He came up with the novel suggestion that since it was impossible now to conduct the large-scale evacuation of Vietnamese who wanted to leave the country, the United States should embark on a campaign to persuade people that it would be in their interests to remain. I told him what 'Nguyen Van Tri' of the National Liberation Front had to say, without, of course, mentioning his name. He took out his pad and scribbled a couple of notes. I didn't pay much attention to it at the time.

As we drove back into Saigon we noticed that the chimney at the American Embassy was belching black smoke. Vietnamese guards around military installations in the city had begun to wear flak jackets.

On all fronts there was disaster; or the signs of impending disaster. The Highland city of Dalat fell for no reason other than that the townsfolk saw Army officers loading their families aboard aircraft to go to Saigon. If it was time for the Army to move, it was time for everyone else.

The worst news of all came from Phan Rang, a charming little port, and Thieu's birthplace, where, on General Weyand's advice, the South Vietnamese had made some sort of an effort to block the southward advance of General Dung's three divisions in II Corps. On 4 April General Nguyen Van Nghi, who had been appointed by Thieu to hold the line here, met General Toan, commander of Military Region 3 at Bien Hoa. Nghi told Toan that to hold Military Region 3 it was imperative that Phan Rang should be held. 'If Phan Rang is lost', he said, 'there will be no way to hold Phan Thiet and Binh Tuy Province and therefore the belt around Saigon will be too thin'.

For the task, General Nghi wanted more resources than Toan or the Joint General Staff were prepared to offer from their dwindling resources. Nghi wanted a full, strong division. Toan replied, 'You ask for a full division. I can find it nowhere for you. But I'll give you the 22nd Paratroop Brigade, then later will send you the 22nd Infantry Division, which is just back from the north and has been reinforced.'

General Toan was still complacent. 'Don't worry', he said. 'The Viet Cong cannot organize a big push now. They have already grabbed too much land. They haven't yet got the necessary forces to attack Phan Rang and the southern provinces along the coast.'

Back in Phan Rang, General Nghi made his own reconnaissance. An attack on Phan Rang posed formidable problems for an enemy force, however large. There were only two possible lines of advance, along Route 1 from Cam Ranh Bay and the north, or along Route 2 from Dalat. Both offered excellent positions for a defending force. The Bellevue (Ngoan Muc) Pass on Highway 2 and the narrow defile through which Route 1 passed in the mountains near the coast were potential death traps for any attacking force.

Nghi deployed his forces to make the fullest use of the terrain. He put blocking forces in the defile on Route 1 and at the Bellevue Pass and dropped commando groups on the peaks of the mountains on a twelve to twenty miles radius from the town. With more troops at his disposal, Nghi looked forward even to taking the offensive, recapturing Dalat and Nha Trang.

Within a week all was in readiness to meet the attack. The air force reported that it had contributed its share and had bombed the bridges and culverts to the west and north.

With engineer forces in the lead to mend the bridges and culverts, followed by tanks and anti-aircraft batteries to provide protection, and with the infantry and artillery bringing up the rear, General Dung's II Corps broke into a number of columns for the march south. In 1962, during an exercise with only four hundred vehicles, the 308th Division had caused so many traffic jams that it could not advance. II Corps, with two thousand vehicles, not only advanced at astonishing speed but also fought on the way. Four days after General Nghi had established his Phan Rang defences, II Corps was knocking at the gates.

On 14 April, North Vietnamese forces struck north and north-east of Phan Rang airport. General Nghi sent a Ranger battalion to counter-attack, but this force was too small for the task and he had

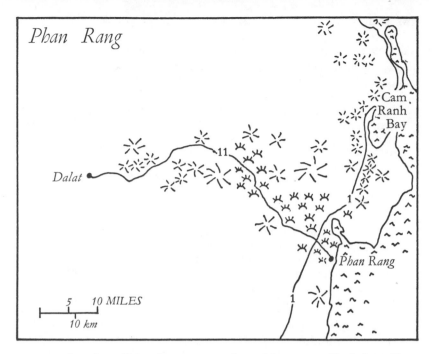

Phan Rang

Dalat

Cam
Ranh
Bay

Phan Rang

5 10 MILES

10 km

to commit a battalion of paratroops from his reserve. Both battalions took heavy casualties.

'I thought this was only a probe on your part, not a real prong of attack', General Nghi told his captors after the fall of Phan Rang. 'Then suddenly at 0300 on 15 April, I got a report from the air force that they had spotted many armoured columns, some having as many as two hundred tanks, rolling south along Route 1.'

The news surprised and shocked General Nghi. Earlier, he had been assured by the air force that the bridges had all been destroyed and that air attacks on the North Vietnamese tank columns had been highly successful. 'There's nothing to fear', Colonel Thao, commander of the air division, had told him. 'We scored many hits and many tanks were seen burning.'

On the morning of 16 April Phan Rang airport came under heavy shell fire. Some of the planes based there for attacks on the advancing Northern column could not land and flew back to Tan Son Nhut. Instead of bombing the advancing enemy, they had mistakenly attacked General Nghi's artillery. When the paratroops along Route 1 called urgently for artillery support, there was no response.

For what it was worth, General Nghi had been given the regrouped 22nd ARVN Division, which was heavily engaged with a small Northern decoy force on the road to Dalat. While it fought desperately to head off what it believed to be the main thrust, the Northern forces in overwhelming strength rolled down Route 1, through the paratroops' line of defence, effectively cutting off the 22nd Division.

Here is General Dung's account:

On 15 April the army corps approached Phan Rang, which the enemy was preparing to defend to the end. A friendly unit had been laying a siege on Thanh Son airfield and the puppet 6th Air Force Division for more than a week. That night the corps' long-range artillery detachments set up their positions along Route 1 and stood ready for action. Meanwhile, many detachments of ground troops supported by tanks formed many spearheads to close in on the airfield and the provincial capital, Phan Rang.

At 0500 on the morning of 16 April our tanks rumbled right into the provincial capital as the artillery batteries of the Corps opened up with continuous barrages onto the airfield and other enemy positions. The 3rd Division of the 5th Military Region also opened fire from the west and north-west on the airfield. Enemy troops panicked when a big force of our tanks suddenly materialized. They sent every armoured car available toward Route 1 in a bid to check our attack. Moving in from different directions, our tanks followed the ground troops, drove through the airfield and battled their way into the centre of the provincial capital. Enemy Rangers and paratroopers, together with their officers, took flight. Confused puppet pilots discarded their flying suits and joined the fleeing puppet infantrymen.

General Nghi's headquarters were at the airfield. Two of the gates to the airfield fell in quick succession, and at the same time the North Vietnamese forces entered the town. Surrounded on all four sides, General Nghi ordered his forces to retreat to Ca Na, about twenty miles south, and regroup. When the general's own car reached the main entrance to the airfield, Northern troops had already taken it. Both Nghi and Brigadier-General Pham Ngoc Sang, deputy commander of the 6th Air Force Division, were captured.

Perhaps a stand might still be made in the narrow passes north of Ca Na. Or so Saigon hoped. But on 17 April an Air America plane scouting over the Bay of Padaran counted twenty tanks south of Ca Na. They were all North Vietnamese.

'Since three North Vietnamese divisions are said to be involved in the major move along the coast, the breakthrough was perhaps to be expected', I cabled to London. 'It is still bitterly disappointing for the government. Since the road south of Ca Na follows the coast for the next five miles, naval gunfire may be able to slow the northern advance. But co-operation between the South's army and navy has not been close in the past six weeks.'

Nothing stopped the advance. Before the print was dry on my

message, Phan Thiet, far down the coast, was already under fire. Nothing the South Vietnamese could do with the military means available could save Saigon now. Nothing else was likely to be available, it was clear. President Ford's Congressional deadline for emergency military assistance for South Vietnam had expired, and now the Americans were concerned not with getting material in but their own people, some 6,000 of them, out.

On the evening of Sunday 20 April I met 'Nguyen Van Tri' and his daughter outside the house of our mutual friend in Saigon. 'How is the military situation?' he asked.

'Surely I don't need to tell you', I said. 'You must know that it is catastrophic.'

'Yes', he replied, 'but I think we have found the solution'.

General Tran Van Don, 'Nguyen Van Tri's' old contact, had taken over as defence minister in the new cabinet on Tuesday 14 April. He found the military situation hopeless. Every South Vietnamese division outside Saigon was held in check by three or more divisions. The battle for Xuan Loc was about to end, and there was nothing in the way of effective resistance that could be organized.

On the afternoon of 19 April, General Toan, the Military Region 3 commander, tried to see Thieu to explain to him that resistance would no longer be possible after 22 April. Thieu refused to see him. But on Sunday 20 April, he did see General Don, who told him the same thing.

Don had continued to see 'Nguyen Van Tri' during the week. 'Nguyen Van Tri' claimed that he had been asked by the Front to ensure the security of Saigon. If Thieu would stand down as president and Don became acting president, with himself as prime minister, a ceasefire could be arranged within forty-eight hours. The North Vietnamese forces would not enter Saigon.

Hanoi was clearly unhappy with the prospect of being placed in a situation where it would be obliged to settle for something less than absolute military victory. On behalf of the Politburo, Le Duan sent the following message to Dung and Tho: 'The military and political conditions are ripe for launching a general offensive against Saigon. We must take full advantage of every day in attacking the enemy from all directions without delay; and if we fail to do this, we will be in a disadvantageous military and political situation. Timely action is the firmest guarantee for complete victory. You must instruct our men in all directions to act in time . . . The opportunities facing us now demand that we act most quickly. By firmly seizing these great opportunities, we will surely win complete victory.'

Tho, Dung and Pham Hung met on 22 April after the arrival of the message from Le Duan to consider the final plans. They needed no reminder of the need for haste.

Thieu had long been aware of Don's contact with 'Nguyen Van Tri' and approved of it. Yet neither he nor Don was fully satisfied with his credentials, although 'Nguyen Van Tri' had now produced a cabinet list. Ever since the formation of the Can government, pressure had been mounting on Thieu to stand down as the one remaining barrier in the face of a negotiated settlement. If he didn't go now, it would be too late. The Hungarian delegation to the ICCS continued to urge Polgar to hasten Thieu's resignation as the one way of bringing about a political settlement. In Ambassador Martin's words, Polgar 'found it attractive'.

Martin saw Thieu on the morning of 20 April, an hour or two after Don's visit. He went armed with the latest intelligence and battle order reports from the Defence Attaché's Office, and the C.I.A. He said that the military order of battle and the analysis of the comparative forces each side could bring to bear provided a very grim picture. The conclusion was inescapable that, should Hanoi move in for the kill, it would be difficult for Saigon to last more than a month, even with the most skilful and determined defence, and probably not more than three weeks. He said that while it was his opinion that Hanoi wanted Saigon whole, and not a pile of rubble, one could not escape the possibility that it might elect the latter if there was no move toward negotiations.

He said that the military situation was very bad, and the Vietnamese people held Thieu responsible for it. The political class, both his supporters and his enemies, did not believe he could lead the country out of its present crisis. Almost all the generals, though they would continue to fight, believed defence was hopeless unless a respite could be gained through the beginning of the negotiating process, and they did not believe such a process could begin unless the President left, or took steps to see that the process began immediately. If he did not go soon, Martin added, it was his feeling that the generals would ask him to go.

Thieu asked whether his resignation would have any effect on the vote in Congress.

Martin replied that it might have changed some votes some months earlier, but it could not change enough now to affect the outcome. The important thing was perhaps the effect it would have on the other side. Martin personally thought it would make little difference. Hanoi would be opposed to any strong leader. They would insist on a much weaker man, if they were really interested in negotiating, but his colleagues felt it might buy time, which was now the essential commodity for Vietnam.

Thieu had still not made up his mind next morning, which was a morning I shall not lightly forget. It began with an alarmed call from one of 'Nguyen Van Tri's' friends. One of the top men in his proposed cabinet had been arrested. My friend had been told that the BBC, quoting the *Daily Telegraph*, had broadcast my account of 'Nguyen Van Tri's' plan. Did I think there was any connection?

My next caller was an acquaintance in the palace, which was very disturbed about the report I had sent out the previous evening. He thought he should see me. Since he was very much worried about his own future, and I was also indebted to him for help in the past, he wanted to warn me that there was talk of taking me in for questioning. Like many others, also, he wanted to know if I could help him get out. I said I didn't think I could, but I would have no chance at all if I was to spend the next few days in the lockup.

He had scarcely gone when I had a call from someone in the C.I.A. Could he come and talk to me?

By all means. In fact, I thought, in view of what I had just heard, it might be encouraging to have some influential company.

Keyes Beech arrived in my room just before the man from the C.I.A. put in an appearance. The conversation was rather difficult to conduct. The C.I.A. wanted to know 'Nguyen Van Tri's' identity. I said I was sorry but I couldn't oblige. He referred me to what I'd said at Bien Hoa the previous week and said that the C.I.A. had a similar report to mine, that time was desperately short, and that he needed to check on credentials. But the C.I.A. was also protecting its sources. He wasn't prepared to name his man.

I said there was a good deal of concern about the arrest early that morning of one of the men named for 'Nguyen Van Tri's' cabinet. Was this to be the beginning of a general roundup of all involved? He checked for me and found that the arrest was coincidental, which I passed on, putting an end to some agitation in a number of Saigon homes.

With the ground softened, we agreed on a compromise. We would exchange the man's occupation, an unusual one, and if we came up with the same answer we would exchange names. It was, of course, one and the same man. He had an impeccable revolutionary background, was a close friend of Nguyen Huu Tho, of the National Liberation Front, and had done some time in prison for his support of the peace movement.

As for my own situation, my c.i.a. visitor thought it might not be a bad idea to consider leaving Vietnam quickly. He would let me know. He was as good as his word. He phoned after lunch to say he thought I should stick around. Interesting things would happen later in the day.

My courage failed me. I did not dare to add to my previous night's message that Thieu had finally agreed to resign, but I had no doubt.

Although Thieu had agreed to go, he had rejected the Don-'Nguyen Van Tri' solution and baulked at handing over to Big Minh. Instead, he handed over to Tran Van Huong, the vice-president, an old, poetic, ancestor-worshipper. The Constitution had been preserved by the succession of the vice-president, whose only idea was to make peace as quickly as possible and on almost any terms. 'I am no de Gaulle', he said. 'You can call me a Petain if you like.'

That was not enough for Hanoi. In demolishing Thieu they had broken only one pillar of the government in Saigon. In their enclave at Tan Son Nhut, the Provisional Revolutionary Government representatives, in reality cosvn employees, whose functions theoretically were to assist in carrying out the terms of the Paris Agreement, were derisive. 'This farce cannot deceive anyone', said Major Phuong Nam, who was in daily radio communication with Le Duc Tho and General Dung through cosvn. 'Decidedly it cannot change the situation, and cannot help the United States avoid heavier defeats.' He described Thieu's resignation as a 'ridiculous puppet dance, a clumsy, deceptive trick manipulated by the United States in order to maintain the traitorous Thieu clique without Thieu'.

Instead of providing a chance to negotiate something short of unconditional surrender, Thieu's resignation led to a political crisis of catastrophic proportions. On the afternoon of 22 April Prime Minister Can told Don, his defence minister, that it was his turn to lead the government. He intended to resign as soon as the curfew was lifted at 7 a.m. the next day. Don consulted the military leaders during the afternoon and the majority appeared to favour his appointment. 'Nguyen Van Tri' also approved. It was expected that Huong, who was in frail health, might resign after the formation of a new cabinet and hand over constitutionally to Tran Van Lam.

Two and a half hours after the cabinet had resigned, however, Jean Merillon, the French ambassador, called on Huong and informed him that Thieu's resignation and the proposed cabinet changes did not go far enough to satisfy the North Vietnamese. Hanoi insisted not only on the removal of Thieu but also on the abandonment of the Constitution under which he was elected. Specifically, Hanoi wanted General Duong Van Minh as head of state.

The news staggered the military, although Minh's name had been bandied about for days. They were prepared to accept Don, who was popular, and, despite his association with 'Nguyen Van Tri', apolitical. They were not prepared to accept Big Minh, who was regarded with something very close to contempt.

President Huong also reacted badly to the proposal. The result was that two days after Thieu's resignation South Vietnam had a government of one frail, if dogged, old man.

So far as I knew on the evening of 23 April none of this was known to other correspondents. My original information was that the United States, France and North Vietnam were all a party to the agreement that Huong should stand down in favour of Big Minh. Since it was clearly a matter of substance whether the United States was involved, I checked with the American Embassy. 'I'm not sure that I'll be able to find out', said John Swenson, when I talked to him late in the afternoon. 'It could be that Washington is keeping that one to itself.'

Around 7 o'clock in the evening he phoned to say that although the United States was aware of the discussions that were taking place, it had had no part in them. I cabled accordingly.

Late that night I had a call from an old American friend. 'Do you know what's going out of this place tonight?' he asked.

'What do you mean?' I replied, thinking in terms of refugees, or evacuation.

'Big Minh', he said.

I replied that I knew about it. He doubted if I did. Polgar, the c.i.a. station chief, had invited the *New York Times*, the *New Yorker*, *U.S. News and World Report* and the *Los Angeles Times* for dinner, and had briefed them about the Big Minh deal. The United States, he told them, was fully involved.

Next morning I remonstrated with John Swenson. He was apologetic. 'Polgar was one of the people I checked with', he said.

On Friday 25 April, Don asked 'Nguyen Van Tri' whether, in the face of the imminent North Vietnamese attack on Saigon, the Front would support a Don government, in which Don himself was prime minister and defence minister, and Nguyen Xuan Oanh, deputy premier and minister of economic affairs. Oanh, one-time Harvard lecturer, former governor of the Bank of Vietnam, briefly acting prime minister, had, in recent years, been devoting himself to the production of movies.

'Nguyen Van Tri' was willing to support Don but only if he could guarantee security within Saigon, and asked for a 24-hour stay while he got in touch with the Saigon-Cholon committee of the National

Liberation Front, who were at that time somewhere in Long An province. That night Don and Oanh saw Ambassador Merillon and told him what was contemplated, and passed word, also, to the American Embassy.

This time the Front wanted 'Nguyen Van Tri' as prime minister. He swore that he could halt the attack on Saigon, and that no one else could succeed, least of all Big Minh. Don reported all of this to Huong. But it was not to be. The c.i.a. and the French, responding to Hanoi's pressure, wanted Big Minh, and the Southern Communists' desperate bid for a meaningful say in the affairs of South Vietnam had come to an end. Nothing now would stop the Northern tanks from driving into Saigon.

3. The Ho Chi Minh campaign

Some South Vietnamese leaders were still far from persuaded that there should not be a last ditch stand. Dr Dan wanted to fight. 'We can blow the bridges', he said, 'block the roads and turn Saigon into a fortress'.

'No one is making any preparation to blow the bridges', I said. 'The anti-tank ditches and obstacles that are going up round the city are useless. They wouldn't stop a tricycle with a resolute six-year-old in the saddle.'

He found this scarcely credible. 'If what you say is correct', he said, 'these are things that can be put right. We can still mine the bridges'. It was inconceivable, he believed, that Saigon could be abandoned without a fight. And he found it hard to comprehend that there was nothing left to fight with. But eventually a visit to Ambassador Martin persuaded him of the hopelessness of the situation and that he ought to make plans to leave.

Ky still wanted to fight, also. He saw Huong in the palace to ask him to appoint him commander of the armed forces. 'I can't do it', Huong said. 'Perhaps in a few days I might be able to appoint you my special assistant for military affairs.' There were very few days left.

General Van Tien Dung had enough force at his disposal now not only to destroy all government forces that stood in his path, but Saigon, also. The problem was not to win the war–it was already won–but to preserve the spoils of victory.

While his IV Corps, now reinforced by an additional regiment, and drawing also on the services of the 325th Division, was battering the 18th ARVN Division into the ground, Dung was making his preliminary moves to isolate Saigon, and to prevent the other divisions in Military Region 3, or the three divisions in Military Region 4 (in the Mekong Delta), which were still relatively unscathed, from moving to the defence of the capital.

The 25th ARVN Division had been fighting hard and well around Tay Ninh. Its officers were hurt that no one came to see it perform. Dung decided against launching an attack directly against Tay Ninh, since this might result in the destruction of the Cao Dai's Holy See, but decided to implant an irremovable obstacle on the road between Tay Ninh and Saigon. One regiment of the 316th Division crossed the Saigon River well above the city. From the outskirts of the Tra Vo rubber plantation, and for a considerable distance along the road to Saigon, it formed a barrier that the 25th ARVN Division could not pass.

Five North Vietnamese divisions, the 3rd, the 5th, the 7th, the 8th and the 9th, were already at their jumping off points, ready to move. Three independent regiments, the 16th, the 88th and the 24th, were also ready. The 10th Division had been left behind at Cam Ranh Bay to clean up. Dung ordered up fresh transport from the North and told the divisional commander to commandeer cars, buses and trucks to get the troops to the Saigon front on time.

South-west of Saigon, in Kien Tuong Province, the North Vietnamese forces were ready to cut Route 4, thus ending any hope Saigon may have had of getting reinforcements from the Delta.

To the north-east, Dung's II Corps had taken Ham Tan, the provincial capital of Binh Tuy Province, about a hundred miles from Saigon. This removed the last government strongpost on the coastal road and an early attack on Phuoc Tuy Province, and the seaport of Vung Tau, where about 4,000 Marines, for what they were worth (Colonel Dong told me they weren't worth anything and ought to be disbanded), had been regrouped. It also meant that within two or three days ships using the Saigon River would come under artillery fire, thus closing one of Saigon's two commercial links with the outside world. The second was Tan Son Nhut airport, on which the big guns were also moving.

In a letter dated 21 April and delivered by hand in an envelope marked urgent, the Australian Embassy issued what it described as a final warning to Australians still living in Vietnam. 'Further to my letter of 17 April, the present security situation in Saigon now compels me to warn you of the desirability of leaving the country without delay',

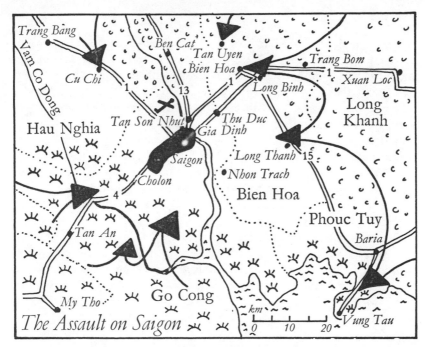

The Assault on Saigon

wrote Ambassador Geoffrey Price. 'Unless you plan to stay in Saigon regardless of the consequences, I strongly suggest that you should now plan to leave.'

A very large crowd filled the gracious Roman Catholic cathedral at the top of rue Catinat one morning. For the first time in living memory Catholics, Buddhists and Cao Daiists met together in a religious ceremony. They prayed for a political end to the war–and for peace.

I sat next to a pretty young Vietnamese woman, with a fair-haired girl, aged about four or five, the child, I guessed, of an American father. The young woman wept as she prayed.

Although there were many tears, impending disaster had also brought for the first time a sense of need and a unity that had not existed before. To see a Buddhist flag lying on the altar of the Catholic cathedral laid to rest much of the bigotry and lack of understanding that had kept the followers of the two religions so far apart. I wondered what might have happened if something like this had occurred in the past.

Outside the cathedral members of all participating faiths handed out leaflets calling for an immediate end to the fighting and the establishment of the national council for reconciliation. The leaflets also called on the United States, the Soviet Union and China–Red China was the wording–to bring about a political solution to the war and real peace.

For some days now I had had three addresses. I had booked a room in the hotel that housed UPI and its cabling facilities. I kept my room at the Continental for daytime work and the nights when I did not need either to cable after curfew, or was unable to get to Dacao, where I was staying with an old friend, Le Van Duyet. Duyet was married to an Australian girl. She wouldn't take her young children and leave for Australia because she was sure that if she did Duyet would be unable to get out. She had no intention of losing him.

Duyet had a top job with the government telecommunications, and was most unlikely to be granted a passport which, according to Ky, now cost $20,000, payable to General Quang, President Thieu's special adviser.

Duyet had been educated in Australia, was about to be granted Australian citizenship and, with or without passport, was not going to be left behind by the Australian Embassy when it left, whatever the rules laid down by Canberra. I had the firmest assurance on this point, and was utterly convinced, but won my point only when I agreed to move in when the family took off. Often I failed to turn up before curfew, of course, and sometimes Duyet stayed in his office all night, but we nevertheless maintained close communications.

On Sunday 20 April, he spent his weekly day off distributing medicines and rice to Cambodian refugees in a camp outside Saigon. The authorities could no longer hope to provide adequately for their own refugees, and the Cambodians were at the far end of a very lean line. With subscriptions from his friends, Duyet had bought enough rice to give one entire camp at least one good meal.

There was a chance for him to leave Saigon the following day–without an exit visa, of course. 'I can't', he said. 'I've got a most important meeting'.

I argued that it might be his last chance, that once he had gone the meetings would have to manage without him. He was adamant.

Two days later another chance occurred. Duyet agreed to go. My part in the arrangements was simple and minor. All I had to do was to turn up at his house in a large American car, carry out his bags as if they were mine, and put them in the boot. Then together we would go to a rendezvous point near Tan Son Nhut airport. We were to be at the rendezvous point at 1.30 p.m. The plane left at 2.30 p.m.

I arrived fifteen minutes early to find that Duyet had gone–with all his baggage. I went back to the Continental. He wasn't there. I phoned the rendezvous point. He wasn't there.

At about 1.50 I got to the rendezvous. Still no sign of him. Two o'clock passed and he still hadn't appeared. At 2.05 he turned up in his own car–with his parents, his sister and brother-in-law and their children.

'I can't leave them', he said.

I told him there was only one place aboard the plane, that nothing he could do would get the others aboard, that heartbreaking as it might be he would have to leave them behind.

'Well, then, I'll get them on the American airlift', he said.

I pleaded again that he would miss his plane. He was not to be dissuaded.

As he drove off, the Australian car which was to whisk him through the guards on the Air America terminal turned up. I was decidedly unpopular. 'You mean to say you just let him go?'

'But what was I to do?'

The minutes sped by. We'd given up all hope that Duyet would make the plane, when, drenched with sweat, and alone, he returned. Somehow he had talked the entire family into the American airlift. He didn't have time to explain. And he caught his own plane just as the doors were closing on the RAAF flight to Bangkok. Vietnam lost a good man and Australia gained one.

By the middle of the week the North Vietnamese had pushed along Route 1 almost to Trang Bom. The 18th Division was breaking under pressure.

I had lunch on Thursday with Geoffrey Fairbairn, of the Australian National University, and Luu Tuong Quang, then acting head of the Vietnamese Foreign Ministry. Quang confirmed the dismal news we had heard elsewhere. We left him to go out in the direction of Trang Bom to see for ourselves and arranged to meet at another friend's house for breakfast the following morning.

Once again the road beyond Bien Hoa was jammed with refugees, but this time among them were many soldiers, some with their weapons, some without. They just drifted along. A surprisingly high proportion were from the élite Airborne.

Once, on the way back, two soldiers, still with their rifles and wearing helmets and flak suits, tried to thumb a lift. The driver stopped incautiously and then, thinking better of it, drove off. I had no means of gauging Geoffrey's feelings, but every second I expected to feel the thump of a bullet on the back of the head. I didn't dare look back.

We tried to estimate how many people we saw on a six or seven mile stretch of road. We thought it might have been around 10,000.

All along the way from Bien Hoa to Saigon there were little groups of soldiers, thumbing lifts on buses, or just walking.

I checked with Air Vietnam late that afternoon. A seat I had booked in reserve for Friday had already been sold. Nothing else was available. The time for the final decision had arrived. I could either evacuate with the Australian Embassy on the following day, or chance it with the Americans at the last moment. I decided to go.

At breakfast next morning we tried to persuade Quang to come with us. 'No one in the Foreign Ministry has left', he said. 'We are unique. We had a meeting yesterday and decided that no one would go while there was still resistance'. We shook hands at his car and stiff and erect he drove off to the Foreign Office. He was still there when the North Vietnamese tanks entered Saigon and then, with great daring and courage, made his own extraordinary escape. He, too, is in Australia. What I said of Duyet is also true of Quang.

My concern now was for Tuan and his family. He was confident he would escape. Like many other antiCommunist Vietnamese, Tuan had maintained contact with American Embassy officials. A friend of his, working for the c.i.a., gave assurances that he and his immediate family would go on an early flight. It turned out that prominent people were not allowed to leave until the last moment; so he was pessimistic about his own chances. 'You and I know there will be no last moment', he said. I agreed, but what neither of us knew was that the Russians had assured Washington there would be no move by the North Vietnamese to block the u.s. withdrawal. The Americans would be allowed to leave with whatever dignity they could still muster. This did not apply, however, to all the Vietnamese who had been promised safe passage.

There was so much to be done on my last day and so little time in which to do it. My two defector friends turned up, one with an auto-graphed copy of a book he had written. I assured them they were on the American evacuation list, but told them I could give no guarantee that it would work. The phone rang repeatedly and the room began to fill with old friends, some who knew they were going and some who knew they had no chance of going. The Australian Embassy was taking out the mother of the Vietnamese ambassador in Canberra. She came with an elderly sister, who was staying behind. There was nothing sweet about the sorrow of that parting. Tuan had some gold and planned to rip out the working parts of a camera, so that I could fill it with ingots and carry it out. At the last moment, he decided against the scheme.

Two girls arrived with a box of travellers' cheques– $36,000 worth. I pushed them into my brief case and promised to deliver them safely to a relation outside.

A cousin in Australia had asked me to give some money to a child she had 'adopted', a chore I had overlooked. The son of one of my friends took off to deliver a few dollars. The piastre had lost almost all value, and at the end I was left with thousands to distribute to friends on the hotel staff. Monsieur Loi was there to see me off. 'I fear you will not come again', he said, shaking my hand for the last time.

The assembly point was outside the consulate and opposite Dr Dan's house. I was relieved to see his furniture and pot plants being removed and thought he had gone, but it was just the government reclaiming its property. As deputy prime minister, Dan had a modest house. Out of office, he was also out of home.

It was Anzac Day. This year, for the first time, there would be no memorial service at the war memorial in Phuoc Tuy Province for the Australians who fell in the Vietnam War. During the period that the Australian Task Force was in Vietnam nearly 50,000 Australian soldiers passed through the province. Their security depended not only on their own efforts but on the co-operation of the local people. In most areas, this was freely given and the relationship between the people and the Task Force was exemplary. Scores of officials, ranging from the province chiefs down to village and hamlet administrators, worked closely with the Australians. Now that the moment had come to say goodbye, the Australian Government made no effort to ascertain whether anyone in Phuoc Tuy wanted to leave, and no attempt was made to help anyone escape. The last Hercules flights left Saigon late in the afternoon of 25 April. They carried, among other things, a basket of cats for U.N. officials. Among others left behind were the Vietnamese employees of the Embassy. When the Embassy shut its doors its books were up-to-date as of 6 p.m. on 24 April. These had been prepared by a woman whose own life was thought to be endangered and whose application for evacuation had been rejected by Canberra.

As early as 1 April Geoffrey Price had reported to Canberra that the Embassy would begin receiving requests, on humanitarian grounds, from various categories of Vietnamese, for permission to go to Australia. With no authority to decide for himself, he proposed consideration of a number of categories, including relatives of Vietnamese married to Australians; locally engaged staff and their families; Vietnamese students in Australia who might also ask for their parents to be allowed entry; and possibly Vietnamese in official positions who might regard themselves as potential political refugees. He sought instructions. For three weeks, while the opportunity to help those in need slipped away, he waited impatiently and desperately for the government's decision.

During this period Hanoi exerted strong pressure on the Whitlam Government not to help in the evacuation. Also on 1 April the Foreign Ministry in Hanoi told Mr David Wilson, the Australian ambassador, that the government of the Democratic Republic of Vietnam had no objection to 'true humanitarian' action in the 'Saigon-held or PRG-held zones', but that evacuation plans were not, in fact, humanitarian and did not help the South Vietnamese people or friendly relations between Australia and North Vietnam.

Confronted with these opposing recommendations, Mr Whitlam on 2 April, assumed personal control of Australian policy regarding Vietnamese refugees. Every application for entry required his personal approval. He was not sympathetic. The Vietnamese sob stories, he said once, did not wring his withers.

All the time Hanoi continued to apply pressure on Canberra. On 6 April its chargé d'affaires in Canberra told the Department of Foreign Affairs that his government had been 'surprised' at the Australian Government's decision to make available RAAF aircraft for use in South Vietnam. He said that although the Democratic Republic of Vietnam understood that the planes had been made available for humanitarian reasons, there were other ways of helping the peoples of South Vietnam. Two days later Wilson saw Tien, the Provisional Revolutionary Government representative in Hanoi, who handed him a written request for $2 million for 'initial emergency humanitarian aid to buy goods for our people'.

On 20 April, Price, who was still awaiting Canberra's decision on refugees, predicted in a despatch to Canberra a North Vietnamese victory by the end of April. He reported the imminent or completed evacuation of several other embassies and recommended evacuation of the Australian Embassy by 25 April. Once again he pleaded the case of those Vietnamese to whom Australia was indebted and who wanted to flee. 'The fate of our locally-engaged staff, together with relatives of wives married to Embassy officers, is causing us all much distress', he said in his despatch. 'I am afraid that you must take the decision on this, taking into account the likelihood that we would encounter problems with the local authorities. At the same time I should like discretion to include any who can be included legally (i.e. Vietnamese holding Australian passports).'

His despatch resulted in a meeting between Whitlam and two senior Ministers, Rex Connor and Bill Morrison, on the morning of 21 April. The meeting was also attended by three senior members of the Foreign Affairs Department, Alan Renouf, Hugh Gilchrist and Gary Woodard. The meeting cut Price's recommendations to shreds. It decided that spouses and children (but not parents or other relatives) of Vietnamese students currently in Australia should be permitted to enter Australia; that Australian citizenship formalities and the issue of Australian

234

passports to the spouses of Australian citizens and their children under twenty-one should be completed in an effort to assist them to obtain exit approval from the Government of Vietnam; and that the Embassy in Saigon should refer to Canberra for ministerial consideration on an exceptional basis the case of any Vietnamese with a long association with Australia whom the Embassy considered to be in grave danger. Whitlam indicated that not more than a handful of such cases should be expected and that locally-engaged Embassy staff should not be regarded as endangered because of their association with the Embassy. As a nice little piece of political window-dressing, however, he sanctioned the admission of a group of nuns of the Order of the Congregation of Mary the Queen. Under no circumstances could their lives have seriously been regarded as endangered. Their proper place was in Vietnam looking after their flock.

Price replied to Canberra's instructions that the Embassy was receiving applications from substantially more than a handful of Vietnamese with Australian associations whose lives were considered to be in danger.

The Embassy had been instructed to close down and withdraw on 25 April. When Whitlam saw Press reports (which were quite inaccurate) late on 23 April that Vietnamese applying for Australia were demonstrating outside the Embassy, he ordered Price to cease operations that night and evacuate all staff first thing on 24 April. Price replied that this was impossible, but was told peremptorily that the order was irrevocable. Whitlam, the sole decision maker, had left for a Commonwealth meeting in Jamaica and could no longer be contacted.

For almost all that night Price stayed by the telex, arguing the case with Canberra. He insisted on the impossibility of leaving by the time stipulated, since this would prevent him from discharging the undertakings made to those who had been assured of evacuation by the Embassy. Finally, Canberra capitulated. Since Price was granted no discretion to add any Vietnamese to the small number already approved, it was an empty victory for him and his beleaguered staff, who had worked until they were exhausted to help those deemed to be in danger, only to be thwarted at every turn in Canberra.

On 24 and 25 April the Embassy in Saigon evacuated seventy-eight Vietnamese. Apart from thirty-eight special cases, these were among the approximately 500 applicants (out of some 5,000 who applied), who were approved for entry into Australia. Of these, not many made it. In the last desperate hours that the Embassy remained active, the consular staff gave affidavits and letters to those whom they considered eligible. If they could leave the country and produce evidence of identity, they would be admitted to Australia. Some got to Guam by their own initiative and were then rejected. The letters, they were told, had been issued under Emergency conditions that had ceased to exist.

After the Australian Embassy had evacuated on 25 April, the Foreign Affairs Department in Canberra had a list of 124 names of heads of families, or of unattached individuals approved for entry, who had been left behind. It wanted to pass the list to the American Embassy in Canberra. Instead Bill Morrison, who was acting Minister for Foreign Affairs, ordered that the names should not be given to the Americans but were to be sent to Australian embassies in Manila and Bangkok.

When the list arrived in Bangkok, Price volunteered to return to Saigon on an Air France plane scheduled to leave the following day and to take with him sufficient members of his staff (all volunteers, of course) to ensure that nobody was forgotten. He was instructed by Canberra that neither he nor any members of his staff should return.

The French Embassy agreed to do the job, and Price and his team worked through the night in Bangkok to prepare the list of names and addresses. The list was ready by 5 a.m. and taken to the French Embassy in Bangkok. Air France took off with the list in the hands of a courier–and overflew Saigon. The letters were not delivered.

On 28 April Hanoi issued another warning to Wilson in Hanoi. Huy, a senior member of the Provisional Revolutionary Government, told him that Australia should not participate in the 'forced evacuation' of Vietnamese (as he characterized the u.s. evacuation) and added that Canberra could expect a demand for the return to Vietnam of orphans taken to Australia. Next day, Nien, the North Vietnamese chargé d'affaires in Canberra, told John Rowland, who was acting secretary of the Foreign Affairs Department, that evacuation of Vietnamese from Saigon was regarded by the Democratic Republic of Vietnam and the Provisional Revolutionary Government as an interference in the internal affairs of South Vietnam and asked that it be stopped. Nien also told David Goss, of Foreign Affairs, that the Provisional Revolutionary Government was 'annoyed' at the use of RAAF aircraft for evacuating refugees and asked that it should cease immediately. He warned that relations might otherwise suffer.

The official lack of sensitivity on the part of the Australian government was matched only by a man in East Brighton, Victoria, who sent the following cable to the Embassy in Saigon: 'Please put on RAAF or other one extra half-white girl 5/7 fair condition for travelling who nobody wants with address plates. Family agreed. Use your ability.'

More, perhaps, might have been done if the Embassy had known definitely that it had another day or two to spare. But the Americans on this point were not forthcoming. Ambassador Martin was the only member of the u.s. Embassy staff who knew that the North Vietnamese would allow the Americans to depart unscathed. He kept the information to himself. Two American ships had been waiting at the Newport wharves on the Saigon River to take evacuees. Martin would not authorize their departure. He was afraid that what had happened in Danang would be repeated all over again if the Americans were seen so obviously to be going. Tan Son Nhut airport was a restricted area and therefore an easier place from which to conduct the evacuation. The Vietnamese could scarcely be unaware that people were going, but they would not see them and, in any case, they could not gain access to the field.

Again, there were fewer palms to grease at the airport and fewer people to ask questions about the departure of Vietnamese citizens who had no passports or exit visas.

Few emerged with much credit from these days. At the Canadian Embassy locally-employed staff were told that arrangements would be made for their departure when they came to work on the following day. When they turned up, they found that their employers had locked the doors and taken off, leaving all non-Canadians behind.*

The German Embassy told its local staff that if they could get through, or bypass, Customs and Immigration at Tan Son Nhut they would be taken aboard a Lufthansa flight. An Australian Commonwealth policeman smuggled a couple into the airport and got them to the plane. They were refused permission to board and had to be smuggled out of the airport.

At dawn on 26 April, General Dung and his staff moved from COSVN headquarters to a forward command post at Ben Cat north of Bien Hoa. Here, twenty years earlier, the Australians in their wisdom had set up a dairy farm to provide milk for Saigon, unaware that

---

* With the fall of Saigon, however, the Canadian Government proved much more humane than its Australian counterpart. On 1 May 1975, it announced that it would accept 2,000 refugees taken out by the United States, up to 1,000 refugees from neighbouring Asian countries, and close relatives of citizens or landed immigrants in Canada. This attitude was in sharp contrast to Australian policy under either Labor or Liberal governments. As Opposition leader, Mr Fraser on 3 April 1975, called on the Australian Government to allow 'thousands' of Vietnamese adults to settle in Australia. This appeal was dismally forgotten when the Liberals took office.

their farm bordered on the Maquis D, which had for years been a secure Viet Minh base. For a year or two the cows grazed unmolested. Then both the cows and their armed guards came under repeated attack.

In one attack, eight cows and a bull disappeared, leading to a facetious suggestion in Saigon that the Viet Cong planned to start their own stud farm. On another occasion, the initial reports suggested that not only a gallant guard but also his wife had lost their lives in the defence of the cows. Embarrassed Australian officials wondered whether they should not confer some posthumous honour on the couple, but changed their minds when they discovered that the man had been lured from duty by a local village maiden and that they had died *in flagrante delicto* under the watchtower.

In later years, the farm became a base for the Rangers. Now Dung used it as a communications and command centre to orchestrate the immense armies that were gathering on all fronts around Saigon and to launch what the Politburo had decreed should be known as the Ho Chi Minh campaign. Dung's I and III Corps had closed in on Dong Du, Lai Khe and Ben Cat to the north; II and IV Corps were moving through Phuoc Tuy and Bien Hoa Provinces to attack Vung Tau, Baria, Long Thanh, Long Binh and Bien Hoa.

A key initial move was the advance on the district capital of Nhon Trach at the south-western extremity of Bien Hoa Province. For it was here that General Dung planned to deploy his long range 130-millimetre guns for the bombardment of Tan Son Nhut airport and the Saigon River system. Originally, the plan called for a simultaneous offensive on all fronts on 27 April as a prelude to the final offensive on Saigon. General Le Trong Tan, the commander of the two eastern columns of six divisions (II Corps and IV Corps) had overwhelming strength, but he was not sanguine about maintaining the schedule set by Dung unless he could move ahead of the other formations.

He requested, and received permission, to open his part of the campaign at 1700 on 26 April.

On the afternoon of 27 April, Dung received the following report:

> On the eastern and south-eastern fronts the striking forces have captured Baria, the Long Thanh and Trang Bom sub-districts and part of Nuoc Trong base, but not Bien Hoa, Vung Tau and Nhon Trach. We are not yet in a position to establish gun emplacements for the Tan Son Nhut airport and the river remains open.
> On the south-western front, Route 4 has been totally cut off from Ben Luc to Truong Long crossroads and at the north bank of My Thuan landing stage. The main striking forces, including the 9th Division and part of the 130-millimetre artillery, have crossed the

Vam Co River, and efforts are being made to speed up the river crossing.

On the northern front, I Corps has destroyed a number of enemy fire bases and liberated part of Route 13 from the north down to a point seven kilometres from Thu Dau Mot, enabling us to move in the striking force for an eventual deep thrust.

On the north-western front, III Corps, in one day and night, has destroyed eleven out of the thirteen enemy fire bases, cut Route 22 and Route 1, prevented puppet Division 25 from falling back from Tay Ninh to Dong Du, and is now making active preparations for the annihilation of Dong Du base.

In Saigon the closing ring of steel had forced the Government of Vietnam to play its last card. Big Minh. Like 'Nguyen Van Tri', he was supremely confident that he and he alone could still forestall the North Vietnamese entry into Saigon. Poor old Huong, described by Dung as 'an extremely reactionary civilian quisling'–Thieu was a 'military fascist quisling'–was ready to hand over to anyone whom the Senate and the National Assembly in joint session cared to nominate.

Tran Van Lam saw Minh to determine whether he was still willing to take over and genuinely believed that he could save Saigon from attack. He found Minh calm and supremely confident.

The two chambers met in joint session at 5 o'clock in the afternoon of 27 April. Of the 219 members, 136 answered the roll call, a surprisingly high number in view of the situation and the need so many felt to escape while there was still time.

Lam called in three top security leaders to brief the joint session– General Cao Van Vien, the ARVN chief of staff, Major-General Nguyen Khac Binh, the police chief, and Major-General Nguyen Van Minh, commander of the Capital Military District, on whose shoulders the defence of Saigon would ultimately rest. A division of police was all that was left in reserve. The Republic of Vietnam could fight no longer.

For many hours on the previous day the two houses had debated the constitutional issues without reaching any conclusion. This time Lam gave no opportunity for debate. He said it was a time for decision, not for talk, and put the question: 'Who agrees that President Huong should hand over presidential powers to General Duong Van Minh so that he may seek a way to restore peace in Vietnam?'

Every hand was raised in favour. Thus was the Constitution of the Republic destroyed and the way open for the miracle that everyone hoped would cause the guns to fall silent and the tanks to stop.

It was after curfew when the joint meeting ended and the politicians headed for their homes. On the previous night the North Vietnamese had signalled their presence outside the city with a shower of rockets. On this night there were no rockets. Over Saigon Radio the city, and what remained of the Republic, learned that Big Minh, the man who had overthrown Diem a decade before, was to be their saviour in this hour of greatest danger.

At Loc Ninh and Ben Cat COSVN representatives listened to Saigon Radio, but instead of preparing for negotiations there was now an added urgency to throw all the five columns into action at the earliest possible moment. Early on the morning of 28 April Le Duc Tho and Pham Hung arrived at Dung's headquarters to co-ordinate the plans for Saigon's capture.

For Big Minh and the attempts by France, the United States, Don, 'Nguyen Van Tri' and others to negotiate a political settlement there was only contempt. Wrote Dung:

> U.S. Ambassador Martin and other Western diplomats actively operated backstage in Saigon politics. Pressure from many directions, including the United States, was exerted demanding that Tran Van Huong resign and be replaced by a person who could easily contact the National Liberation Front. Huong wanted to cede his throne only to a member of the Thieu faction. He strenuously clung to the presidential seat to give his underlings enough time to sell exit visas at exorbitant prices and to collect their material assets. We knew that there was someone else at the back of the stage, awaiting his cue. Many complex activities were being undertaken by several sides. The U.S.-puppet clique resorted to many devices, including perfidious manoeuvres to check our troops' advance and avoid total defeat. The U.S. C.I.A. clique in Saigon crept around like a venomous snake to spy and to conduct many insidious plots. It spread a report that Huong would be an interim president and the United States was ready to reach an agreement, was waiting for a reply, and so on.

Not for a second did the Politburo in Hanoi, or Le Duc Tho and Pham Hung, counsel Dung to restrain his forces on the final assault. A message from the Politburo in Hanoi removed any doubt on this issue. After congratulating all units on their exploits in the first two days of the final offensive, it said:

> All cadres, combatants and Party and youth union members are called on to display their highest determination to launch a quick and direct attack on the enemy's last den and to use the powerful force of an invincible army to smash all enemy resistance, combining an offensive with an uprising to liberate completely Saigon-Gia Dinh municipality . . . While concentrating command and guidance to liberate satisfactorily Saigon-Gia Dinh, it is necessary to plan for armed assignments and preparatory tasks aimed at quickly develop-

ing advantageous positions, completely eradicating all residual enemy forces in other areas, especially in the Mekong Delta and on Con Son and Phu Quoc Islands, and totally liberating South Vietnam.

After making due allowances for ideology, and the fiction that the masses were just waiting to rise up to welcome their 'liberators', this does not sound like the views of an organization that was willing to negotiate a political settlement, with or without 'Nguyen Van Tri' or Big Minh.

'Nguyen Van Tri' was right on one point. 'I told you a month ago that Hanoi, and even the Front, will disown any government headed by Big Minh', he said to one of the intermediaries. 'Now, I keep saying the same thing. Minh is a zero, an idiot, and a dangerous idiot.' The same intermediary says, 'My conclusion is that the Americans, who duped the Republic of Vietnam, were duped by Hanoi. About the French, it's difficult to know whether they double-crossed the Americans or were double-crossed by Hanoi. What I can say is that the Vietnamese who worked for French intelligence and are now left behind in Saigon have not been prosecuted. Hanoi rushed its attack on Saigon in a last-ditch attempt to deter an NLF last-ditch attempt to come to a separate agreement with the Americans and Vietnamese nationalists.'*

Confirmation that the North Vietnamese double-crossed the French came in the most bizarre manner. At the Helsinki conference American agents spent an hour and twenty minutes going over every inch of the table where Ford and Kissinger would sit. They even drank some of the water to see if it was poisoned. When the conference got under way, Dr Kissinger filled in spare moments reading incoming messages. A free-lance photographer named Franco Rossi with a telephoto lens snapped away while Kissinger ran through the documents, including one dated 30 July 1975, and marked TOP SECRET SENSITIVE EXCLUSIVELY EYES ONLY CONTAINS CODEWORD. Rossi's film recorded every word of the document, which described the diplomatic state of affairs between Paris and Hanoi, and related information gathered from an 'established C.I.A. source' with excellent access to the French Foreign Ministry's Far Eastern Section for Financial and Economic Assessments. The report said that the French considered themselves 'outrageously deceived by Hanoi's assurances that the Democratic Republic of Vietnam would not invade the South'.

---

* Both Diem and Thieu believed that intelligence collected by French agents (Vietnamese) during the war was passed on to Hanoi. The Vietnamese who helped Terzani write his book, *Giai Phong*, was a French agent, who worked for years for *Newsweek*.

In one of his reports, Dung says that Big Minh had 'come too late'. It is not clear, however, whether he meant to imply that if he had come to office immediately after Thieu resigned there would have been a chance to arrange a political settlement. The weight of the evidence is to the contrary. Hanoi was massively committed and was determined to allow nothing to stand in the way of victory after the Politburo meeting on 25 March.

What was standing in their way on 28 April was not Big Minh but some unexpected resistance. The eastern column under General Tan had failed to take Nhon Trach on 27 April, and the 130-millimetre guns were not yet in position to shell Tan Son Nhut. There was also strong, and unexpected, resistance at Ho Nai, the church-filled town built by refugees from North Vietnam just outside Bien Hoa. The Nhon Trach setback was most serious, because the shelling of Tan Son Nhut was an essential part of Dung's plan to take Saigon with military force but in a way that would cause minimum damage to the city. He wanted Saigon, and he wanted it intact.

The 18th ARVN Division had been all but destroyed at Xuan Loc, together with most of the strategic reserve. The 25th ARVN Division was cut off at Tay Ninh, and the 5th ARVN was at Lai Khe, nearly thirty miles north of Saigon in the camp area once occupied by the U.S. 1st Division. It, too, was cut off.

With the main remaining ARVN assets neutralized, Dung's plan, drawn up originally by General Le Ngoc Hien, and modified and approved by Le Duc Tho, Pham Hung, Tran Van Tra, and, of course, by Dung himself, called for highly selective attacks in Saigon. There was to be no house to house action, no fighting for the city street by street, but five deep thrusts by five main columns to take out five targets–the Independence Palace, the Joint General Staff head-quarters at Tan Son Nhut, the Tan Son Nhut airbase, the Capital Military District headquarters and the Police headquarters.

'If these positions could be removed', said Dung, 'the whole puppet regime would be shaken down. If we could hit these vital points, the puppet army and administration would be deprived of their leader-ship, their defences would fall to pieces and the masses could then rise up . . . Moreover, only by directing our attacks at these main targets could we avoid civilian casualties and hope to spare many economic and cultural establishments and public facilities.' In the event that the government forces succeeded in blowing the bridges on the Saigon and Dong Nai rivers, Dung planned to use pontoons, as well as ferries and 'a whole fleet of river boats, sampans and barges to move part of our troops to Saigon or to take our big guns and vehicles across'.

The morning of 28 April found Big Minh as confident as ever that he had only to put a government together, call for negotiations and the fighting would stop. Unlike Huong, he realized that he did not have much time, hours not days. All day long at his home a succession of visitors came and went. During the day he had succeeded in forming enough of a government to present himself to what was left of the nation as a credible leader with a credible policy.

Once again the members of the Senate and the House of Assembly gathered, this time at the Independence Palace, together with the judges of the Supreme Court, to watch the resignation of Huong and the installation of Minh. It was now just after 5 p.m. General Dung did not have his 130-millimetre guns in place to make the appropriate salute to the new regime. But Lieutenant Nguyen Thanh Trung, who had bombed the Independence Palace precisely twenty days before, was on his way back to Tan Son Nhut airport at the head of a flight of A-37 aircraft taken when Danang fell to the North Vietnamese at the end of March.

Old, trembling Huong, who once years before when he was an aspiring presidential candidate had given me an autographed copy of his poems, could scarcely speak. Turning to Minh, he said, 'Your responsibilities are great, General'.

It was enough. Minh, still confident but not complacent, took his place at the rostrum. 'I accept the responsibility for seeking to arrive at a ceasefire, at negotiations, at peace on the basis of the Paris Agreement', he said. Outside the palace thunder and lighting and torrential rain marked the beginning of the wet season. In a week or two it would be too late for tanks and artillery to manoeuvre. If Phan Rang had only . . . If Xuan Loc . . . If the B52s . . . If Congress . . . If ifs and ands were pots and pans . . . The ceremony ended and the guests dispersed into an evening made fresh by the storm.

Then, as they made their way to their homes, from Tan Son Nhut came the sound of heavy explosions. The palace anti-aircraft guns opened fire. Frightened men with rifles began shooting in the air. The sirens wailed the news of immediate curfew.

At Tan Son Nhut the evacuation was in full swing. About 2,000 South Vietnamese evacuees were in the Defence Attaché's compound waiting to go. Forty plane loads had gone out during the day and another sixty were scheduled for the following day. As Trung's A-37s came in to drop their bombs, the controller in the civilian air tower called on the attackers to identify themselves. 'We are American built', came the reply.

Great damage was claimed for the raid. In terms of material damage, the claims were exaggerated but, as with the attack on the palace earlier in the month, the psychological damage was heavy.

With the bombing attack came the first significant rocket attacks–the 130-millimetre gun crews were still working feverishly to get them into position on the east bank of the Saigon River. The first rocket rounds resulted in the death of two u.s. Marines at the Defence Attaché's Office.

In Washington, President Ford was presiding over a meeting of his energy advisers when an aide handed him a note informing him of the death of the Marines. An hour later the National Security Council met in the Roosevelt Room in the White House to decide whether it was now time for the final evacuation of Americans to begin. One C-130 had been set on fire either by rockets or by the bombing attack and three South Vietnamese Air Force planes had been shot down not far from Tan Son Nhut. Under pressure from Congress not to delay the evacuation, President Ford decided to wait just a little longer.

As dawn broke over Saigon, two C-130s were approaching Tan Son Nhut to begin, or to await orders to begin, the evacuation flights for the day. Two South Vietnamese C-130s attempted to take off surrounded by crowds of armed Vietnamese demanding passage. One C-130 was blocked by a car that was parked in front of it on the runway, and the second by an F-5, whose pilot had abandoned it under fire with the engine running just after he had landed.

General Homer Smith, the senior American officer at the Defence Attaché's Office, was still trying to land the C-130s in the air over Tan Son Nhut. The planes came down to 16,000 feet and were beginning their fourteen-minute landing approach when Smith learned that North Vietnamese ground forces were less than half a mile from the airport. He called off the landing and phoned CINCPAC in Pearl Harbour to report that the situation was getting out of control.

Fifteen miles to the south-east the 325th North Vietnamese Division was now making up for lost time in Nhon Trach. Behind the tanks and the infantry came the long-barrelled 130-millimetre guns. Saigon awoke to a blaze of light in the south-east and the double explosion as the shells–304 in the first barrage–left the guns and roared across the outskirts of the city to Tan Son Nhut.

Early the previous evening Ky had sought out Erich Von Marbod, u.s. Deputy Assistant Secretary of Defence, to enlist his support for a plan to continue the war from Can Tho in the Mekong Delta. The answer was No.

Unable to sleep, Ky made his own last contribution to the war during the night when he went up in his helicopter to inspect the damage and assess the chances. When he saw it was impossible for the fighter-bombers to use the airfield, he called up Can Tho, where the local air commander agreed to send four planés with 750-lb bombs. Ky directed their attack on the rocket installations. He thought they knocked out one of the biggest sites. But it was a gesture, nothing more.

According to Martin, Ky asked the air force commander at Tan Son Nhut to fly out all serviceable aircraft to Thailand, or the Philippines, as soon as the opportunity presented itself. The order, perhaps the request, appears to have come from Von Marbod himself, since Ky knew nothing of it until he was told by the station commander.

Martin was among those who had been awakened from his sleep by the thunder of the 130-millimetre guns. He was also called by General Smith from the airport, who told him that he no longer saw any hope of continuing the evacuation by fixed-wing aircraft.

To satisfy himself that this was no longer possible, Martin made a brave, and foolhardy, inspection of the base. By this time the North Vietnamese ground forces weie on the outskirts of Tan Son Nhut, and the sound of gunfire was distinct and near. Martin concluded that it was no longer possible to continue using the field for large aircraft taking many passengers. Back in the Embassy he took an incoming call from Kissinger. 'Let's go with option four', (helicopter evacuation) Martin told him. Kissinger called President Ford to pass on the recommendation. The President immediately set in motion the final evacuation by helicopter to the U.S. 7th Fleet, which had been waiting offshore for many days.

At his home in Tran Quy Cap Street, Minh busied himself with Vice President Nguyen Van Huyen and Vu Van Mau, the prime minister, with the plans for a ceasefire. It was decided that a delegation should immediately call on the Communist officers at Camp Davis (Tan Son Nhut) to start the negotiations. The delegation met with a cool reception. The terms, it was told, had been stated on 26 April: the disbandment of the 'puppet' armed forces and the police and an end to all American intervention. The delegates left to report back to Minh, having assured the Communists that the new government would issue a statement on the basis of the 26 April demands, with a view to settling the military problems at a two-party conference at Tan Son Nhut and the political problems in Paris.

Even now, Minh did not despair. Vu Van Mau phoned the U.S. Embassy with the request that the Americans should all leave Vietnam within twenty-four hours. He learned that they were on their way.

The North Vietnamese forces were also on their way–in. The

artillery barrage on Tan Son Nhut had just ended when ground forces from II Corps made contact with the sappers who had seized control of the Dong Nai bridge on the previous day to prevent government forces from blowing it up.

III Corps had attacked and destroyed the 25th ARVN Division's positions at Trang Bang and Dong Du, and was now ready to join with I Corps in the attack on Joint General Staff Headquarters.

Tan Uyen had fallen to I Corps.

To allow the Americans to go in relative peace–and to avoid the possibility that even at this last hour the B52s might be brought in to protect the evacuation–Dung ordered his 130-millimetre guns to cease fire and, for the time being, to abandon the bombardment of Tan Son Nhut.

Shortly after noon the Americans began to take their leave. Twenty-one years before the French had retained at least some dignity when they left Hanoi. There was precious little dignity left in this helter skelter. Promises, pledges were mostly forgotten. In the Foreign Ministry, Quang called the American Embassy repeatedly to ascertain what arrangements were being made for those who had so loyally stayed at their posts. He was brushed off by junior officers. Nine Supreme Court judges, who had been promised they would be evacuated, were forgotten. Tran Van Lam, who, on request, had supplied a list of all Senators whose lives might be endangered if they remained behind, was told that he had to cut the list to two–and that there was no room for families. He chose two bachelors.

All of the Vietnamese Government's secret agents who had been planted in the Viet Cong apparatus, together with their case officers and leading district police officers, were asked to gather at police headquarters to be evacuated. All were left behind. Almost all the Phoenix programme officers, whose task had been to destroy (very successfully) the Communist cadre infrastructure, were also left behind.

A group of USIS employees had been promised a flight out if they worked to the last. They were not alerted until their employers had retreated behind the only two secure areas in the city able to take evacuation helicopters–the U.S. Embassy and the U.S. compound at Tan Son Nhut. 'We went to the Embassy and could not get in', said a senior American official's secretary. 'We drove to the airport and could not get in. We went to the other American compounds but everyone had gone.'

In the Seventh Day Adventist Hospital an old friend lay dying of cancer. A mutual friend phoned from Bangkok through the military circuit, and our friend answered the phone. There were only three people left in the hospital, all of them patients, he said. They had been told to get themselves cyclos and go home, but they were not well enough to move. He had been left with no drugs to ease his pain. I hope he died before his liberators discovered who he was.

Outside the American Embassy thousands of Vietnamese clamoured for entry and a place on the helicopters now shuttling backwards and forwards from the 7th Fleet. They got a rifle butt for their pains. Members of the Japanese Embassy and the Japanese Press corps were refused admission, along with the Koreans, although all had been promised that they would be evacuated.

Dung took calculated risks that day. He had suspended the bombardment of Tan Son Nhut by the 130-millimetre guns, but he still intended to adhere to his timetable for the capture of Saigon. There was always the chance that things would go wrong and American planes return to the attack. He was ready for this contingency. Every Army Corps, all of them now within a radius of about ten miles of the city, was amply equipped with SAM missiles. The situation was now far beyond the point, however, where any action the United States might contemplate, short of nuclear war, could save Saigon.

During the night of 29–30 April, the U.S. Navy proposed calling an eight-hour halt in the evacuation. It wanted time to sort out those who had already been lifted out of Saigon by helicopter, and to start with a new batch at 8 a.m. Wisely, Martin refused to agree, and all night long the shuttle continued. All night long, also, the five Northern columns continued to advance.

Headquarters of the 25th ARVN Division was at Cu Chi, once the headquarters of the U.S. 25th 'Tropical Lightning Division'. The headquarters were heavily mined and protected with barbed wire. The T54 tanks broke through the defences and over-ran the headquarters, capturing the divisional commander.

The 5th ARVN Division had its headquarters at Lai Khe on Route 13. On the morning of 30 April the division lost radio contact with Military Region 3 at Long Binh. Brigadier-General Le Nguyen Vy, the commanding officer, decided to mobilize all his vehicles and to try to make a dash for Saigon. He was hit by Dung's I Corps and the division was annihilated. Vy committed suicide.

The North Vietnamese III Corps captured Bien Hoa and the headquarters of Military Region 3 at Long Binh and sent the 7th Division over the untouched Dong Nai River down the road to Thu Duc, where the remains of the 18th ARVN Division were preparing to make their last stand in front of the Saigon River. It was no match for the tanks of II Corps and the 7th Division and collapsed.

To the east, the 325th Division had begun to cross the Saigon River and to enter into the 9th Precinct. And on the west the Joint General Staff area had been over-run.

Still the helicopters continued to fly out from the roof of the American Embassy. Determined not to contribute in any way to a panic situation in Saigon, Martin had refused to send out his personal possessions while there was still time. His wife remained with him. 'Her contribution to stability was enormous', Martin believed. 'Had we begun to pack our household items, the signal would have been all over Saigon. So all our small collections of things that were of great sentimental importance to us remained untouched.' Martin allowed his wife eleven minutes to pack. They walked back to the Embassy together, but Martin had no intention of leaving himself until he was assured that the several hundred Vietnamese to whom he was personally committed had been flown out. Among them was Tran Van Lam.

Bitterly criticized by some of his disloyal staff, and dismissed by much of the media with contempt, he had not done enough, but at least, in the face of almost total panic reflected in the messages coming in from Washington, he had done his courageous best.

This was not quite how General Dung saw it. He wrote:

The departure of Code 2–Code 2 was Martin's secret name–and Lady 09–Lady 09 was the name of the helicopter that whisked him away to the east sea–marked the tragic defeat of the U.S. imperialists after thirty years of military intervention and adventure in Vietnam. At the height of the war of aggression in Vietnam, the U.S. imperialists used 60 per cent of the entire infantry force of the United States, 58 per cent of the U.S. naval forces, 50 per cent of the strategic air force, 15 out of 18 aircraft carriers, 800,000 U.S. troops, including those stationed in satellite countries participating in the Vietnam War, and more than a million puppet lackey troops. They mobilized as many as six million U.S. troops, dropped more than ten million tons of bombs and spent more than $300 billion. The end result of all this was that the U.S. ambassador had to crawl onto the roof of the Embassy building to escape.

It was an unkind comment, but the scene at the gates of the Embassy was not one that Americans will care to remember. Marines guarding the building had to use tear gas and rifle butts to hold back the surging crowds. As the Marines withdrew, floor by floor, toward the roof they were followed by angry, vengeful mobs. Marines used so much tear gas down the lift wells that even the helicopter crews were affected.

The American withdrawal did not precipitate the panic that had marked the end in Danang and Nha Trang. But it did set off a rampage of looting of American homes, offices and the PX warehouses. It also marked the beginning of a massive flight of Vietnamese who wanted to escape. Dung had made an error in his calculations. He assumed that the 130-millimetre guns at Nhon Trach would close the Saigon River. For large ships there was no escape, but during daylight hours on 29 and 30 April, and again during the two nights, scores of small boats, loaded down with refugees, set sail down the river. The lucky were picked up by American and other ships. There were degrees of luck, however. In many cases the river boats were too frail and unseaworthy for use beyond Vung Tau. Many of the boats that passed this point and the artillery of Dung's II Corps sank in the waves. Again the more fortunate escapees found places, at least to stand, in open ammunition barges that sometimes drifted for days before being rescued. Many people died on the barges. 'I saw a woman give birth to a child while standing on the body of someone who had already died', said one member of a Vietnamese family who had fled clutching a paper issued by the Australian Embassy on 25 April, virtually promising that if they could get away from Vietnam and identify themselves, they would be admitted to Australia. When they got to Guam, they were told they were not wanted.

For Minh and his new government the evacuation of the Americans again seemed to hold the promise that even now something could be done to hold back the Northern forces. Late that afternoon he sent another delegation of three to Camp Davis to try to arrange a ceasefire.

Night fell when the discussions were continuing and with it came the renewed North Vietnamese assault. It was very timely. About 0200 hours the delegation at Camp Davis reported to Dung:

> A three-man delegation of the Saigon administration came to see us about a ceasefire. Comrade Vo Dong Giang [the senior officer] received them and confirmed our views and standpoint outlined in the government's 26 April statement. After the talk, they asked for permission to leave the camp. After we told them that our artillery was now bombarding Tan Son Nhut airport fiercely, and that it would be better for them to stay and spend the night at the camp, they finally agreed to stay with us. They are now in an underground shelter with us.

Better still, from Dung's point of view, the telephone lines to Camp Davis had been cut. Minh's emissaries could neither return nor phone. 'The puppet leaders were impatiently awaiting the return of their three envoys', Dung wrote. 'They were perplexed and embarrassed, phoning each other to inquire about the whereabouts of their envoys.' All the time, of course, the Northern advance went on.

At 10.20 a.m. on 30 April Saigon Radio broadcast a message from Minh:

I believe firmly in reconciliation among Vietnamese. To avoid needless bloodshed, I ask all soldiers of the Republic to put an end to all hostilities and remain where they are. The military command is ready to make contact with the army command of the Provisional Revolutionary Government to achieve a ceasefire. I furthermore ask our brothers of the Provisional Revolutionary Government to cease hostilities on their side. We are waiting here for their representatives to come and discuss an orderly transfer of powers.

Minh's 'brothers' in the Provisional Revolutionary Government had no say in the matter. The Laodong (Workers) Party of North Vietnam was calling all the shots. In effect, Minh's broadcast was a surrender. Hanoi regarded it as a trick.

To Dung's headquarters at Ben Cat came an urgent and immediate message from the Politburo whose members had heard the broadcast in Hanoi: 'Continue the attack on Saigon according to set plans, have the troops advance with the strongest impetus, liberating and occupying the entire city, disarming enemy troops, dissolving the enemy's administration at all levels, and completely smashing all enemy resistance.'

Dung immediately issued an order of the day to all army corps, military regions and units:

1. The army corps, military regions and units must continue to attack rapidly designated areas and objectives in the city and nearby;
2. Call on enemy troops to surrender and turn in all weapons, and capture, detain and concentrate enemy officers of field grade and above;
3. Wherever the enemy resists, our troops must immediately attack and annihilate him.

Dung's order of the day was unnecessary. Minh's broadcast had already destroyed what was left of the Republic of Vietnam. I Corps occupied the Joint General Staff headquarters. III Corps took Tan Son Nhut. IV Corps occupied the Ministry of Defence building, down the street from the American Embassy. A troop of tanks from II Corps rolled down Thong Nhat. The lead tank fired a shot in the air as it passed the cathedral, accelerated to smash through the iron gates of the Independence Palace and came to a halt in front of the steps. The war was over.

In the command post at Ben Cat, where the Australians had once raised their Jersey cows, Le Duc Tho, the Nobel Peace Prize winner, and Pham Hung embraced.

Part four

And beyond

1. The morning after the war before

Nai Jom Saenpo was fifty. His face had began to dry out and wither like an apple left too long on the tree, though his eyes were still bright and penetrating and his jet black hair showed no signs of grey. He sat cross-legged on the floor of his open-fronted shop among the dusty bottles of soft drink, packets of matches, bundles of bark, hand-woven bolts of cloth and half a dozen tins of sardines that he offered for sale. A checked blue and white sarong tucked loosely around his waist revealed a wide expanse of richly tattooed thigh.

Across the dusty track from Jom Saenpo's shop was the schoolhouse and the sandbagged headquarters of the police and military detachments stationed in Pontum village. In the background, green and inviting in the afternoon sun, were the slopes of the Phuphan mountains which run through Nakae district and the province of Nakhon Phanom in north-eastern Thailand.

The Phuphans' shady streams abound with fish. Their forests are filled with game–and with elusive bands of Communist insurgents, one of whom is Jom Saenpo's son, the eldest of his six children. There are about 300 families in Pontum village where, because of his shop, Jom Saenpo makes a better living than most. About a hundred families have contributed a son or a daughter to the insurgency.

'Why did your son go to the hills?' I asked.

He shrugged his shoulders. 'I do not know why. Perhaps he has gone to Vientiane, or to Bangkok, and not to the jungles at all.'

'You know he is in the mountains', interrupted Lieutenant Kanit

Pipithirunkarn, a strongly-built officer, dressed in camouflaged uniform, who for two years had been hunting the insurgents. 'You know he is there.'

The lieutenant was not threatening. He was merely stating the fact, and Jom Saenpo nodded. The lieutenant and his troops from the sandbagged military post were his bread and butter, his best customers, and his friends. But they were not privy to his secrets.

'I mind my own affairs', said Jom Saenpo. 'I don't bother about other people'.

He was, nevertheless, a proud man. 'A long time ago', he said, 'when I first came here, there was only forest. I started to cut the forest and to make a clearing. I made this village. At first there were very few families and there was much sickness. My brother died of cholera. The people were very poor.'

'Has the government helped the people of the village?' I asked.

'Yes', he replied, 'the government has helped very much. Now there is no cholera. There are roads and this year we have fertilizers and the biggest rice crop we have ever had.'

'Why, then, do the people support the insurgents?'

'He knows everything', said Lieutenant Kanit, 'but he will not talk'.

'I am afraid', said Jom Saenpo. 'I am afraid they will come and kill me'.

'Isn't it better here than in the mountains?'

Lieutenant Kanit answered. 'It is good in the mountains', he said. 'There is much wild boar. I eat pig every day.'

'You don't need guns', said Jom Saenpo, pointing to his crossbow hanging on the untreated paling wall behind him. 'With the crossbow I can shoot boar.'

'The insurgents help with the rice harvest', said the lieutenant. 'They are helping now and they will claim their reward. Everywhere they are helping, and because they are helping no one will talk. When they go against the insurgents they have cause to be afraid.'

His point was well made. During the night the insurgents had called at the house of a pregnant woman in the village of Dong Thong and asked for food. When she refused to give it to them, they shot her down.

Lieutenant Kanit suspected a trap, and his suspicions were warranted. By jeep a detachment of police was on its way to Dong Thong. The insurgents lay in wait, killing four policemen and wounding nine others.

Here at Pontum where we were talking they had also come in the night, not to kill this time but to spread their crude, hand-printed leaflets in the village. In content and appearance these did not vary much from the type of propaganda that used to be common in the Mekong Delta when the insurgency there was in its infancy. They were laboriously hand-printed in big letters. In the name of the Liberation Army of Thailand they called on the people to overthrow the government of Thailand and to kill the Americans. To show the proper ideological orientation, they were complete with hammer and sickle.

'Only the insurgents get information', said Lieutenant Kanit. 'Every time we go out on patrol the people pass the news. We look and look but we never see.

What do you expect when these people have sons and brothers and husbands and fathers in the hills?'

Ten years have passed since the Thai Government discovered the classic indicators of an incipient insurgency in the district of Nakae. They found that hard-core cadres had been at work in the villages, organizing cells, building training sites and beginning with the familiar assassination of school teachers, village headmen and police informers. To Bangkok's dismay, the area chosen by the Communists for what appeared to be a tentative attempt to create a 'liberated' area in the north-east was also the location of two of the government's most highly regarded counter-insurgency programmes, one involving a multi-ministerial Community Development Unit team and the other the Royal Thai Army's Special Operations Centre.

In Bangkok before I headed to the north-east the word was that things were better generally and in the Nakae district, in particular. Things were indeed indefinitely better in terms of effort and material achievement. The deeply-rutted, meandering ox-cart tracks, inches deep in dust during the dry season and feet thick in oily mud in the wet, had been replaced in many areas by all-weather roads. Transportation used to be so difficult in the 1960s that many people in many places had never been to the district capital. Buses ran to few villages and hundreds of thousands of the perhaps fifteen million people in the sixteen north-eastern provinces had never seen a car, or a truck. The only difference among the so-called village schools was the degree of poverty. Though four years of primary education was theoretically compulsory, many villages had no schools and many schools had no regular teachers.

Today, the progress is demonstrable. New and prosperous towns have sprung up through the north-east. Dams bring water for irrigation and electric light to regions which used to be so poor that even the oil lamp was unknown.

Yet Captain Khluan Sariboot, the assistant district officer, who had been in Nakae for a year, seemed less sanguine than many of his seniors in Bangkok that improvements in the way of life also meant improvement in security. Despite the road improvements, he thought many were still very bad. Two villages in the Phuphan mountains could not be reached by road at any time, and during the wet season it was extremely difficult to travel to about half the remaining hundred in the district. The population of Nakae district was about 30,000, and one doctor, at district headquarters, could not cope with the needs of the people. In twelve of the mountain schools the only teachers after all the improvements had been made were policemen. Thirty-one villages still had no schools at all, and there was no high school at this time, even at the district level.

'The insurgents prey on the illiteracy of the people', he said. 'Though there are not many of them in the mountains, there are enough for them to operate in teams of thirty to fifty men.'

This was not enough to give the insurgents the initiative when large concentrations of government forces swept through the area. The insurgents simply disappeared. But always they came back. Pontum village, where Captain Khluan made his headquarters, not only had a police and military post, it was also defended by one of the twelve security teams in Nakae district. Even that was not enough to deter the insurgents.

The captain pointed out of the window of his headquarters to a clump of bamboo no more than a hundred yards away and perhaps half that distance from Jom Saenpo's shop. 'That was the scene of my third ambush', he said. 'Only a month ago they were waiting for me with carbines as I came out of the headquarters in my jeep. It was just after dusk, about seven o'clock in the evening. I was very lucky to get away'.

When the harvest was gathered, Captain Khluan expected more ambushes to come. Unmarried and then thirty-seven, he was philosophical about it, although he knew, and everyone else knew, that his life expectancy could not be regarded as high.

The story of Nakae district is atypical. There are many other areas in north-eastern Thailand where the people live in absolute security, but all around the frontiers the pressures are mounting. The situation is not becoming better but worse. The Thai forces are stretched dangerously thin. Now, with tough Communist neighbours with debts to settle, the situation could easily become critical. In all of Nakhon Phanom Province there are only two companies of troops to supplement the village security forces. Everywhere the complaint is the same: there just aren't enough resources for all the tasks that ought to be done.

In the north, 60,000 Meo tribesmen, who have entered Thailand in the past fifty years or so, have fallen out with Bangkok. With the best of motives and the most impolitic of methods, Thai officials tried forcibly to resettle the tribesmen in lowland country and to uproot their crops of opium poppies which in December and January of each year turn the hillsides into a blaze of color.

West of Bangkok, in Ratburi province, a small group of insurgents is at work, with the Burma border providing a sanctuary in times of trouble. Further south, where the isthmus comes to its narrowest point and the road and railway to the central and far south are highly vulnerable, another insurgent group has made its appearance. Two separate insurgent forces have erupted with bloody violence in the south. One is under the direction of the Malayan Communist Party. It operates in the four southernmost provinces and across the Malaysian border. For all practical purposes, it governs there.

Dr George Tanham, once the u.s. Embassy's adviser on counter-insurgency operations, and the leading American authority in his field, was adamant about keeping the American military out of the firing line in Thailand long before the United States had become disenchanted with the Vietnam War. He even succeeded in keeping American military advisers far from any tactical position. This, and of course the fact that the Americans have withdrawn their forces, will ensure that Thailand will never become another Vietnam. It does not ensure that Thailand will not succumb to revolutionary insurgent forces armed and trained and encouraged from beyond its borders.

Thailand is a microcosm of South-East Asia. 'There is probably no other area in the world so richly endowed with diverse cultural strains', Cora Du Bois wrote years ago. Stanley Karnow found the mixture of races and culture a source of enigmatic charm. 'Here are orange-robed Buddhist monks, begging bowls in hand, filing between the serpentine eaves of a gaudy Bangkok temple', he wrote. 'There among the wild orchids and towering trees of a Laotian mountain jungle go Meo headhunters, stalking deer and wild boar with primitive flintlocks. A lissom Vietnamese girl in billowing silk pantaloons, her black hair cascading to her waist, cycles down a Saigon boulevard; a Royal Khmer dancer, performing amid the great stone faces of Angkor, pantomimes a Hindu myth as ancient as Athens.'*

No Royal Khmer dancer exists any longer to pantomime anything, but the picture was true enough, perhaps more what we like to imagine South-East Asia to be than the reality, a picture postcard of the wish-you-were-here variety. For South-East Asia is also people who

---

* Stanley Karnow, *South-East Asia*. Life World Library, New York, 1962.

work from daylight to dark, or can find no work at all. It is people grown weary from malnutrition and disease. It is a mortality rate of 50 per cent among Vientiane's children. It is the poor with matted hair and unwashed hands grubbing for food among the garbage dumps in the city slums that so often lack all facilities, including clean water, and the drains and services to remove excreta and garbage.

It is a region where the most careful economic plans are wrecked by the population explosion. South Vietnam had a population of ten million when the Geneva Agreement was signed in 1954. The population had doubled, despite the awful losses caused by the war, when General Van Tien Dung's tanks broke down the gates of the Independence Palace twenty-one years later. Thailand, with a population of about forty million, will have eighty million to care for in twenty-one years' time. The Philippines, just on forty million, will double in twenty years. Indonesia's population will double to 245 million in twenty-seven years and Burma to some fifty-five million in thirty-two years.

With the growth in population, there has also been a drift to the cities. Jakarta had a population of about 400,000 when it won its independence. Today it has grown to about four million. Over a period of years there I watched with dismay the proliferation of a colony of people who lived, bore children and died in unused water pipes within two minutes' walk of the city's most expensive hotel. The slums in Manila are among the worst in the world. So are the slums of Bangkok. Too often the revolution of rising expectations has become one of diminishing expectations. The product of the slum is unhealthy, uneducated, untrained and often unemployable. And the results, beginning with juvenile delinquency, are increases in the rate of unemployment, lawlessness and crime.* The mental deprivation of the slums, as we have seen in Calcutta, becomes self-perpetuating, for the children of those who have suffered nutritional and educational shortages have no equipment to escape from the environment in which they are brought up.

To the insurgency potential in the rural areas of Thailand must also be added, therefore, urban frustration and disillusionment. The succession of military leaders who ruled Thailand until October 1973, were corrupt and known to be corrupt. The most effective of them all, Field-Marshal Sarit Thanarat, found time to put away a tidy fortune variously estimated between $36 million and $90 million and to maintain first, second and minor wives and concubines on a scale that

---

* There are about 13,000 murders in Thailand each year.

258

had not been matched in Thailand, publicly at least, since Prince Itsarate, who filled the post of Second King, wrote to the Bangkok Calendar a century ago to make clear that King Monghut's family was not larger than his own. King Monghut claimed only twenty-seven wives, thirty-four concubines and seventy-four others who had been presented to him by their fathers as maids of honour; Prince Itsarate, who had been credited with only twenty-four wives, claimed that he had at least a hundred and twenty.

Sarit liked a pretty face and every time a new one appeared on television, on the screen, or at a beauty competition, his agents made an offer. The duties were light and the rewards agreeable. He preferred to work surrounded by ten or a dozen pretty girls. Since he did not care for them to bathe in public, he built them a private pool at the back of his house, provided them with their own transport from a private garage of fifty-one cars and rewarded the favourites with land titles and homes.

His family financial empire was widespread and highly complicated. At its centre was his second wife, Vichitra, well known as a keen businesswoman. Sarit's half-brother, Sanguan Chandrasaka, directed the State lotteries. Another brother ran a gold shop from which the lottery directors recovered $650,000 after Sarit's death. A jute company depended, in turn, on the gold company for financial support. And so it went on.

With glee the Bangkok press published every word while Sarit's mortal remains lay in a golden urn awaiting burial. Anyone in Thailand who was not aware of corruption in high places was fully briefed now. The contumely cast on the late field marshal also fell on his successors, General Praphas Charusathien and Field Marshal Thanom Kittikachorn. With singular political sagacity, Sarit had acted as match maker in the marriage that wed Thanom's son to Praphas' daughter, but in the end this marriage of convenience served only to discredit the three families and in October 1973, when they used brute force to put down a students' revolt, the King moved to hurry the leaders into exile and to pave the way for the introduction of democratic government.

The collapse of the military junta, with all its anti-Communist restrictions, led to dramatic changes in Bangkok. Bookshops which had never dared to sell a Communist book were now filled with Mao and Marx and Ho Chi Minh. Almost openly students went off to Laos for training by North Vietnamese instructors in insurgency. From southern China the Voice of the People of Thailand continued to advocate a 'relentless struggle against the enemies of our nation'.

As the SEATO capital, Thailand had once been the most enthusiastic South-East Asian backer of the American effort in Vietnam. Thai forces fought overtly in South Vietnam and covertly in Laos, and much of the bombing of North Vietnam was carried out from American bases in Thailand. For a long time it was unthinkable to the Thais that the Americans could lose the war in Vietnam. The prospect that they might–and eventually did–contributed greatly to the fragility of the democratic apparatus established after the flight of Praphas and Thanom.

For nearly three years, two brothers, Seni and Kukrit Pramoj, alternated in the political leadership of the country. Both tried to bend, now left, now right, with the new breeze blowing through South-East Asia.

'What else can we do? What else can we do?' Seni Pramoj asked. 'Bamboos bend with the wind. But it's more than a breeze now, it's a storm.'

'Can you bend with such a wind?' I asked.

He sighed. 'Can or cannot, we must try.'

In 1941, when he was a young minister in Washington, Seni did not bend when the message came through from Bangkok to declare war on the United States, and I reminded him of this.

'I didn't bend because my situation was favourable', he replied. 'I took the message from Prime Minister Pibul Songgram and went to Cordell Hull. I told him that I was instructed to declare war but didn't see any reason why I should. We had no *casus belli*, no cause for war, and it was all silly, very silly. Mr Hull looked a bit shocked and said, "You know what you are doing?" '

Seni laughed with pleasure as he recalled Hull's surprise. 'I said, "Yes, I think so." Cordell Hull hummed a bit and replied, "Mr Minister, since you won't declare war, I don't know how to declare it all by myself." And so that is the way it was. It was all a great help.'

Thailand's special relationship with the United States dated from this decision of Seni's. Thailand allied itself with Japan at home and Seni refused to declare war on the United States abroad and all worked out very well indeed. The breeze blew from the east and west and Thailand bent gracefully. This time the gale Seni spoke of proved too strong for the new democratic plant which was torn out by the roots.

'Before there was talk of the United States leaving South-East Asia', said Seni, 'I didn't go to Russian cocktail parties. Now I find that their vodka and caviar taste better every time'.

But the taste of vodka, the establishment of diplomatic relations with China, the expulsion of American bases, the acceptance of humiliating conditions from North Vietnam as the price for establishing relations, the phasing out of SEATO, and all the other bending acts performed by Bangkok contained no assurances that Thailand would be left to shape its own destiny free from interference from abroad. The government promised to declare war on corruption and to bridge the deep gulf, social, economic, physical and even racial, that separated Bangkok and the rich, rice-growing central plains from the vulnerable border regions. But democratic government, though well-intentioned, was weak. Back on unauthorized private visits to upset it came first Praphas and then Thanom. Their return one after the other exposed the full frailty of the government. When students protested violently, there was bloodshed on the campuses, a coup d'état and a return to strongly anti-Communist government, which promised to be more authoritarian than any Thailand had known in the immediate past. One extremely discouraging sign was the exodus of students and left-wing workers and intellectuals who by-passed the police nets and fled to Laos and the North Vietnamese training schools in insurgency and revolution.

One important, but perhaps temporary, plus for the government was the shock wave that accompanied the tens of thousands of refugees from Cambodia, Vietnam and Laos into Thailand. Although there have been similarities in the goals pursued by the new leadership of the three Indo-China states, their time schedules, and their methods, have been separate and distinct. Aware of 'bloodbath' charges, the Vietnamese chose to be tough but discreet. The Khmer Rouge had no interest or concern in what anyone else thought of their methods. They quite literally swept the blackboard clean. They were not content to change the old society. They eradicated it. When the war ended on 17 April 1975, Cambodia had a population of about seven million people. The Khmer Rouge controlled the countryside. The government had mostly controlled the cities. This meant that slightly more than half the population had been living in government controlled areas, slightly less under the control of the Khmer Rouge. The proportions were in the approximate ratio of four to three. Of the four million about half were children under the age of fifteen. These were spared the execution squads and were taken over by the state. Of the other two million approximately one million have been executed, or have died from hunger, overwork, exposure or disease. They have not died by mischance, but by a calculated programme of what a French reporter, Jean Jacques Cazeaux, of Agence France Press called 'genocide by natural selection'. Everyone who had been living in government areas was regarded as a prisoner of war–and potentially expendable. Everyone who had worked for the old regime, or who had profited from his work under the existing society, or who was a significant part of that society, was an enemy of state.

The Khmer Rouge celebrated their victory by emptying the cities and towns. They came into Phnom Penh and at gunpoint drove out the population. Sydney H. Schanberg, of the *New York Times*, who was there to see it, reported:

> In Phnom Penh two million people suddenly moved out of the city en masse in stunned silence–walking, bicycling, pushing cars that had run out of fuel, covering the roads like a human carpet, bent under sacks of belongings hastily thrown together when the heavily-armed peasant soldiers came and told them to leave immediately, everyone dispirited and frightened of the unknown that awaited them and many plainly terrified because they were soft city people and were sure the trip would kill them. Hospitals jammed with wounded were emptied, right down to the last patient. They went – limping, crawling, on crutches, carried on relatives' backs, wheeled on their hospital beds.

They went at the beginning of the monsoon season into areas where there was no shelter, where there were no food stocks sufficient even for the needs of the local people, no drugs, no water fit to drink, no sanitation, no medical care, no transport system to take care of those who fell by the road side, no one to bury the dead. In the most highly organized society in the world this sort of exodus would have led to widespread death and disease. In Cambodia, drenched with rain and baked by the sun, only the very hardy survived.

For those who did survive worse was yet to come. For there now began a deliberate campaign of elimination. The officers in Lon Nol's army and their families were killed, along with the bureaucrats. Then, as the months passed, there were further purges: the business men, the lawyers, the doctors, the shopkeepers, the artists and the artisans. In their tens of thousands they were all killed.

Deprived of their children, their money, their freedom, and even of their names, with no payment for their labour, with no possessions that they could call their own, with no means of communicating with anyone beyond their own labour brigade, with only communal mess halls to eat in, the rest were put to work on the land, to plough the fields and to make new canals.

The extent of the slaughter came as a surprise, even to those who had expected absolute ruthlessness. But the Khmer Rouge were not acting on impulse. As early as 1972 they had begun to remodel rural society. In 1973 and early in 1974 they developed what they called low level production co-operation. Groups of ten to twenty families were obliged to turn over their cows, their water buffaloes and their farm tools to the commune. The rice was placed in a common storage building where it was controlled by the village Party secretary, who doled out a monthly ration to each family.

The next step was the total confiscation of all personal property, including jewellery, precious metals, money, watches and other valuables. The Buddhist religion was abolished and all religious ceremonies outlawed. The monks were dragged out of their pagodas along with everyone else to do manual labour. Finally, the children were taken over by the commune. As soon as a child was old enough to carry a weapon he was drafted into the Army.

Today the children are back, as Angka representatives. 'Some are very, very young, about ten years old', said one of the thousands of refugees who have escaped to Thailand. 'They are no less dangerous. They mingle with the people and are taken for children of the villagers, but if one talks in front of them one is shot.'

Pol Pot, the prime minister, is as unknown to the refugees as he is to the outside world. Prince Norodom Sihanouk has been living under house arrest in Phnom Penh. On January 4, 1978, he issued a statement supporting the government in its war with Vietnam. In any event, he has no role in this new society that is being rebuilt in the labour camps by Angka, the faceless, unknown, ruthless system that has begun to create a new society, and a new man, in the countryside of Cambodia. Throughout 1977, the Cambodian forces clashed repeatedly with the Thais and the Vietnamese in the border areas.

Refugees are sometimes unreliable sources of information. They sometimes colour their stories to suit their audience. They seek comfort and solace and perhaps they tend to exaggerate. But if enough observers talk independently to enough refugees, a pattern will begin to emerge if the refugees are telling the truth. The pattern has emerged from Cambodia. Its effect in Thailand has been to send shivers of fear down the backs of many Thais.

The Pathet Lao have been significantly less brutal in their handling of the situation in Laos, but their performance has put to flight a much larger number of refugees than the official counts reveal, and some 50,000 are believed to be held in labour camps in the North. In the past the Mekong River was a bridge rather than a barrier between the two countries. Most of the people in north-eastern Thailand are ethnic Lao, with the same language, culture, religion and outlook as their cousins across the river. They intermarried naturally and frequently. When the Pathet Lao took over, thousands, even hundreds of thousands, according to Governor Detchard in Ubon Province, crossed the river into Thailand and moved in with relatives. Every day others swell the refugee camps on the Thai side of the river. Their story lacks the horror of Cambodia, but it is real and terrifying for those who have escaped. 'I would rather the Thais shot me than go back', a twenty-year-old girl, who had left her family to escape by night across the Mekong to Ubon, told me.

This is the message the Thai authorities have been spreading among the villages and hamlets of the north-east. It is a message that appears to be understood.

Far to the south in Thailand is the port of Songkla, home for a growing flotilla of Vietnamese boats. More than two years after General Dung's forces captured Saigon, the exodus from Vietnam is continuing. For every boat that escapes with its handful of people an estimated ten others are caught or go down.

In his battle report, General Van Tien Dung laid down the attitudes that would prevail toward the Southerners after the victory was won. 'We had resolutely and mercilessly to destroy these stubborn ring-leaders who were inclined to resist the revolution to the end. But for the broad masses of the people and puppet soldiers we had to open a path to life and not destroy their lives once they threw down their arms, surrendered and freed themselves from the coercion of the u.s.-lackey ringleaders. We fully believed that they would recognize the just cause and successfully receive the education given by the Party and revolution-ary administration.'

To ensure that the 'stubborn ringleaders' would not be able to influence the broad masses, General Dung left nine of the seventeen divisions under his command for the final offensive against Saigon in Military Region 3. Although the scene was one of occasional resistance, dissidence and lawlessness, the counter-revolutionaries had little chance against this sort of opposition. The machinery was fully capable of nipping armed insurgency in the bud.

To anyone familiar with what happened in North Vietnam in and after 1954, Saigon provided few surprises. Three days after the French marched out of Hanoi in 1954 a people's court found a youth guilty of 'serious', but undisclosed, offences. He was shot dead in the street, his body serving for the next twenty-four hours as an example to those who might have defied the new regime.

Government servants of doubtful loyalty who had remained behind in Hanoi found absolution by volunteering for work on the railway that within months was to link Hanoi with China. Others were sent off to political schools (or re-education camps) for three-month courses at which a passing grade in the new theories was a prerequisite for re-employment. Offices, even the post office, closed without warning for the daily indoctrination of staff. The United States was an early target of wrath. 'Think of each rock you crush as an American head' was a slogan posted at a work project outside Hanoi. A large billboard at the far end of the Little Lake in the centre of the city showed Uncle Sam falling off the edge of the world with an A-bomb clutched in his hand. Out in the countryside people's courts tried the 'tyrants' and rich landlords, and many died by firing squad.

So the thought-remoulding process began. Political indoctrination began in the first grade, where six-year-olds were taught slogans and political terms arranged under popular rhymes. The highest honour was to be made one of Uncle Ho's nephews and nieces. In the first ten years, half a million, according to Pham Van Dong, had been awarded the title and granted special responsibilities that included 'looking after smaller children, pasturing oxen, keeping watch over spies, preventing leakage of secrets, and watching strangers coming into the village'.

One evening, just before dusk, in July 1972, a young Viet Cong soldier, who subsequently defected to the government side, was travelling with nine of his comrades to pick up rice along a track in Binh Dinh province. The track was steep and rough and the men were very tired when they reached a hamlet called Kim Son, which was the half-way point on their journey and their staging post for the night. The young Viet Cong, whose name was Pham Chan, had just settled down to rest when he saw coming down the trail an absolutely orderly, apparently self-disciplined, file of children, each keeping the required seven metres between them.

As the children came into Kim Son, Pham Chan counted 126. Some were so young, and so tired, they could not walk and were being carried in hammocks by twenty porters. The rest carried themselves straight and upright, like soldiers on parade, not children.

When the group stopped, Chan talked to the woman cadre in charge and asked how it was possible for such little children–none of the boys or girls looked more than ten–to walk over such a difficult trail when his group of men found the journey exhausting.

The cadre told him that the group had been chosen, with great honour to their revolutionary parents (who would continue the fight against the u.s.-Thieu clique), to join the select band of Uncle Ho's nephews and nieces and to train as future cadres for service in the South. They did not have to walk much further. Waiting a little distance ahead were the trucks that would take them to North Vietnam.

That evening, after the cadres had prepared an evening meal for the children, every child in turn was asked to stand up and tell the group if during the day's march he or she had failed to keep the rules. Did they keep the required seven metres distance apart? Did they talk or cry or complain? One by one the small boys and girls stood up to tell about the rules they had broken and promise never to do it again.

Early the next morning the children marched out to keep their rendezvous with the revolution.

I heard the story from Donald Rochlen who had been in Binh Dinh to find out what had happened in areas occupied by the North Vietnamese. He was shocked by the story. The essence of the system, as it was developed in North Vietnam, was to catch the children when they were very young, to make them aware of their role in the society and to do this before anyone else had a chance to fill their minds with superstitions and religious dogma.

From the second grade onward, political training became more systematic and was directed toward developing a high degree of political consciousness. People everywhere were organized into cells and groups that met to review the activities of their members. At the Hanoi Teachers' College, for example, cells met every night after work for fifteen minutes. No student could hope to escape the exercises in self-criticism.

Like it or dislike it, the system worked. Because of it, North Vietnam did become what it was supposed to be–a strong rear for the war in the South. Now, with the war won, the process of re-educating the South had to begin, and obviously people's courts, the elimination of 'tyrants' and counter-revolutionaries, re-education camps, and the indoctrination of Southern children for future service in their home areas, were the way to go about it.

On 25 May 1976, Saigon published new regulations for the re-education and punishment of former government officials and others who had not been reformed through labour in the re-education camps. Article 5 of the regulations explained that:

> Officers and functionaries who have made progress in the re-education centres may, with the guarantee of their families and the agreement of the local administration, be authorized to return to their families. Following administrative surveillance of from six months to one year's duration they may be restored their civil rights. If members of their families have taken part in or rendered services to the revolution, their requests will be given priority consideration and the duration of their administrative surveillance cut down. The same applies to the aged and sick persons or those who had retired prior to the liberation, or women expecting babies or having children of less then three years of age.

Section C of the regulations dealt with those 'who must continue their re-education or must be brought to trial'. The section was divided into three parts and read:

> 1. The soldiers, non-commissioned officers and officers of all armed

forces, including the para-military organizations, functionaries of all grades, if they do not belong to the categories described above, must spend three years in a centre of re-education. Those who are really found to have made progress will be authorized to return to their homes and to recover their civil rights earlier than the regulation time.

The die-hard agents of the former regime who have committed crimes against the people and who show themselves to be obstinate at the political courses will be brought to trial at tribunals.

2. Those who, having committed crimes against the revolution or against the civilian population, fail to report to the revolutionary authorities, hide or conceal themselves in any way, including the assumption of a false designation of their grade in the former army, or who take refuge in churches, pagodas, schools etc., and clandestinely sabotage the revolution, will be severely punished by law. If, however, they report to the revolutionary authorities and own up their crimes, they will benefit from a reprieve of their penalty.

3. Those who have committed numerous crimes against the revolution or against the population and have zealously served the u.s. imperialists, and now, following the day of liberation, seek to leave the country in the wake of their masters, will be punished by law. Not included in this category are those who, duped by enemy propaganda and taking fright, have fled abroad.

These regulations are neither more repressive, nor more benign, in character than past experience indicated. On 19 January 1969, Australian troops of the 1st RAR captured a document dated 30 September 1968, issued by the Armed Security Forces, Security Agency, COSVN. It was typical of many such documents found during the war and set out guidelines for use not only during the war but after victory had been won. 'We must counter the aggressive war not only in the present but also in the future, even when our fatherland is completely liberated', the document said. 'The people's struggle will continue to take place, fierce and complicated, especially the struggle against spies, reactionaries, henchmen of the u.s. imperialists, reactionary elements in religious communities and ethnic minority groups. The Armed Security Forces will still have to display high determination to provide security for the revolutionary government and territory. It must also suppress the counter-revolutionaries.'

Part of the re-education process is the people's court at which those singled out for special punishment are brought to trial. These courts are much less a means of eliminating 'tyrants' and 'counter-revolutionaries' than they are an instrument for making the people participate in the revolution. The court consists of a judge, a prosecutor and a clerk, but no defence attorney.* Crowds ranging from a few hundred to a

---

* The faculty of law has been closed at the University of Saigon.

few thousand are brought together to attend the court, to listen to the charges and to respond when the judge says, 'What do the people say? Shall we kill him or release him?' Cadres scattered through the crowd shout, 'Kill him', and the people, if they don't want to come under suspicion themselves, take up the cry. Once they have participated in this way, of course, they are deeply involved.

The leniency policy is an essential part of the system. Death sentences may be suspended while the man under sentence is given the chance in reform-through-labour to repent and absolve himself of his sins.

Nevertheless, compared with what happened in Cambodia, the North Vietnamese takeover has been relatively benign. It was not at all benign for the more than two hundred thousand *hoi chanh* who had defected during the war to the Southern side. They were sent back to their former units for punishment. Thousands are known to have been killed; it is not known whether any are alive.

It was not at all benign for senior officers and civil servants who went to the re-education camps. These were modelled on the Chinese reform-through-labour camps, with similar methods of indoctrination. Those undergoing re-education were required to begin by writing their life histories, mentioning by name all those they had been associated with. By cross checking, and by reference to the government files, which fell into the North Vietnamese hands intact, the cadres could pick up the discrepancies and force new confessions. Together with this ideological reorientation went hours of hard physical labour and very little food. One former major who escaped with two others from a camp near Nha Trang and eventually from Vietnam by small boat said in Thailand that labour included mixing human excreta by hand to provide fertiliser for the camp vegetable garden. No washing facilities were available other than the water in a canal, and no knives and forks or chopsticks were provided at meals. Most of the inmates suffered from dysentery, and were often forced to kneel on the parade ground to be beaten by cadres.

For minor officials and junior officers the courses were often quite brief. For senior officials and officers the period is now beginning to run into years. Even the Third Force people have not escaped. I last saw Tran Van Tuyen, one of the founders of the Vietnam Boy Scouts movement, president of the Protection of Human and Public Rights Association, and a bitter critic of Thieu, when he was sitting on the steps of the National Assembly building in Saigon, holding a picture of Thieu with a large cross through it and a slogan in English and Vietnamese, 'Thieu Must Go'. He was taken off to a re-education camp, where he refused to work. His wife thinks he will stay in the camp for ever. Father Thanh, who fought corruption under Thieu, is described as a fascist and is under detention. So is Tri Quang, the Buddhist monk who was once regarded as a Communist.

For the first year Saigon managed to live on its fat. Gold and currency had to be turned in, but the people were left with their personal possessions, which they sold to the North Vietnamese troops and the waves of carpetbaggers who came from Hanoi to wonder at the wealth of the Southerners. There came a time, however, when there was nothing left to sell. People could no longer afford petrol for their cars, and were afraid to put their names on the rice ration list for fear of attracting attention and being sent to one of the 'new economic zones'. A wave of suicides swept the country.

Unemployment jumped from about one million to three million. Inflation soared. And gradually the screws were turned harder. In the countryside, no one was allowed to go to a neighbouring village without written authorization, or 'papers'. Families were required to unite in groups of three to observe, and to report on, the behaviour of the others. As part of the process of showing signs of genuine revolutionary tendencies–and to win clemency for relations in the re-education camps–people were encouraged to renounce their private property. Religion was not persecuted but strongly discouraged. A French priest described the new tuition methods in a convent. The infant children were told to pray to God for sweets. They prayed and nothing happened. Then they were told to pray to Ho Chi Minh–and a shower of sweets came through the windows.

The chief pilot on the Saigon River, who waited for nearly eighteen months for his chance to escape, spoke of the deep suspicion with which the new rulers of South Vietnam regarded everyone, even their allies. Although most of the ships going up the river were Russian, no one was allowed ashore in Saigon. Every pair of binoculars, every telescope, every camera on every ship had to be sealed as soon as a ship entered the river. Every ship going down river was searched from bow to stern for stowaways. Books were banned and burnt. Radio and television and the movies ceased to provide entertainment, only propaganda. All the old political parties and organizations were banned.

To convert the people of the Roman Catholic community of Ho Nai near Bien Hoa, the Communists staged a number of people's courts, with real criminals brought to trial. When the people refused to pass sentence even on a known murderer, the cadres closed the churches.

Armed resistance remains sporadic, unorganized and apparently diminishing, but passive resistance continues and is a source of serious concern to the authorities. 'For a new-born revolutionary power to be lenient with counter-revolutionaries is suicide', was the view held by Truong Chinh, the second ranking member of the Politburo, in 1945. Under his guidance the terror in North Vietnam began in 1953 and continued until Ho Chi Minh decided, in 1956, that the excesses had gone too far. Yet Truong Chinh, despite his temporary eclipse two decades ago, still holds his place in the Politburo, which cannot afford to be more tolerant than it was twenty years ago.

If there has been none of the mass butchery that took place in Cambodia, there has been a selective programme designed to eliminate marked men, not only 'tyrants' and counter-revolutionaries but members of the political organizations. If all the *hoi chanh* have been killed–and this is reported by refugees–then the number of executions is much higher than anyone has guessed. Add to this the number in re-education camps awaiting trial and Vietnam does not emerge as a model that non-Communists neighbours would care to follow.

Seeking to shore up its own defences by borrowing from the Vietnamese the concept of re-education camps, the new Thai dictatorship is endeavouring to meet totalitarian threat with totalitarianism. One fundamental difference between Thailand and the three Indo-China states under their new rulers is that it lacks the machinery to impose its will in this way. Unlike Cambodia and Vietnam, it also remains wide open to external pressures and subversion from beyond its borders. It is also shaky, as the attempted coup in March 1977 demonstrated.

One of the few useful legacies of the Soekarno era in South-East Asia was the maintenance of diplomatic relations between Hanoi and Jakarta. These had been established as a suitable gesture of anti-Americanism during the first heady days of Soekarno's final year of 'living dangerously', as he called it. Despite the vigorously anti-Communist approach of the Soeharto regime, it was wisely decided in Jakarta that these ties should not be broken. Thus, when ASEAN (the Association of South-East Asian Nations) came into being in 1967, with Indonesia, Singapore, Malaysia, Thailand and the Philippines as members, the Jakarta-Hanoi relationship provided the five non-Communist powers in the organization with some sort of communications link, however tenuous it may have been, with the power that was soon to loom so formidably in South-East Asia. After the Vietnam War ended, Indonesia wasted no time in recognizing the Provisional Revolutionary Government of South Vietnam, and promised to support its entry into the United Nations.

Within days of the end of the war, Nguyen Hoa, the active North

Vietnamese ambassador in Jakarta, was busy telling not only the Indonesians but all ASEAN members that they had nothing to fear from the Communist takeover in Saigon, that Vietnam would be too busy with domestic reconstruction to worry about extending its influence into the rest of South-East Asia and had no interest in exporting revolution.

At the same time, he hinted discreetly, and not so discreetly, that Hanoi would be very displeased with any concerted action by the ASEAN powers to embark on measures that could be interpreted as a reaction against the Communist takeover. From Hanoi, Professor Usep Ranuwijaya, the Indonesian ambassador, reported in much the same way. When the official Hanoi press lambasted Thailand, and soon included Indonesia in its hostility, he argued (though scarcely with much conviction, one imagines) that it would be an error to interpret press opinion in Hanoi as being identical with the views held by the government. The professor saw Pham Van Dong for a talk lasting several hours and emerged from the meeting convinced that the new Vietnam harboured no hostility to ASEAN. Only five days later, however, the *Quan Doi Nhan Dan*, the Vietnamese Army newspaper, launched one of its bitterest attacks on ASEAN and claimed that the United States was attempting to use it 'with Indonesia as a main prop, to rally all pro-American reactionary forces to oppose the revolutionary movement in South-East Asia'. If this was scarcely an encouraging pipe-opener for the ASEAN summit meeting which was about to be held in Bali, the leaders when they met held out the olive branch, expressing their readiness to develop fruitful relations and mutually benefical co-operation with the Indo-China countries. Moreover, they were at pains to make absolutely clear that they had no intention of attempting to make ASEAN any sort of military substitute for the dying SEATO. Pushing aside the olive branch, Hanoi, through *Nhan Dan*, the Party newspaper, and as authoritative in its own way as any statement made by Pham Van Dong, replied by attacking Thailand as the 'chief instrument of U.S. imperialism's evil designs in Indo-China', and Indonesia's aggression in Portuguese Timor.

This sort of ambivalence has continued ever since, with assurances often followed by threats. The situation deteriorated sharply after the military coup in Bangkok. In the vulnerable north-eastern provinces the North Vietnamese have a ready-made justification for any move they may eventually feel obliged to take against Thailand–a harassed Vietnamese minority, anything from 50,000 to 70,000 in number, who have been openly pro-Communist ever since the days Ho Chi Minh lived there from 1928 to 1930 and, as a principal Comintern agent, used the region as a base for planting the seeds for Communist revolution in South-East Asia.

For nearly a quarter of a century, in my own personal knowledge, the Vietnamese in Thailand have been a worrying irritant, and sometimes a real nightmare, to the government in Bangkok. In 1953 Field Marshal Pibul Songgram, then prime minister of Thailand, decided to make a personal investigation of the Vietnamese in the north-east as a prelude to resettling them in less sensitive areas. He abandoned the project in the town of Nong Khai when Vietnamese women lay down in the streets, blocking the ministerial motor cavalcade, while some even cut their throats in further protest.

A repatriation programme made little progress and was suspended when it was discovered that some of those who had returned to Hanoi were making their way back to Thailand again for purposes that caused the Thais great concern. With Laos no longer a buffer, the Thais believe they have even more reason for concern. Even the possibility of an eventual overt North Vietnamese attack against Thailand is not altogether discounted. Playing war games in Bangkok, the experts discovered that two North Vietnamese divisions would be sufficient for the task.

While he was busy preparing for the offensive in South Vietnam, General Van Tien Dung found the time to address himself to 'Some Problems of combining Economic Development with the Consolidation of National Defence'. It was published in *Hoc Tap* and *Tap Chi Quan Doi Nhan Dan*, and also in *Nhan Dan* and the *Quan Doi Nhan Dan* in December 1974. This unusual spread must be interpreted as having stamped the article with the Party imprimatur, especially since its publication preceded by one day the all-important meeting of the Politburo in Hanoi on 18 December, when final plans for the new offensive in the South were reviewed.

The article was essentially forward looking, with the coming military campaign peripheral to the main theme: the post-war creation of major industrial and military power in Vietnam. Dung admitted quite freely the debt that Hanoi owed to fraternal Socialist countries for their military and economic assistance. From this he drew the conclusion that Vietnam was now obliged to accept similar responsibilities: 'In the course of receiving and using the fraternal countries' assistance, our people are bound to contribute to consolidating and developing international solidarity and unity among the fraternal countries and parties, to defending the Socialist system and increasing its strength and to accelerating the world revolutionary trends . . .' There was to be no reduction in force strength Army units were told that they had to 'eliminate the bad habit of considering their participation in labour and economic development as a temporary task'. They had to organize their production activities in accordance with their labour task, 'while meeting the Army's requirements for building, achieving combat readiness and engaging in combat'. New arsenals would be built to produce modern weapons.

Since Dung began the 1975 offensive absolutely confident of victory, and the article took a long-term view, it was significant that he anticipated only a limited period of peace. It was necessary, he said, to work out air defence and evacuation plans while carrying out economic activities. And he mentioned plans to build in peacetime 'a number of important shelter projects and underground shelters for very important installations'. 'Why?', one may well ask. Because there are dangers, perhaps, in fulfilling the 'internationalist obligations' that Dung so often refers to? The South-East Asians, in general, and the Thais, in particular, can scarcely be blamed if this is what they fear.

How free the Vietnamese may feel to move is another matter. When the Thais were in China to establish diplomatic relations with Peking after the end of the Vietnam War, they voiced their concern about Vietnamese intentions. They were told not to worry. If the Vietnamese attacked, the Thais could count on the Chinese for assistance.

One day in July 1975, Valerian Skvortsov, *Pravda*'s Indo-China correspondent, was wandering about the streets of Saigon taking pictures when he attracted the potentially unfriendly attention of a four-man military patrol.

Pointing at himself, he shouted 'Soviet' in Vietnamese. If he had shouted that four months earlier he might have got a bullet in his back, if anyone had understood what he was saying. But times had changed. Some minutes later the patrol's lieutenant approached him and asked him in what Skvortsov described as pretty fair Russian where he came from in the Soviet Union. One thing led to another. Soon they all found themselves in the bar of the Majestic Hotel having a drink, where Skvortsov learned that the lieutenant had been trained in Rostov-on-Don.

Skvortsov found all this sufficiently interesting to record it in a long article. It was perhaps more interesting than he suggested.

Thousands of North Vietnamese were trained in the Soviet Union during the war, but the general assumption was that they were technicians in specialist units who needed to learn Russian to master the sophisticated equipment they were receiving. That a junior officer leading a military police patrol of four men in Saigon should speak Russian, and have been trained in the Soviet Union, is remarkable.

It also helps to explain why the Chinese would be unwilling to see any further Vietnamese expansion in South-East Asia.

The last shot had only just been fired in the Vietnam War when the Chinese leaked a report that the Russians had asked Hanoi for the use of Cam Ranh Bay as a naval base. In denying the story, Hanoi said that of course any friendly Socialist state would be welcome to the use of its facilities.*

That the Soviet Union and Vietnam were determined to remain the closest of friends became apparent when Le Duan led a delegation to Moscow in October 1975, for discussions with Brezhnev and other members of the Central Committee of the Communist Party of the Soviet Union. In view of the determined effort the Vietnamese had made for so many years during the war to maintain a balance in their relationship between Peking and Moscow, the communique issued at the end of the talks was an extraordinary document. There was no outright denunciation of China, but the discussion covered areas of specific Chinese interest, including those where Chinese and Russian interests collided. The statement that 'the two sides held completely identical views on the matters brought to discussion', could only have been interpreted in Peking as a rebuff.

Vietnam has not become a Soviet satellite, but perhaps it feels some measure of security in associating itself more closely with the distant bear while keeping some distance from the dragon next door.

One result of this is that the bitter antagonisms between the Soviet Union and China–and they are both national and ideological–have spilled over into South-East Asia. China has a foothold in Cambodia, and the bi-monthly flights from Phnom Penh to Peking provide the new regime with almost its only contacts with the outside world. Peking even provided a plane–and the advice–that prompted a Cambodian delegation to go to Bangkok for discussions.

The Voice of the People of Thailand, based in southern China, still broadcasts its propaganda to the Thai insurgents, but the flow of arms and other aid to the guerrillas from China has diminished appreciably in recent times.

But can China really afford to divorce itself from the Communist insurgents who have hitherto looked to it for guidance, training, direction and at least some material support? Does it not run risks to its own future security in allowing primacy in the art of people's war to pass to General Dung, who can legitimately claim to have fought,

---

* A more recent report is that the Russians are building a submarine base near Haiphong.

and to have defeated, the most powerful nation in the world?

Of one thing we can be certain: the era of peace and neutrality for South-East Asia, widely acclaimed by foolish men, did not begin when the North Vietnamese tanks rolled through the gates of Independence Palace on 30 April 1975.

There has been no demobilization of the North Vietnamese armed forces. The military draft has continued in the northern parts of the country and, after reunification, was extended to the South. American estimates of the military booty that fell into General Dung's hands are around the $6 billion mark. Not all of it could usefully be absorbed into the Northern military machine, dependent as it has become on Soviet equipment, and much was worn out.

Frequent reports that the surplus has been sold abroad to terrorist organizations and sovereign governments cannot be substantiated, and have, in fact, been denied by the governments said to have been concerned. Relatively small quantities of arms that have turned up in Thailand and Malaysia are believed to have been obtained from smugglers and gun runners in the business for profit and not for ideological purposes, although Thai insurgents have received larger– but still not very large–quantities of supplies direct from the Pathet Lao.

The Vietnamese now see themselves as, and are, in fact, a major force in Asia. They are the only people in the world who have ever engaged the United States in a major war–and won. They have perfected the doctrine of protracted-conflict revolutionary war. They borrowed from the teaching of Mao and improved his technique beyond recognition. When Giap and Dung claim they have made a new development in the art of leading a revolutionary war, no one can contradict them. There were doubtless many occasions on which the United States could have won the war, but, within the rules that Washington laid down, it fought and lost. That loss has contributed significantly to the decline of the United States as a super power. Its defence line in South-East Asia to which, rightly or wrongly, it once attached such importance, has collapsed. No force, or combination of forces, in South-East Asia could stand up against the Vietnamese today. They won the war. They won the right to be heard. And they will be heard.

Acknowledgments and notes on sources

In telling the story of what happened and why during the closing fifty-one days of the war, nothing was more useful, or more important, than Senior General Van Tien Dung's (the D is heavily interlarded with z and the u is soft) account of the last great North Vietnamese offensive that began with the attack on Ban Me Thuot on 10 March 1975, and ended with the fall of Saigon on 30 April. This was published by the newspaper *Nhan Dan* in Hanoi, beginning on 1 April 1976, and concluding on 22 May. I have drawn on it heavily.

I have also made extensive use of the testimony of Ambassador Graham A. Martin before the special sub-committee on investigations of the Committee on International Relations, u.s. House of Representatives. Douglas Pike provided vital material about North Vietnam's psychological warfare. For years in gathering material on which the book is based I was enormously indebted to my friends Bui Anh Tuan and Dr Phan Quang Dan. Nguyen Ngoc Phach, who served as a staff officer on the Joint General Staff, read the book in manuscript form and picked up some of my errors. My wife read and re-read the manuscript and suggested many important additions and changes. Tran Van Lam was the source for the Nixon letters and the background to the Paris Agreement. Several most helpful sources I have reason to believe are dead. Other are undergoing 're-education'. I shall not add to their problems by mentioning their names.

The notes on the chapters in the book are not intended to be comprehensive. Since for reasons of their personal security I cannot indicate all sources, I have limited the notes on sources to information that is new, or little known.

Part one: The beginning of the end

1. General Dung's beautiful road to war

The two major sources are General Dung and Tran Van Lam. General Dung documents the date on which Hanoi decided to resume full-scale war in the South and the events leading up to the battle for Ban Me Thuot. His articles are unique. Nothing remotely approaching the detail was published by Hanoi during the war. In fact, for many years Hanoi sought to convey the impression that it was not involved in the South, and that all the fighting was being done by indigenous Southerners. Dung's articles from 1 April to 14 April cover the period of this chapter. Tran Van Lam supplied the information about the Paris Agreement in interviews in Saigon in mid-April 1975, and in Canberra in September and November 1976. For further detail on Russia's advice to North Vietnam to 'go for broke' see page 605 of the Vietnam-Cambodia Emergency, 1975, Part III Vietnam Evacuation: Testimony of Ambassador Graham A. Martin. For Le Duan's role see Vietnamese Communism, Its Origins and Development, by Robert F. Turner, Hoover Institution Press, 1975, pages 178–180.

2. The Highland rout

Dung and Lam are again principal sources. Pike supplied the material on dich van. Martin's message to the State Department Ref. (A) Saigon 15729 (B) State 281471 and the full text of the inter-faith pastoral letter appear on pages 552–555 of Martin's congressional committee evidence. The shooting in and outside Ban Me Thuot was described by an eyewitness interview in Saigon on 20 April 1976. Since he is presumably still in Vietnam, his name cannot be disclosed.

3. The fall of Danang

Colonel Van Cao Dong, who commanded the government's Regional Forces in Military Region 1, provided the details of the fall of Hue and Danang in interviews in Saigon on 3 April and 7 April 1975. General Dung's articles filled in the North Vietnamese background.

Part two: The end of the beginning

1. The French bow out

For details of Lansdale and Conein's activities in Vietnam during this period see *The Pentagon Papers*, pages 54–66. The Joint Chief of Staff's recommendation for a greater role in Vietnam, *ibid.*, pages 153–154. Conein was the principal source of information for the account of the coup.

2. The Americans bow in

For unrestrained American optimism during this period see Situation in Vietnam, Hearings before the Sub-Committee on State Department and Public Affairs of the Committee on Foreign Relations, United States Senate, 86th Congress, 30 and 31 July 1959, including statements by Elbridge Durbrow, pages 9–98, and Lieut-General Samuel T. Williams, pages 18–117. For a full account of the building of the Ho Chi Minh trail after May 1959, see *Vietnam Courier*, Hanoi, July 1976, page 12. The article leaves no doubt that the construction of the trail was intended to bring about the reunification of the two Vietnams by armed force in which 'the duty of the North was to give support to this struggle which would be full of hardships and difficulties'.

3. And out

Peter Young's The Military Situation Within South Vietnam, dated 9 July 1967, and classified SECRET. It consists of ten foolscap pages of single-spaced type.

4. South Vietnam's golden age

'The signature was Nixon's but the words were Kissinger's' – Tran Van Lam, interview, Canberra, November 1976.

Part three: The end

1. 'The invisible star of the Milky Way'

Douglas Pike's unpublished Anatomy of Deceit is the source for Vietnamese Communist efforts to manipulate public opinion throughout the world. North Vietnam's battle order outside Saigon comes from General Dung in *Nhan Dan*.

2. The battle for Saigon begins

The presidential correspondence between Ford and Thieu was backgrounded by Tran Van Lam. Martin's comments on the agent's report from COSVN appear on page 583 of his testimony to the Congressional committee. His talk with Thieu, *ibid.*, pages 544–574.

3. The Ho Chi Minh campaign

The evacuation of locally-engaged staff, Foreign Affairs Department, SA2187 and SA2456. Hanoi on evacuation, DFA, Memo 166 from Hanoi. Details of planning and execution of the final offensive against Saigon, General Dung in *Nhan Dan*, 18–22 May 1976; Minh's confidence, Tran Van Lam interview.

Part four: And beyond

1. The morning after the war before

Regulations issued by Saigon authorities for the re-education and punishment of former government officials and others, *Vietnam Courier*, Hanoi, July 1976, pages 10–11. Conditions in Vietnam after the fall of Saigon from Donald Rochlen's debriefings, Bangkok, August–September 1976; letters from Vietnam to relatives and friends outside and from refugees and deportees. See Jean Bourdarias, 'Communists Tighten Control and Surveillance', *Figaro*, Paris, 26 September 1975; Giorgio Torchia, 'Vietnam: The Great Shell Game', *Tempo*, Rome, 30 April 1976; also 'Conspiracy of Silence Regarding the Persecutions', *ibid.*, 30 April 1976; also Fox Butterfield, 'Vietnam One Year Later: A Major Transformation', *New York Times*, 30 April 1976. He writes, inter alia, 'People of an entire social class of perhaps a million people . . . have been dispossessed. They have been stripped of their jobs, their state housing, their savings, and, if they were disabled or retired, their pensions'. Genocide in Cambodia has been thoroughly documented. See Jean Barre (once a close confident of Prince Norodom Sihanouk), 'Refugee Reports Cambodia in the Hands of the Little Chiefs', *Journal de Genève*, 4 March 1976; Jon Swain, 'Cambodia is Convulsed as Khmer Rouge Wipes Out a Civilization', *Sunday Times*, London, 18 April 1976; Lewis M. Simons, 'Cambodia Palace Bomber Defects', *Washington Post*, 4 May 1976; Sydney H. Schanberg, 'Cambodian Reds Are Uprooting Millions', *New York Times*, 9 May 1975; Jean Pouget, 'Cambodia, the Insane Experiment of a New Order',

Figaro, Paris, 31 May 1976; Jean Bourdarias, 'Cambodia: The Calvary of a People', *Figaro*, 15 October 1975. Children at Kim Son, Donald Rochlen, Binh Dinh Report No. 1, 10 September 1972, pages 17–18. John Barron and Anthony Paul, 'Murder of a Gentle Land', *Reader's Digest*, February 1977.

Index

Ea Yong, 35
Eden, Anthony, 110
Elections: and Ho Chi Minh, 84; as part of treaties, 8, 178; in South Vietnam, 97, 110, 111, 112, 154
Energy crisis: effect on South Vietnam villages, 10–11; effect on U.S. military aid, 8
Evacuations, 217; of Americans from South Vietnam, 221, 232, 244–46, 248; of South Vietnam, 202, 210; of Vietnamese from South Vietnam, 232, 233–36, 237, 243

Faas, Horst, 201
Fairbairn, Geoffrey, 231
Faure, M. Edgar, 105
Ferguson, Michael, 56
15th parallel, 13
Filipinos, 104
Fonda, Jane, 16
Ford, Gerald R., 188, 207, 221, 241; and evacuation of Americans, 244, 245; requesting aid from Congress, 44, 210, 213
Francis, Al, 76
French, 23, 36, 54, 95; and Bao Dai, 86; at Dien Bien Phu, 15, 25, 41, 93, 99; and Cambodian independence in 1945, 83; and Ho Chi Minh, 15, 83, 85, 86; and Indo-China War, 80, 84, 85, 87, 90; and Laos, 92–93; and North Vietnam, 15, 212, 241, 264
French Army, 6
French Embassy: and Australian evacuees, 236
French Union, 84, 88

Garvey, Paul, 126
Geneva Agreement, 23, 97, 100, 102, 103, 109, 110, 254; ending Indo-China War, 15–16
German Embassy: and evacuation of Vietnamese, 237

Geronimo, 47, 49; as Phnom Penh blockade run survivor, 14
Gia Dinh province, 190
Gia Kiem, 215
Giam, Hoang Minh, 185
Giang, Vo Dong, 249
Giap, Vo Nguyen, xvii, 15, 18, 85, 93; and Indo-China War, 90; and 1975 offensive, 25, 32, 34, 35, 36, 41; and Saigon offensive, 195; and Viet Minh, 80
Giau, Tran Van, 90
Gilchrist, Hugh, 234
GKR, 53. See also Cambodia
Goss, David, 236
Gracey, Douglas, 83
Graves, Hubert, 96
Green Berets, 122
Guerrilla warfare, 19, 61, 135; and Ho Chi Minh, 15, 80; U.S. ignorance of, 108, 118; and Viet Minh, 89, 90
Gumbleton, Thomas, 16, 21
GVN, 53. See also South Vietnam

Habib, Philip, 44, 207
Haig, Alexander, 211
Haiphong, 17; closed by Geneva Agreement, 104; French bombing of, 85; and Soviet submarine base, 274 n
Hai Van Pass, 54, 68
Halberstam, David, 117, 205
Hammer, Ellen, 79
Hai Hung, xiv
Ham Tan, 228
Han, Cao Hao, 172
Hanh, Vo Huu, 56
Hanh Dong (South Vietnam), 132
Hanoi: elections push in, 110; as secretive to diplomats, 26; under Viet Minh, 81, 97–98
Harkins, Paul, 118
Hau Bon, 61
Helsinki conference, 241
Hickey, Gerald, 182

FEB 19

CONNETQUOT PUBLIC LIBRARY

0621 9100 409 915 6

959.704
WARNER.
Certain victory.

017102

lnv 82

9.95

Connetquot Public Library
760 Ocean Avenue
Bohemia, New York 11716